IMAGES
of America

THE LINCOLN HIGHWAY ACROSS ILLINOIS

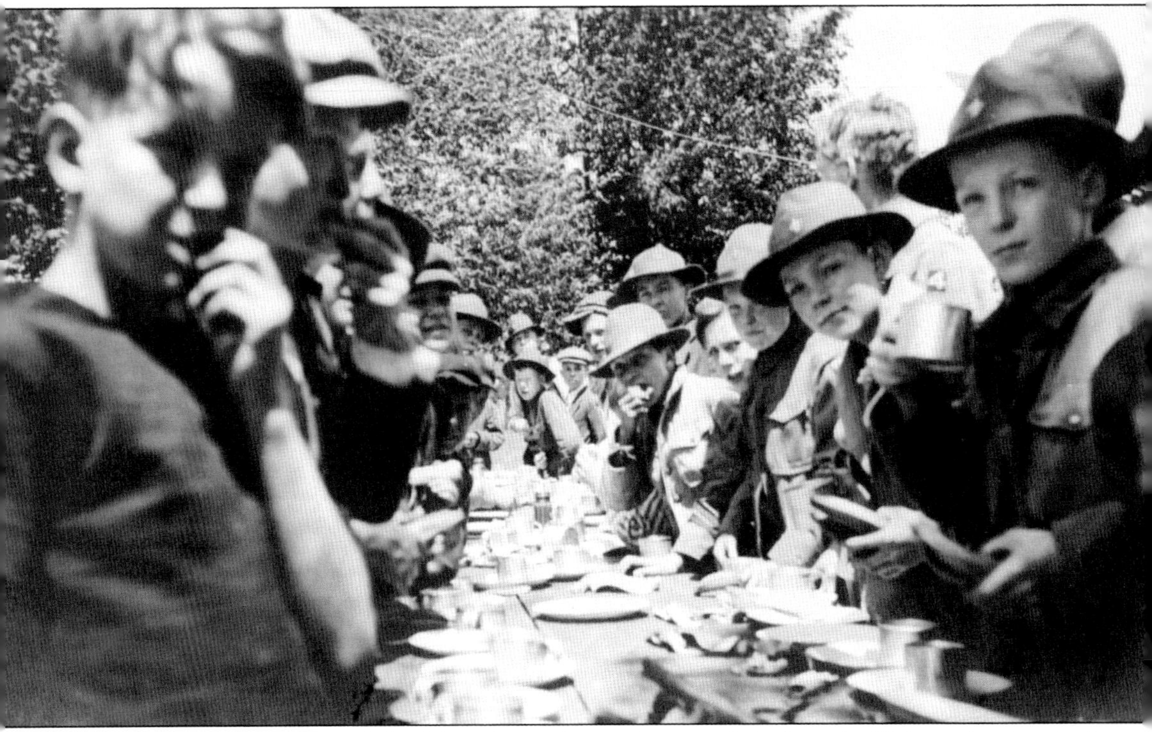

Affectionately known as "The Main Street Across America," the Lincoln Highway has inspired many tourists, travelers, and towns along the coast-to-coast roadway to keep the legacy of Carl Fisher's pioneering spirit alive. Since his death in 1939, the Lincoln Highway has remained a persistent memory in the minds of many. One such reminder of the old road is a few of the original Boy Scout markers that can still be found in places along the route. This image of the Boy Scouts enjoying some lunch after working hard along the highway in Illinois helps to show how important this old roadway has been to every citizen in the nation. (Courtesy of the University of Michigan.)

On the Cover: Much like the automobile assembly line transformed the nature of the workplace, the automobile revolutionized the entire transportation system in America. By the end of the 1930s, cars, trucks, and buses had almost completely replaced the horse-drawn vehicles that were still commonplace a generation before. To accommodate the increase in traffic, thousands of miles of new roads were built during the 1920s, and other routes, including the Lincoln Highway, were improved. This image shows an automobile along the Lincoln Highway about a mile west of Franklin Grove. Notice the sign to the left that indicates that this section of roadway was built by auto fees. (Courtesy of the University of Michigan.)

IMAGES
of America

The Lincoln Highway across Illinois

David A. Belden and Christine O'Brien
Foreword by Kay Shelton

ARCADIA
PUBLISHING

ISBN 978-0-7385-9358-6

Published by Arcadia Publishing
Charleston, South Carolina

Printed in the United States of America

Library of Congress Control Number: 2013933263

For all general information, please contact Arcadia Publishing:
Telephone 843-853-2070
Fax 843-853-0044
E-mail sales@arcadiapublishing.com
For customer service and orders:
Toll-Free 1-888-313-2665

Visit us on the Internet at www.arcadiapublishing.com

Contents

ACKNOWLEDGMENTS

The publication of this book would not have been possible without the assistance and support of Kay Shelton and the Illinois Chapter of the Lincoln Highway Association. Area historical repositories and residents also provided help, material, and support: the University of Michigan and the Lincoln Highway Digital Image Collection; Michigan State University Libraries; the Will County Historical Society; Kim Shehorn-Martin, Joliet Historical Museum; Sam and Lynn Reichert; Patricia Thomson; Robert Horras; and Russell S. Rein. A large portion of the vintage and archival Lincoln Highway images used in this publication came from the Transportation History Collection of the Special Collections Library at the University of Michigan.

Several people at Minooka Community High School have also been helpful with local histories, materials, equipment, and expertise, and to the following individuals I am grateful: Debbie Dobson, Karen Turk, Glenda Smith, Dave DiLorenzo, Robert Williams, Stephanie Ledesma, Sherry Harris, and especially Christine O'Brien for helping decide on the cover image. I also want to thank Lisa Wright and Evangeline Stephenson for assisting me with obtaining the research for this book. Both were extremely helpful in organizing and securing materials throughout the project. I also want to thank Jen Gabel for her time and help in obtaining images around Aurora.

I would also like to especially thank Russell S. Rein for his time and assistance in providing background material, images, and guidance on this project. This book would not have been possible without the use of Rein's digital collections. And a very special thank you to Christine O'Brien for providing numerous contemporary images of the Lincoln Highway and for providing her time, input, expertise, patience, and friendship in helping to proofread and edit the text for this book. For that I am grateful.

The production and preparation for this book would never have been possible without the dedication of students in my local history classes. I wish to thank Aaron Alexander, Camille Arroyo, Mishel Daletski, Ryan Fleming, Nicolette Krzywanos, Tara O'Shea, Gary Parker, Ian Pershey, Rico Sally, Macey Scranton, Joseph Sheppard, Jessica Smeets, Victor Turpin, Chad Van Meter, and Dylan Warnicke.

Finally, I wish to acknowledge the help and assistance of Jeff Ruetsche, Amy Perryman, and Kelsey Jones at Arcadia Publishing. Thank you for all your time and support on this publication. I also would like to thank Paige Stratemeyer, who originally had the idea for a Lincoln Highway book across Illinois.

FOREWORD

Close your eyes and imagine what it was like to drive an automobile 100 years ago. Many roads were made of dirt that turned into a sticky mud after a rain. Some roads had planks—flat boards laid across dirt. Imagine what the automobile was like 100 years ago; many had no roof nor headlights. In an open car with no roof, drivers and passengers wore goggles to keep the grit and dust out of their eyes and long coats called dusters to keep the dust from damaging their clothing. Early automobiles had no air-conditioning, no heat, and no radios. Flat tires were common without paved roads and before technological improvements in tire design.

In those early days of the automobile, the Lincoln Highway became the first coast-to-coast highway in the United States developed on improved roads. Established in 1913, the Lincoln Highway stretches from Times Square, New York City, to the shadow of the Golden Gate Bridge in San Francisco. Envisioned by Carl Graham Fisher, the Lincoln Highway is the world's largest memorial to Pres. Abraham Lincoln. Fisher was an entrepreneur involved with manufacturing headlights for automobiles, he developed the idea of the Indianapolis Motor Speedway and owned it with partners, he drove the first pace car for the Indianapolis 500 in 1911, and he was an early promoter of Miami Beach in Florida.

Partnering with other automobile industry pioneers like Henry Joy, president of the Packard Motor Company, and Frank Seiberling, cofounder of the Goodyear Tire & Rubber Company, Fisher imagined a coast-to-coast highway to show the public that it would be possible for people to drive automobiles across long distances. Fisher also knew the key to encouraging more people to buy automobiles was having good roads. Who would want to drive an automobile on muddy roads? The Lincoln Highway Association (LHA) formed to organize mapping out a route from New York City to San Francisco for the Lincoln Highway and to gather private donations to be used for road improvements. The goal was to have the highway finished in time for travelers to use it to attend the Panama-Pacific International Exposition in San Francisco, otherwise known as the 1915 World's Fair.

In 1913, very few roads were paved, so not everyone in the general public outside large cities had first-hand knowledge of the benefits of driving on paved roads instead of dirt roads. Paving over 3,300 miles of road could not be done overnight—it would take too much labor and financial funding, so the LHA constructed Seedling Miles. The Seedling Miles were meant to show samples of how pleasant driving an automobile could be compared to getting stuck in the mud. The LHA chose particularly muddy sections to pave with concrete. Paving a mile-long section gave automobile owners the experience of driving on a good road.

In Illinois, the LHA organized the paving of the first Seedling Mile outside Malta in 1914. That particular stretch of the Lincoln Highway was in a low area where spring rains pooled into a muddy mess. The LHA collected private donations from local people, including one farmer who donated because he understood that a paved road would make it easier for his horses to pull his wagon of grain into town. The LHA combined donations with a pledge of barrels of cement from the Portland Cement Company to pave the Seedling Mile. After the paving of the Seedling Mile, automobile drivers traveled to Malta to try out the smooth road, especially enjoying how fast they could drive on it. Some people brought their roller skates and went skating on the road.

Elsewhere in Illinois, another Seedling Mile outside Morrison in Whiteside County showed people on the west side of the state what an improved road was like. Toward the east-central part of the state, the charitable community of Mooseheart, established by the Loyal Order of the Moose, already paved a near-mile-long section of the Lincoln Highway with over 1,000 volunteers at its entrance on April 15, 1914. Gov. Edward Dunne shoveled the first spade of dirt at Mooseheart to start the paving process. He declared that day Good Roads Day throughout Illinois and traveled the Lincoln Highway westward, stopping at several communities to give speeches about the importance of improved roads. Without a microphone and loudspeakers, by the evening on Good Roads Day in 1914, the governor's voice became hoarse from having to shout so the throngs of people in the crowds could hear.

Paving the road did not happen overnight, although the Lincoln Highway did inspire communities such as Ashton to pave all of its roads in town. By 1919, when a young Army lieutenant colonel named Dwight Eisenhower participated in the first transcontinental Army convoy across the Lincoln Highway, not all of it was paved. The purpose of the convoy was to test the durability of US Army vehicles and how fast they could travel, and it also tested the quality of roads and bridges. The heavy trucks sometimes became stuck in mud and damaged wooden bridges. Eisenhower's bad experiences with mud and broken bridges on the Lincoln Highway, and later seeing the Autobahn in Germany during World War II, helped convince him to sign the Federal-Aid Highway Act of 1956, which created the interstate highway system.

The Lincoln Highway was an integral part of improving the driving experiences of the American people, and the State of Illinois continued to be a leader. Illinois was the first state to have the entire length of the Lincoln Highway paved. An early leader of the LHA was William G. Edens, who never learned how to drive an automobile himself but was a banker for the Chicago Central Trust, and he understood how to finance large infrastructure projects from his earlier days working for the railroads. Edens was the Chicago consul for the LHA and the Edens Expressway, which is Interstate 94 in the Chicago area, named for him because of his work on financing road improvements.

In 2013, a century after the establishment of the Lincoln Highway, this "Father Road" remains a vital part of the American experience. The invention of the automobile in the 20th century reshaped how and where Americans lived and where they could work. The automobile was more than just new technology that added convenience to daily life such as the radio, television, or the microwave. The automobile completely changed opportunities for travel. The LHA helped show people that driving could be a good experience. I hope you enjoy reading about this wonderful part of American history.

—Kay Shelton
State Director, Illinois Chapter, Lincoln Highway Association
and National President, Lincoln Highway Association

One

Early Road Travel

Less than 100 years ago, there was no single road that stretched across the United States. There were many wagon trails that existed out West, and a network of roads and turnpikes in the East, but traveling between the coasts was a directional challenge. Few people had even imagined that it could be possible to create a single cross-county route that could be traversed and named from east to west. Even when the idea for the Lincoln Highway was envisioned in 1913, it was not a new road, just someone's idea of roads and trails that could be connected together to link the coasts of the nation.

When Carl Fisher envisioned the road in 1913, he wanted something more than just a road. He wanted a road that would bring Americans together to create something special, something artistic, something that would instill pride in all Americans for generations to come. Soon, the Lincoln Highway would be the most celebrated road of its time and would be rightly described by many as "American's Main Street." While the creation of such a route was the main crusade for the men involved in the road's founding, the idea for such a route would also help America out of the mud.

Soon after the idea for the first transcontinental road was announced by Carl Fisher and the Lincoln Highway Association, communities across the nation began to make plans for road improvements. Local good roads clubs had been formed around the country, and the thought of a coast-to-coast route created a movement to connect towns and communities across the nation with new and improved roads. It was not until the Federal Aid Road Act of 1916, however, that the national government provided some highway funding to improve the country's road system. While the Lincoln Highway Association's main objective was to encourage local communities to help fund additional paving projects that would reach the Seedling Miles from either side, it would take a few years for the government to increase its role in road improvement.

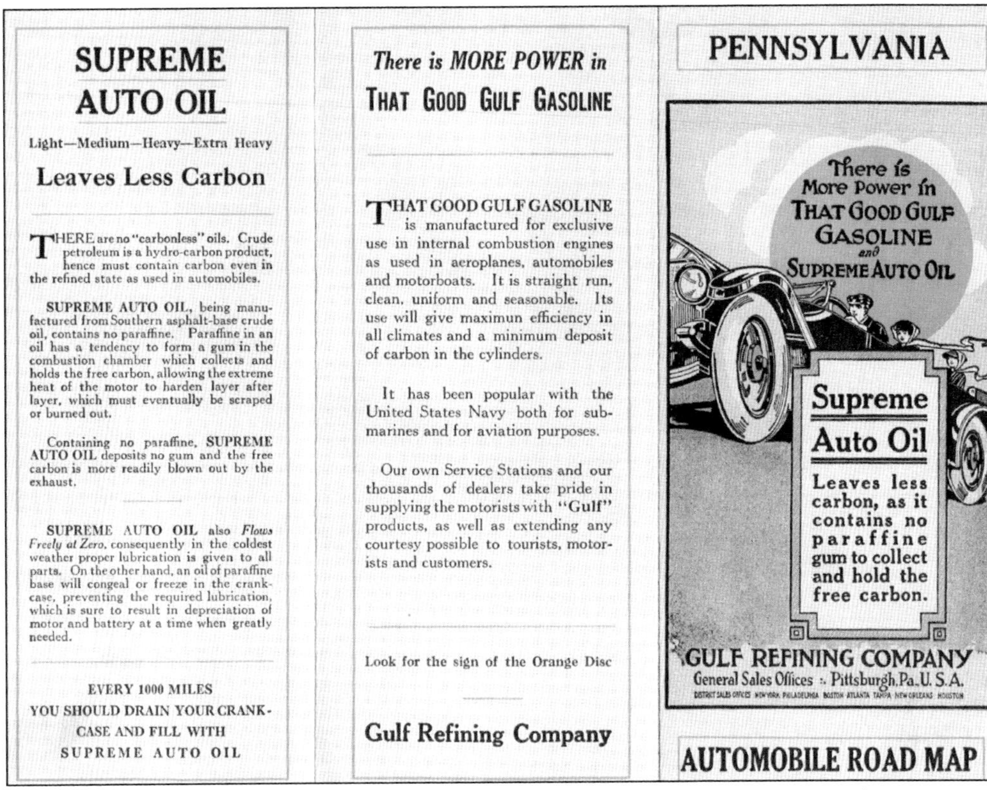

Navigating by automobile at the dawn of the 20th century was a difficult proposition, because maps appropriate for this new form of transportation were essentially nonexistent. An early solution was the creation of the route guide, which helped motorists travel the network of unmarked local roads. Early guidebooks were useful visual tools for the travel enthusiast, and by 1915, automobile manufacturers, tire companies, and some motor hotels began passing out less-detailed and complimentary maps to their customers. These free map resources would help to spark an advertising frenzy, which would catch the attention of petroleum refiners. The top image is a 1918 Gulf Refining Company automobile road map for the state of Pennsylvania. The bottom image is a road map for Oregon and Washington that was produced by the Northwest Refining Company of Montana.

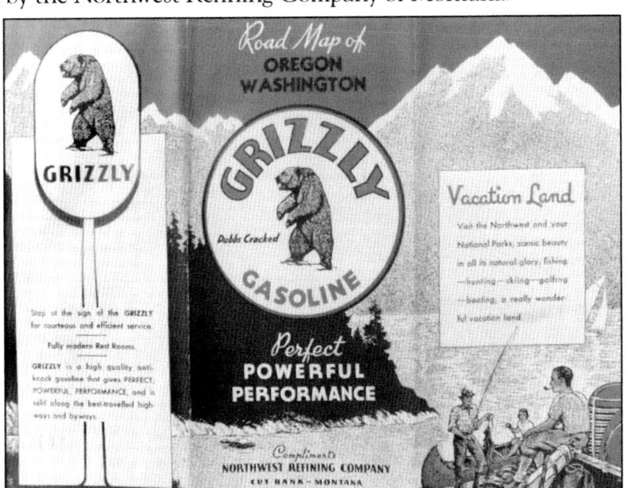

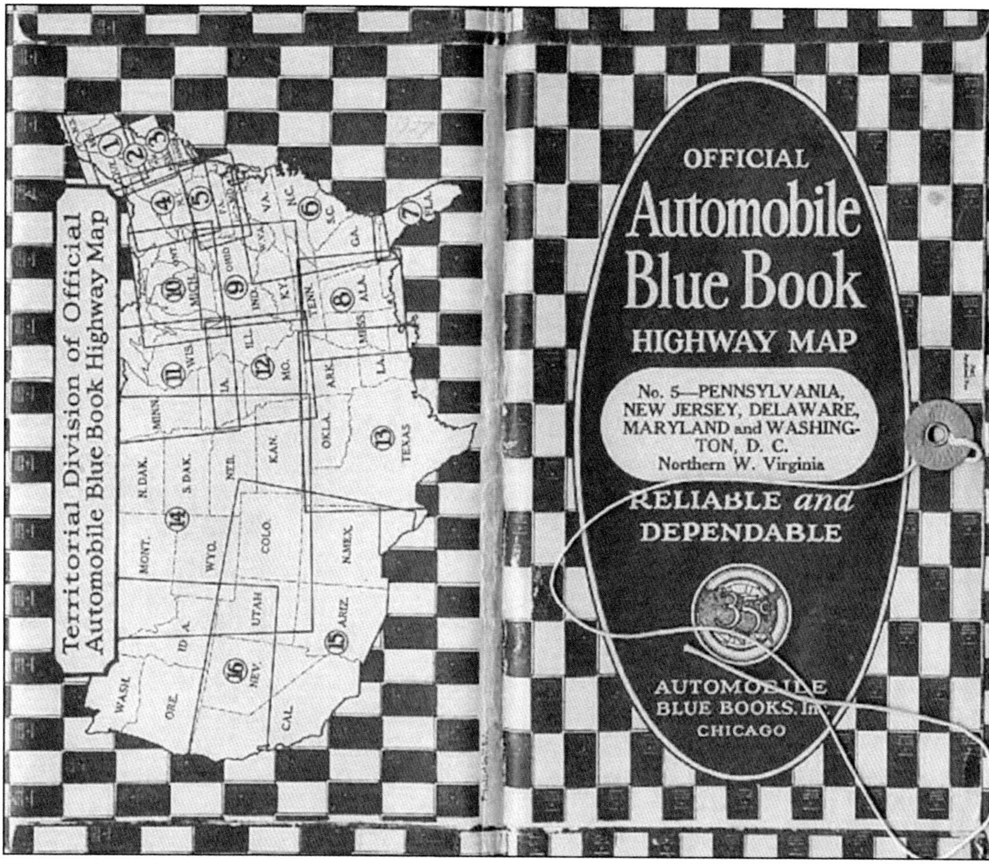

During the early years of road travel, the pioneering motorists traveling over the crude roads found routes that were poorly marked, if marked at all. Becoming lost while attempting to navigate the early roads was common. In the late 1890s and early 1900s, state road books, route books, automobile road guides, and route lists were regionally available to aid the motorist. By 1915, as roads were improved, organizations such as the Automobile Association of America introduced road guides in an effort to aid and assist their members. The *Official Automobile Blue Book*, shown in the top image, is an example of an early automobile road guidebook. The image on the right shows a typical map with available roads that would be found in the publication.

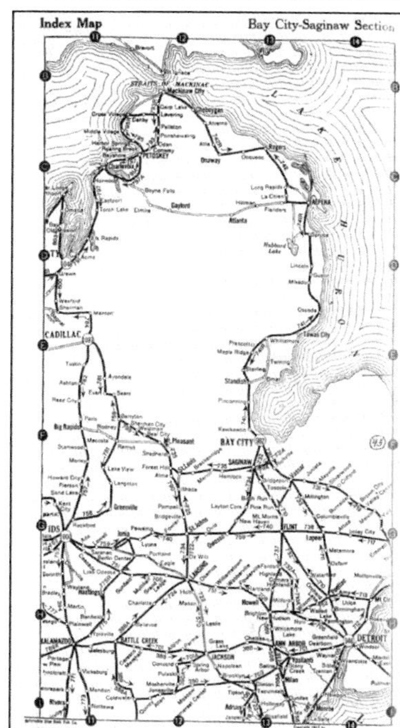

Even with the early route books and road guides, it was still difficult for the early motorist traveling along the Lincoln Highway. The early methods for showing the auto road tended to be descriptive in words and pictures. Typical entries in these automobile guides were often confusing and left travelers navigating using local landmarks, rivers, statues, cliffs, and man-made structures. A typical entry might read: "Enter Washington Park, curving slightly right and immediately taking left fork at open square, passing refectory building over to right." The image on the left shows a typical page and route entries in the *Official Automobile Blue Book.* The bottom image shows similar route entries found inside a *Goodrich Tires Route Book.*

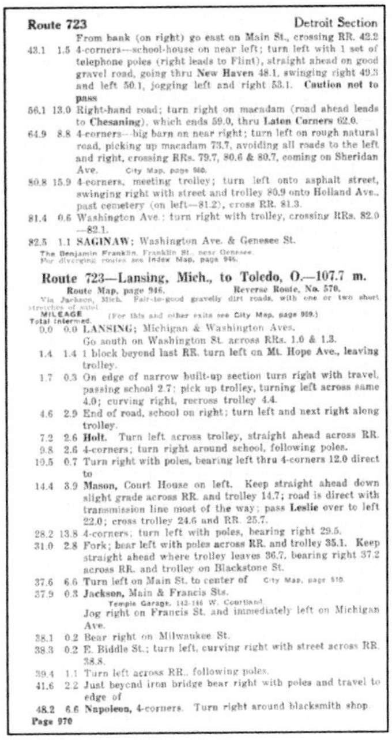

Route 723 Detroit Section

From bank (on right) go east on Main St., crossing RR. 42.2

43.1 1.5 4-corners—school-house on near left; turn left with 1 set of telephone poles (right leads to Flint), straight ahead on good gravel road, going thru **New Haven** 48.1, swinging right 49.3 and left 50.1, jogging left and right 53.1. **Caution not to pass**

56.1 13.0 Right-hand road; turn right on macadam (road ahead leads to **Chesaning**), which ends 59.0, thru **Laton Corners** 62.0.

64.9 8.8 4-corners—big barn on near right; turn left on rough natural road, picking up macadam 73.7, avoiding all roads to the left and right, crossing RRs. 79.7, 80.6 & 80.7, coming on Sheridan Ave. City Map, page 980.

80.8 15.9 4-corners, meeting trolley; turn left onto asphalt street, swinging right with street and trolley 80.9 onto Holland Ave., past cemetery (on left—81.2), cross RR. 81.3.

81.4 0.6 Washington Ave.; turn right with trolley, crossing RRs. 82.0—82.1.

82.5 1.1 **SAGINAW**; Washington Ave. & Genesee St.

The Benjamin Franklin, Franklin St., near Genesee.
For diverging routes see Index Map, page 946.

Route 723—Lansing, Mich., to Toledo, O.—107.7 m.

Route Map, page 946. Reverse Route, No. 570.

Via Jackson, Mich. Fair-to-good gravelly dirt roads, with one or two short stretches of sand.

MILEAGE (For this and other exits see City Map, page 959.)
Total Intermed.

0.0 0.0 **LANSING**; Michigan & Washington Aves. Go south on Washington St. across RRs. 1.0 & 1.3.

1.4 1.4 1 block beyond last RR. turn left on Mt. Hope Ave., leaving trolley.

1.7 0.3 On edge of narrow built-up section turn right with travel, passing school 2.7; pick up trolley, turning left across same 4.0; curving right, recross trolley 4.4.

4.6 2.9 End of road, school on right; turn left and next right along trolley.

7.2 2.6 **Holt.** Turn left across trolley, straight ahead across RR.

9.8 2.6 4-corners; turn right around school, following poles.

10.5 0.7 Turn right with poles, bearing left thru 4-corners 12.0 direct to

14.4 3.9 **Mason,** Court House on left. Keep straight ahead down slight grade across RR. and trolley 14.7; road is direct with transmission line most of the way; pass **Leslie** over to left 22.0; cross trolley 24.6 and RR. 25.7.

28.2 13.8 4-corners; turn left with poles, bearing right 29.5.

31.0 2.8 Fork; bear left with poles across RR. and trolley 35.1. Keep straight ahead where trolley leaves 36.7, bearing right 37.2 across RR. and trolley on Blackstone St.

37.6 6.6 Turn left on Main St. to center of City Map, page 510.

37.9 0.3 **Jackson,** Main & Francis Sts.
Temple Garage, 142-146 W. Courtland.
Jog right on Francis St. and immediately left on Michigan Ave.

38.1 0.2 Bear right on Milwaukee St.

38.3 0.2 E. Biddle St.; turn left, curving right with street across RR. 38.8.

39.4 1.1 Turn left across RR., following poles.

41.6 2.2 Just beyond iron bridge bear right with poles and travel to edge of

48.2 6.6 **Napoleon,** 4-corners. Turn right around blacksmith shop.

Page 970

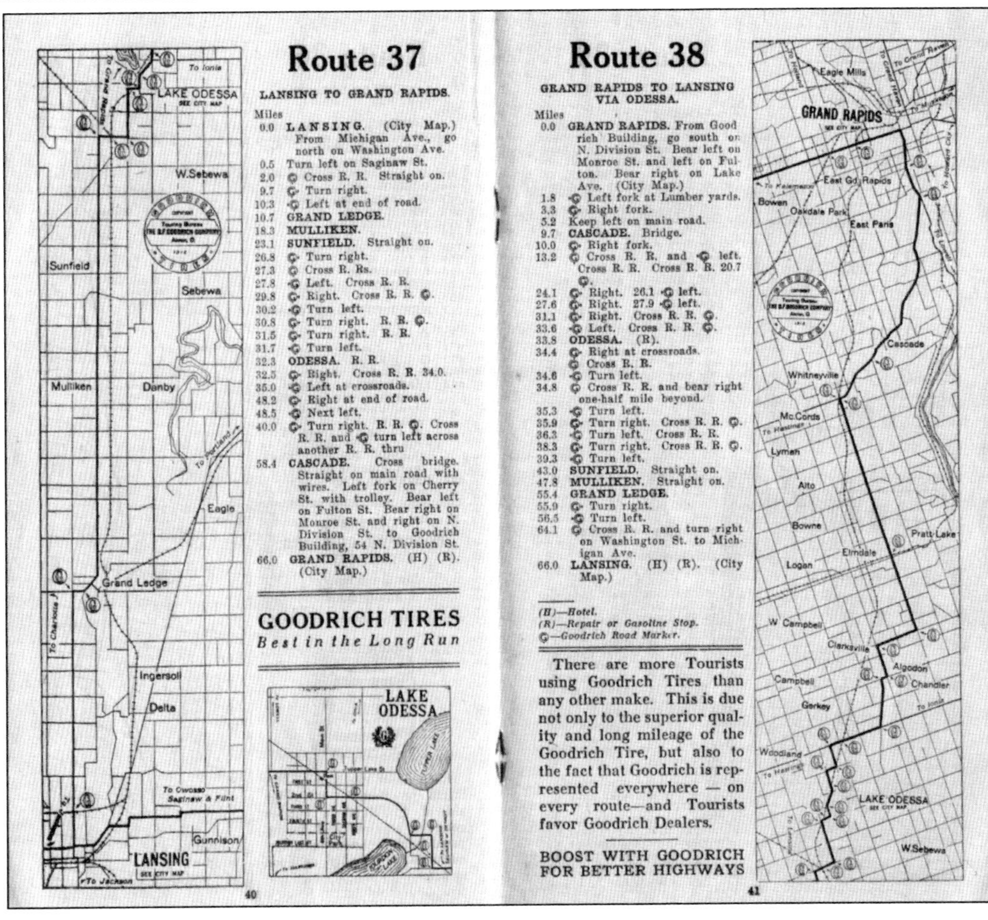

Route 37

LANSING TO GRAND RAPIDS.

Miles
0.0 LANSING. (City Map.) From Michigan Ave., go north on Washington Ave.
0.5 Turn left on Saginaw St.
2.0 Cross R. R. Straight on.
9.7 Turn right.
10.3 Left at end of road.
10.7 GRAND LEDGE.
18.3 MULLIKEN.
23.1 SUNFIELD. Straight on.
26.8 Turn right.
27.3 Cross R. Rs.
27.8 Left. Cross R. R.
29.8 Right. Cross R. R.
30.2 Turn left.
30.8 Turn right. R. R.
31.5 Turn right. R. R.
31.7 Turn left.
32.3 ODESSA. R. R.
32.5 Right. Cross R. R. 34.0.
35.0 Left at crossroads.
48.2 Right at end of road.
48.5 Next left.
40.0 Turn right. R. R. Cross R. R. and turn left across another R. R. thru
58.4 CASCADE. Cross bridge. Straight on main road with wires. Left fork on Cherry St. with trolley. Bear left on Fulton St. Bear right on Monroe St. and right on N. Division St. to Goodrich Building, 54 N. Division St.
66.0 GRAND RAPIDS. (H) (R). (City Map.)

GOODRICH TIRES
Best in the Long Run

LAKE ODESSA

40

Route 38

GRAND RAPIDS TO LANSING VIA ODESSA.

Miles
0.0 GRAND RAPIDS. From Goodrich Building, go south on N. Division St. Bear left on Monroe St. and left on Fulton. Bear right on Lake Ave. (City Map.)
1.8 Left fork at Lumber yards.
3.3 Right fork.
5.2 Keep left on main road.
9.7 CASCADE. Bridge.
10.0 Right fork.
13.2 Cross R. R. and left. Cross R. R. Cross R. R. 20.7
24.1 Right. 26.1 left.
27.6 Right. 27.9 left.
31.1 Right. Cross R. R.
33.6 Left. Cross R. R.
33.8 ODESSA. (R).
34.4 Right at crossroads. Cross R. R.
34.6 Turn left.
34.8 Cross R. R. and bear right one-half mile beyond.
35.3 Turn left.
35.9 Turn right. Cross R. R.
36.3 Turn left. Cross R. R.
38.3 Turn right. Cross R. R.
39.3 Turn left.
43.0 SUNFIELD. Straight on.
47.8 MULLIKEN. Straight on.
55.4 GRAND LEDGE.
55.9 Turn right.
56.5 Turn left.
64.1 Cross R. R. and turn right on Washington St. to Michigan Ave.
66.0 LANSING. (H) (R). (City Map.)

(H)—Hotel.
(R)—Repair or Gasoline Stop.
—Goodrich Road Marker.

There are more Tourists using Goodrich Tires than any other make. This is due not only to the superior quality and long mileage of the Goodrich Tire, but also to the fact that Goodrich is represented everywhere — on every route—and Tourists favor Goodrich Dealers.

BOOST WITH GOODRICH FOR BETTER HIGHWAYS

41

Automobile clubs, road and highway associations, and other travel-related organizations sponsored or published road guides during the first three decades of the early 20th century. Such publications included the *Automobile Green Book*, official guide book of the Automobile Legal Association of Massachusetts; *King's Official Route Guide*, published by Sidney J. King of Chicago, Illinois; the *Interstate Automobile Tourists' Guide*, published by F.S. Blanchard and Company of Worchester, Massachusetts; and the *Official Automobile Blue Book*, published by the Automobile Blue Book Publishing Company of New York. The image on the right shows the front cover of the 1915 *Automobile Blue Book*, Middle West version. The bottom image is the cover of the 1916 *Goodrich Tires Route Book* for Michigan. This version also includes guide instructions for traveling a route from Chicago, Illinois, to Cleveland, Ohio.

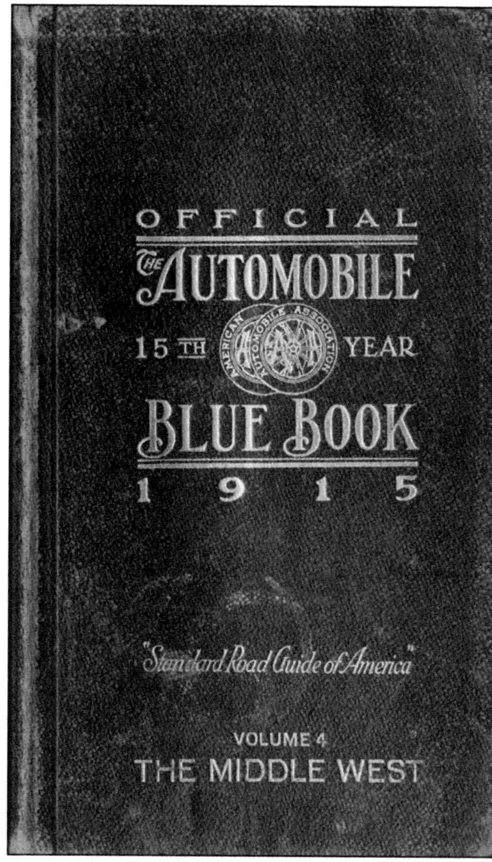

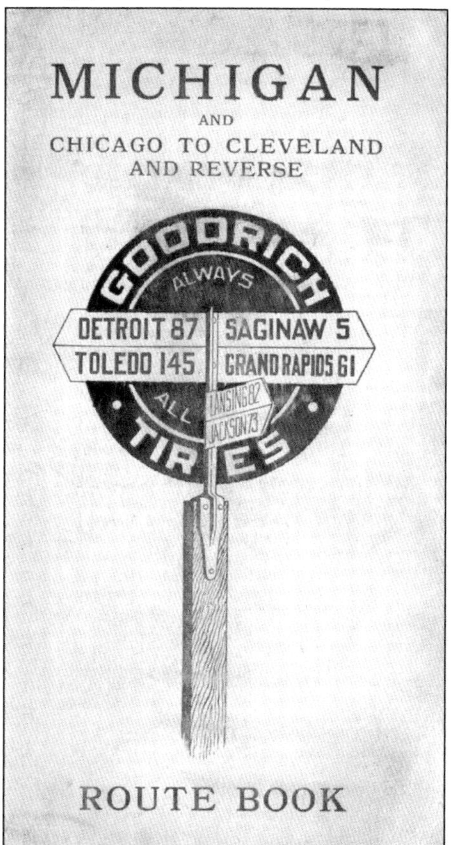

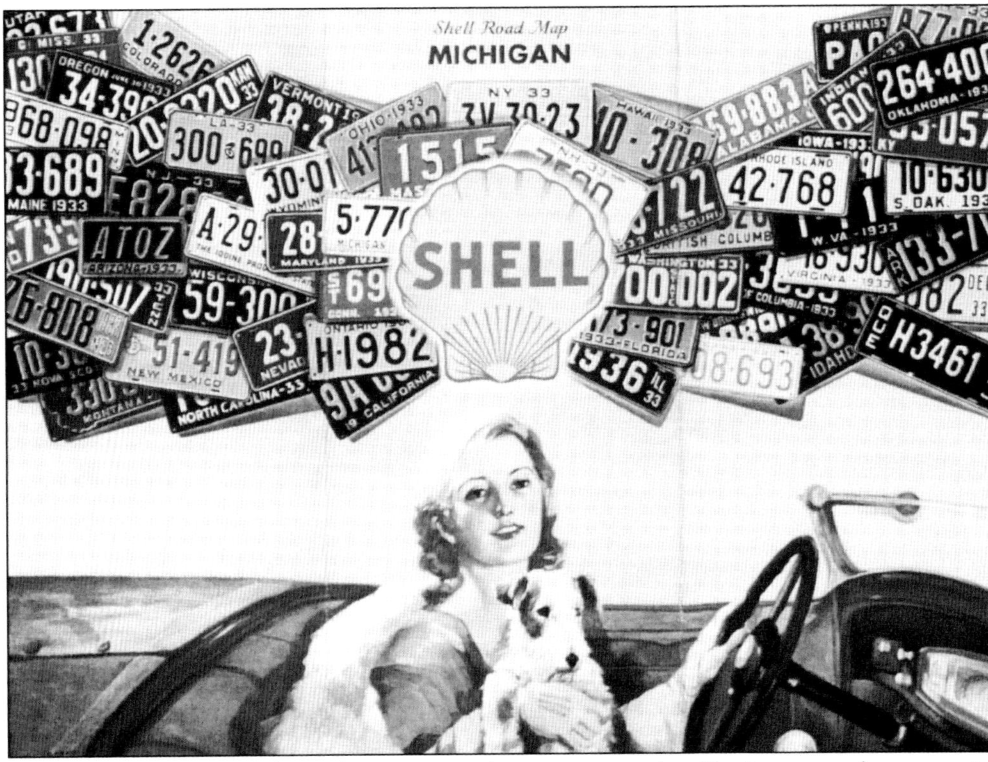

After 1910, the automobile age began to accelerate as a parade of businesses and commercial organizations began to offer brand name promotional maps and guides to the motoring public. By 1912, oil companies, such as Vacuum Oil Company, the Union Oil Company of Los Angeles, and the Monarch Oil Refining Company, were offering free, or nearly free, maps to their customers. The Gulf Oil Company has long proclaimed itself to be the sole initiator and developer of the first free oil-company road map. Prompted by the suggestion of William B. Akin, a local advertising man from Pittsburgh, the company mailed out thousands of free Allegheny County, Pennsylvania, maps to registered motorists in the county. The success of this marketing idea led Gulf Oil and other oil companies that joined the fray to produce more detailed and colorful maps for motorists. These Shell Oil Company maps from the early 1930s are typical of those produced by oil companies during this era.

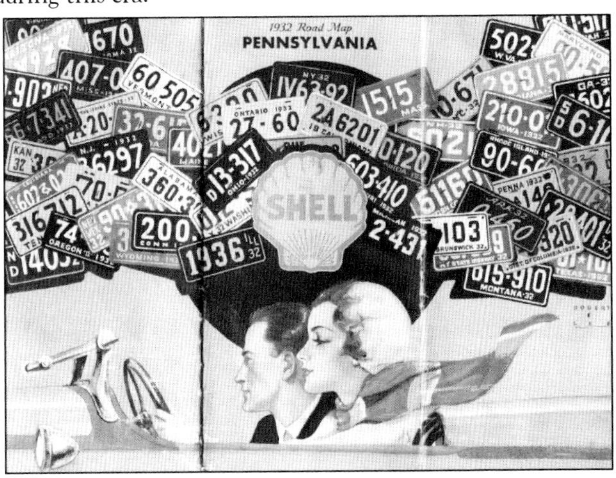

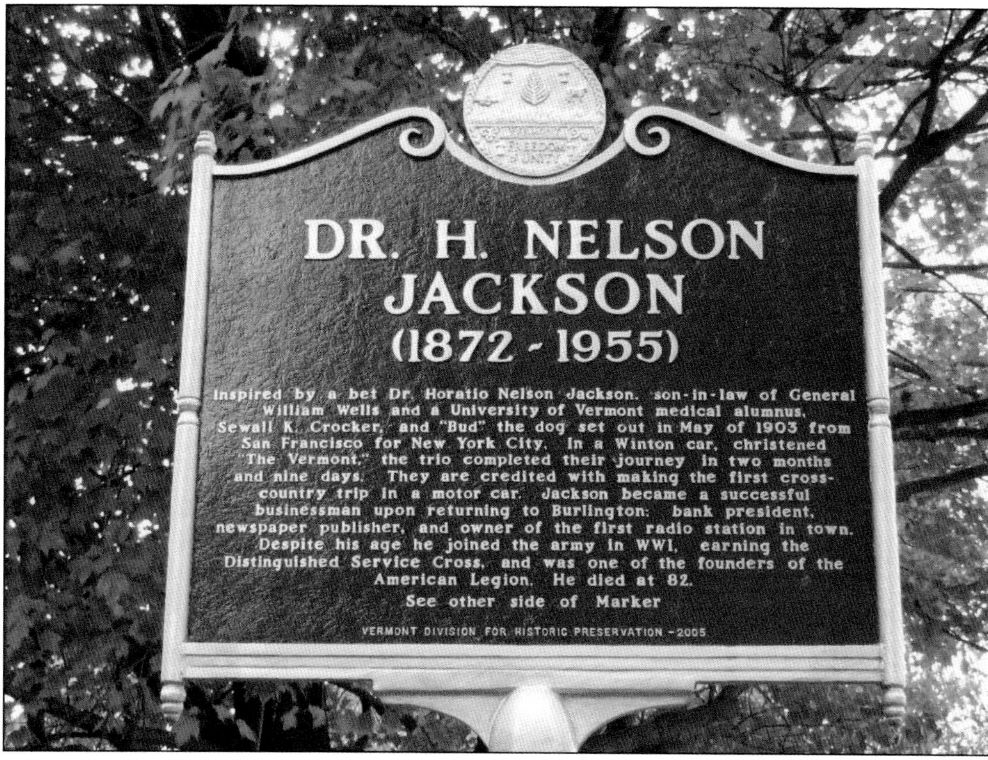

When Dr. Horatio Nelson Jackson completed the first transcontinental crossing by automobile from San Francisco to New York in 1903, the United States was in the midst of the golden age of railroads. Most people had yet to actually see an automobile or even drive one of these unique "horseless carriages." Dr. Jackson, his mechanic Sewall K. Crocker, and a light-colored bulldog named Bud spent 63 days on their historic trip, traveling over 4,000 miles. Their journey took more than two months because the roads at the time were in poor condition at best in certain locations and nonexistent in others. They had difficulty navigating because road maps and signs were extremely rare. The top image shows a historical marker commemorating Jackson's cross-country trip located near the corner of South Willard and Main Streets in Burlington, Vermont. The bottom image shows the typical dirt road conditions that Jackson experienced along his journey.

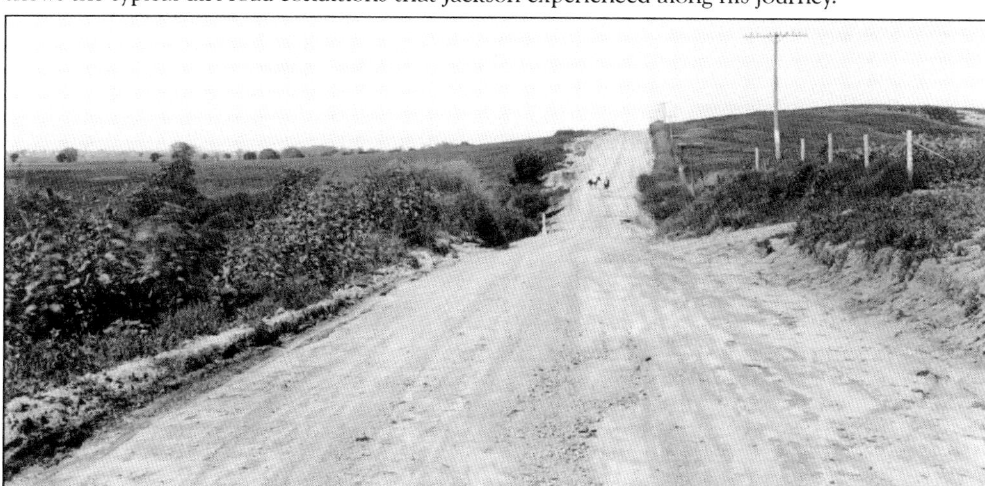

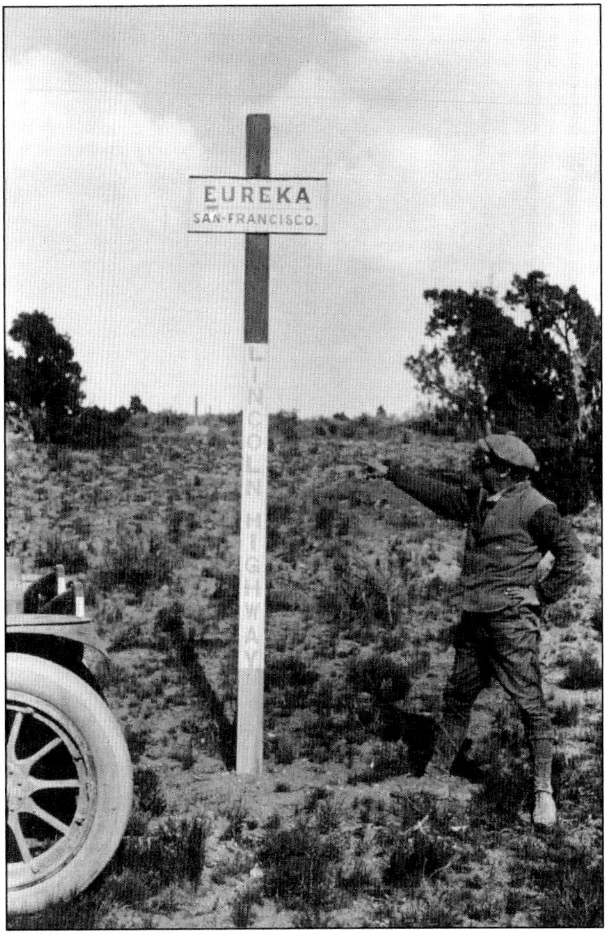

After the success of Dr. Horatio Nelson Jackson's transcontinental trip and the publicity that followed his endeavor, the automobile and distant travel became part of the public consciousness. Soon, other automobile adventurers set out on local and distant journeys, often testing their endurance, navigation prowess, and dexterity. With the increasing popularity of automobile touring came the need for navigation aids, as early adventurers were accustomed to geographic route-finding, which was often local in scope. People knew how to navigate on foot or by horse and buggy from prior experience or mental maps. As a result, road signs were not needed and rarely found in the local landscape. A trip by automobile, however, required navigation aids. In time, road signs became common sites along roadbeds, and before standardization, they were as unique as the locations they represented. These images show typical road signs in the early years of the Lincoln Highway.

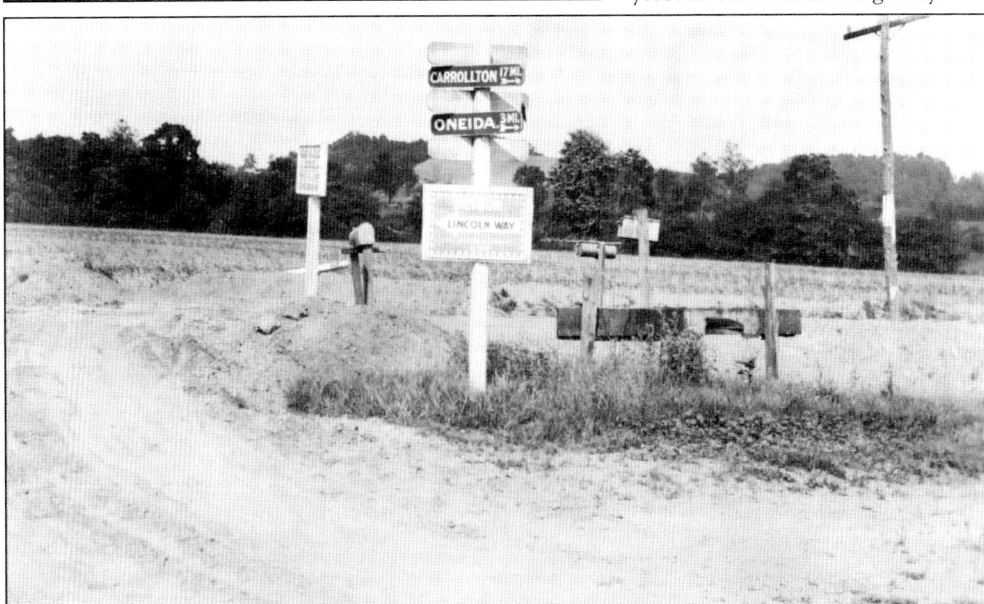

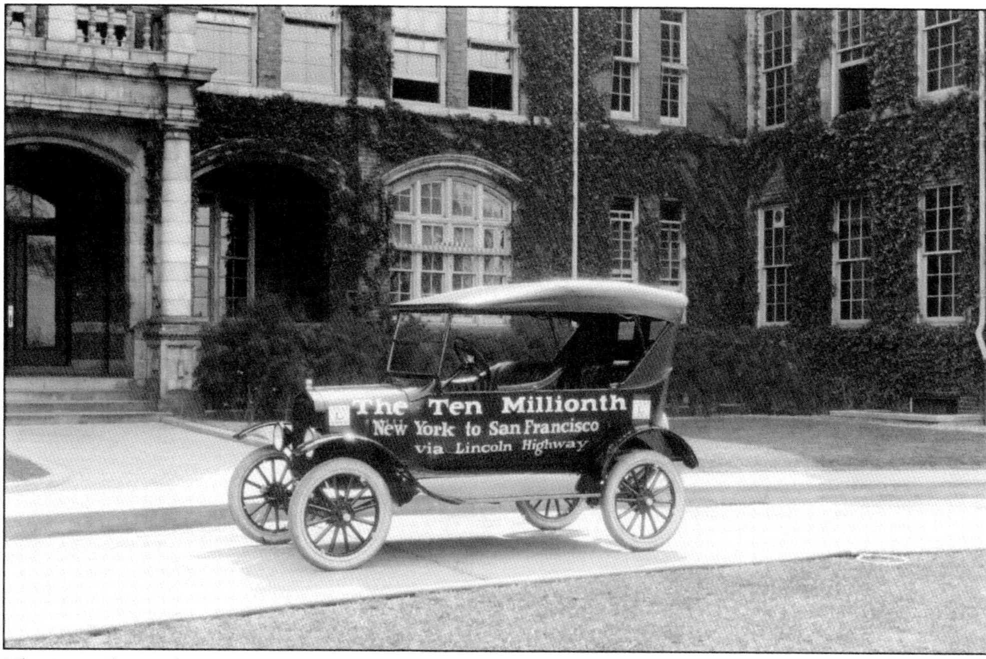

The Lincoln Highway was America's first transcontinental interstate highway that was planned to be used by automobiles, trucks, and motorcycles. The idea of constructing such a road was radical for the time not only because it was considered a major technological undertaking but also because the idea originated in the private sector, not in the government. The concept was first proposed by Carl G. Fisher, who was an entrepreneur with big ideas. In 1909, his Indianapolis Motor Speedway became a huge success after it was paved with over 3 million bricks, and it was inaugurated with the first Indianapolis 500 motorcar race on May 30, 1911. Within a decade, Americans would take the roads as millions of automobiles were manufactured to meet the demand. In 1924, Henry Ford produced his 10 millionth Model T. As a publicity stunt, the car was painted with Lincoln Highway lettering and driven on the highway from New York to San Francisco by Frank Kulich, a well-known racing star. These images show the official 10-millionth automobile.

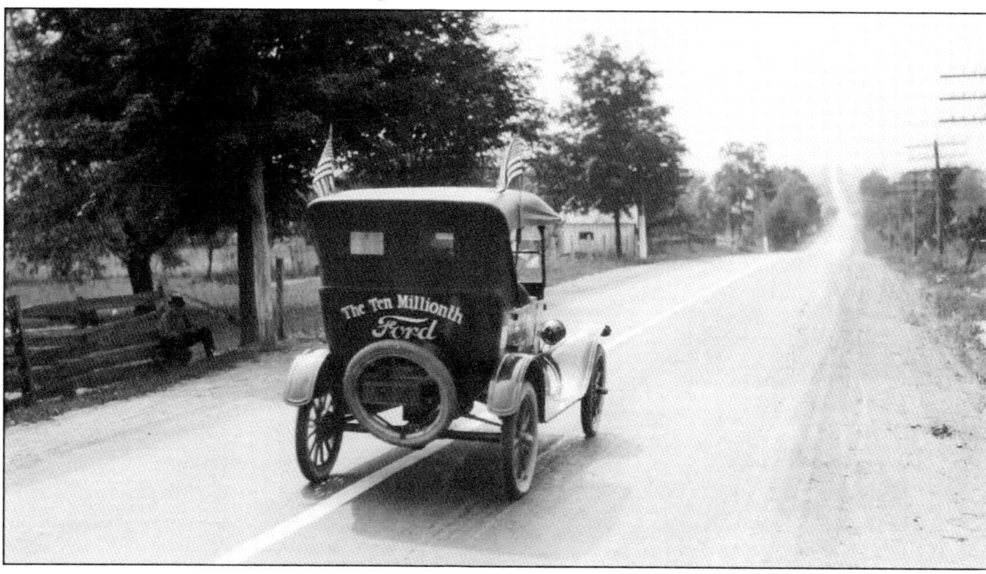

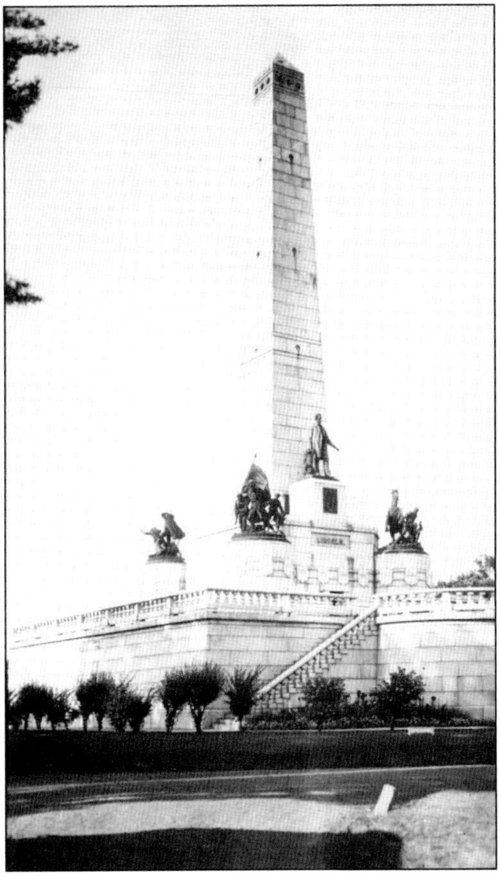

By 1912, Fisher conceived the idea of creating an automobile-friendly, gravel-surfaced road spanning across America from New York to San Francisco. He referred to his dream highway as the "Coast-to-Coast Rock Highway." Fisher embarked on a promotional tour across the county to secure private financing for his dream, which he estimated would cost in excess of $10 million and take two years to build. By 1913, a group of automobile executives formally established an organization to help make Fisher's idea a reality. That organization was chartered as the Lincoln Highway Association and adopted a goal to "immediately promote and procure the establishment of a continuous improved highway from the Atlantic to the Pacific." The image on the left shows a view of Abraham Lincoln's tomb in Springfield, Illinois. The bottom image shows a Lincoln Highway memorial fountain located along the roadway in Creston, Illinois.

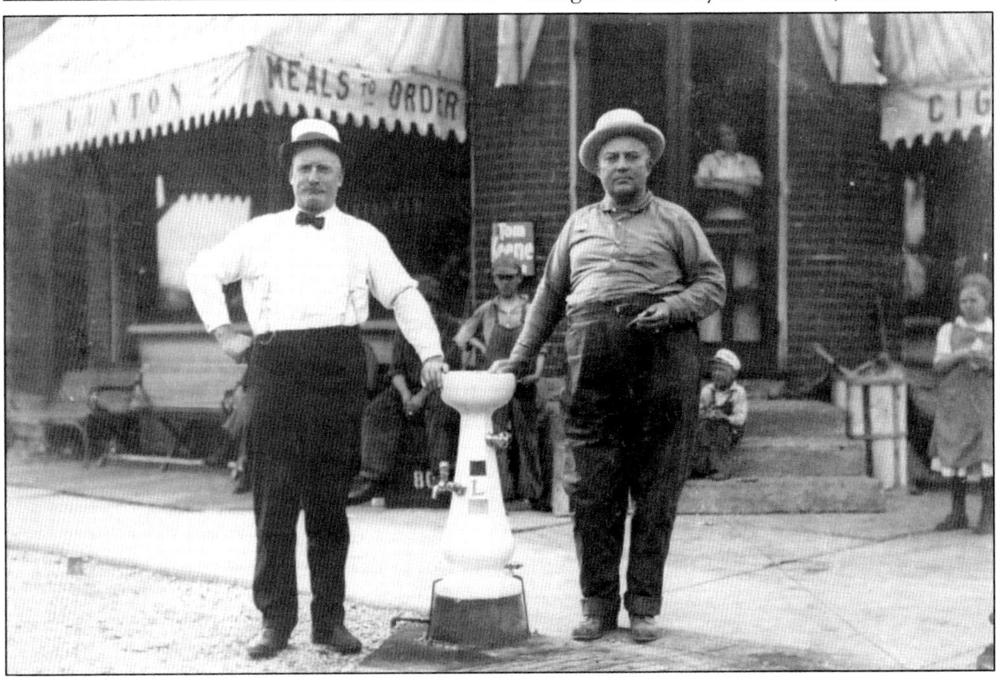

In 1913, a group of visionary businessmen from the automotive industry formed the Lincoln Highway Association. Led by Henry B. Joy and Carl Graham Fisher, the association—which was made up of representatives from the automobile, tire, and cement industries—led the charge for the creation of a publicly funded road that stretched from New York to San Francisco. The goal of the association was the planning, funding, constructing, and promoting of the project. Traveling through 13 states and stretching nearly 3,400 miles, the Lincoln Highway would become the first transcontinental highway in America. The right photograph is of Carl Fisher, and the bottom photograph is of Henry Joy.

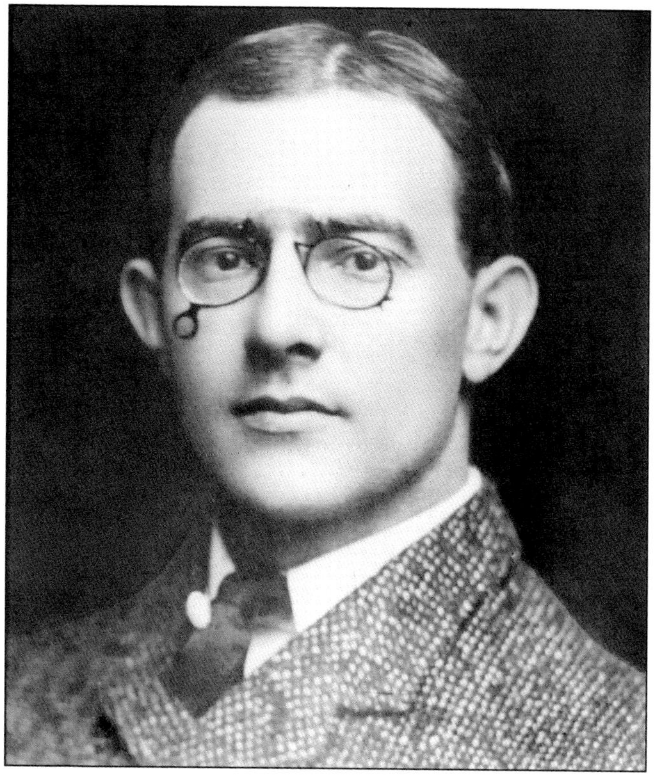

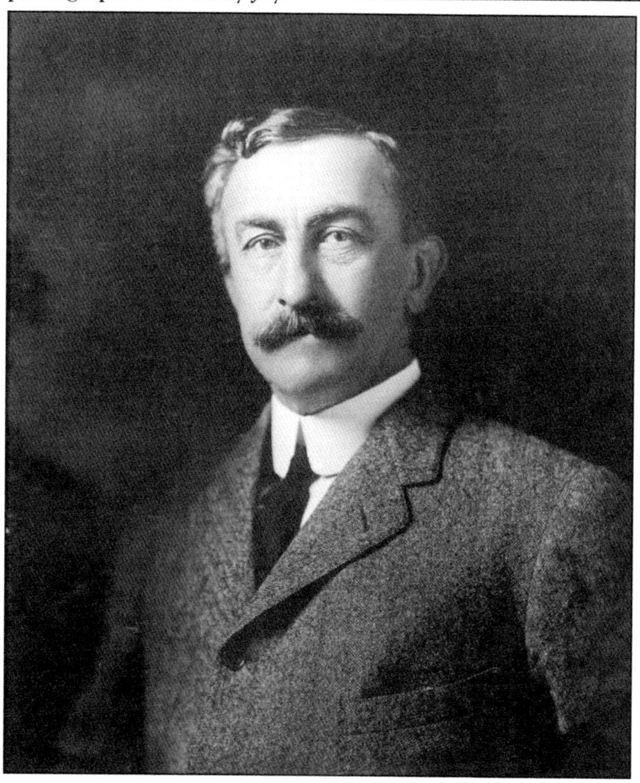

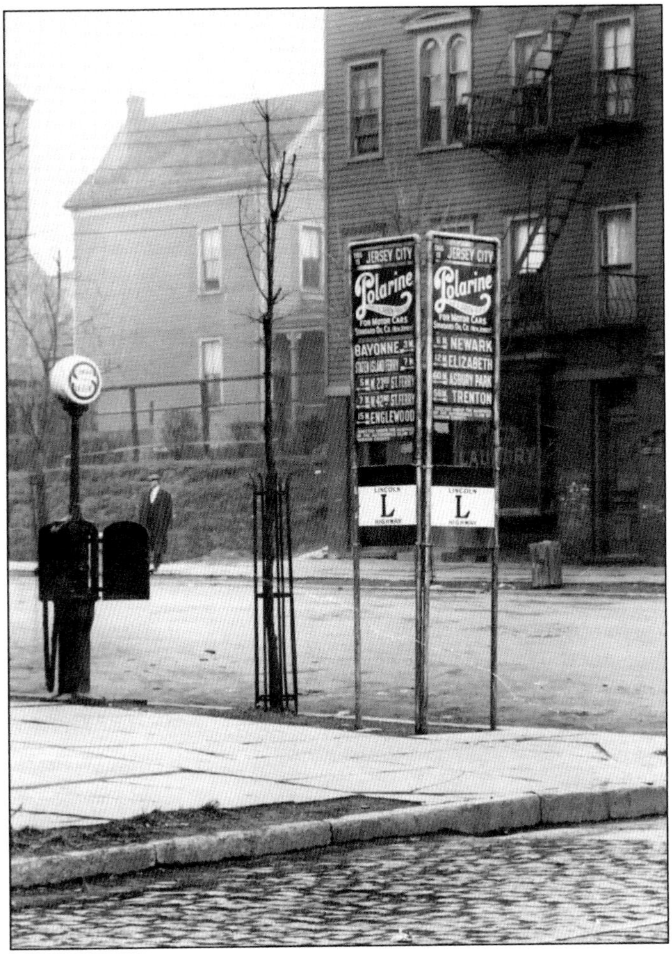

Soon, many donors did contribute or pledge donations to help build the road, but the Lincoln Highway Association (LHA) had hoped to target Henry Ford, one of the wealthiest men in the country, to help fund the project, as he was the nation's largest manufacturer of automobiles and trucks. Ford's refusal to donate to the LHA or to any road-building projects effectively ended the LHA's plans for actually constructing the gravel coast-to-coast highway. Ford believed that government, not private individuals or American companies, should support the construction of the nation's roadways. Instead, the association needed to approach the idea for a coast-to-coast roadway by using existing roads and label them Lincolnway or the Lincoln Highway. These images show typical highway markers used to identify the roadway during the 1920s.

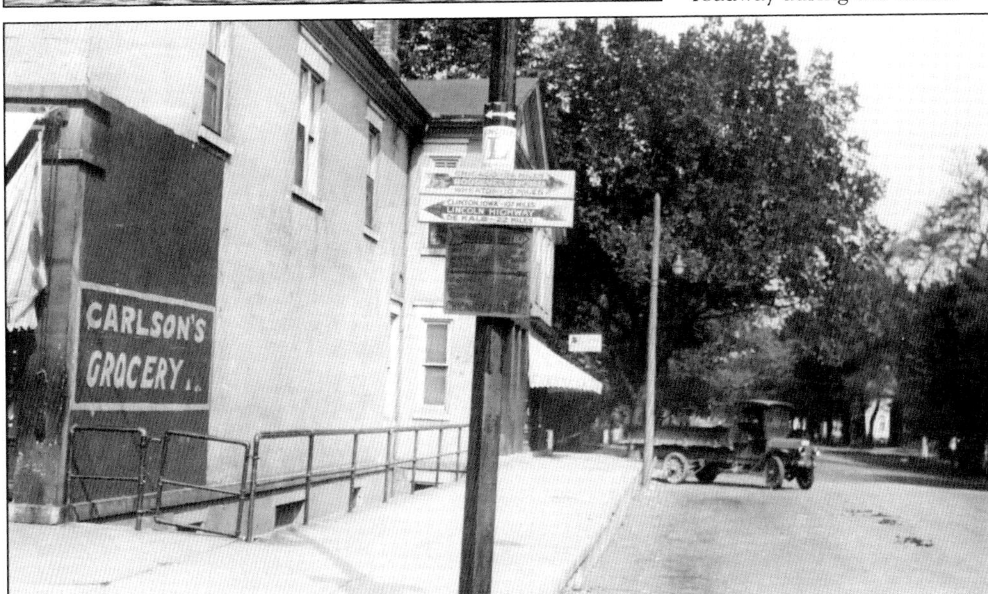

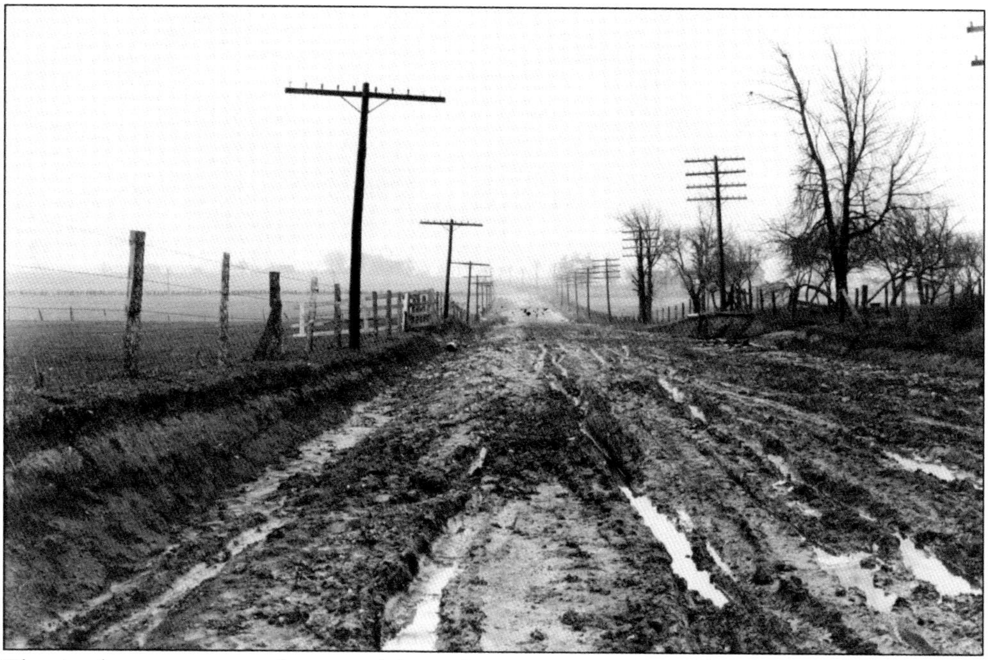

The simplest answer to early automobile road construction was to allow automobiles to use old, well-worn wagon roadways. While this was certainly a cheap solution, it did not address the larger problem of providing good roads for the traveling public. Unimproved roads were rough and unsafe, and often the extent of roughness was clear to all drivers. Many would travel with a shovel to help fill in a rut in the road or dig out the automobile, as was often the case, especially in wet conditions. The above image showing a muddy, rutted road 14 miles east of the Illinois border in Indiana was a common site in the early years on some sections of the Lincoln Highway. The bottom picture shows a typical dirt road section of the highway looking east near the state line.

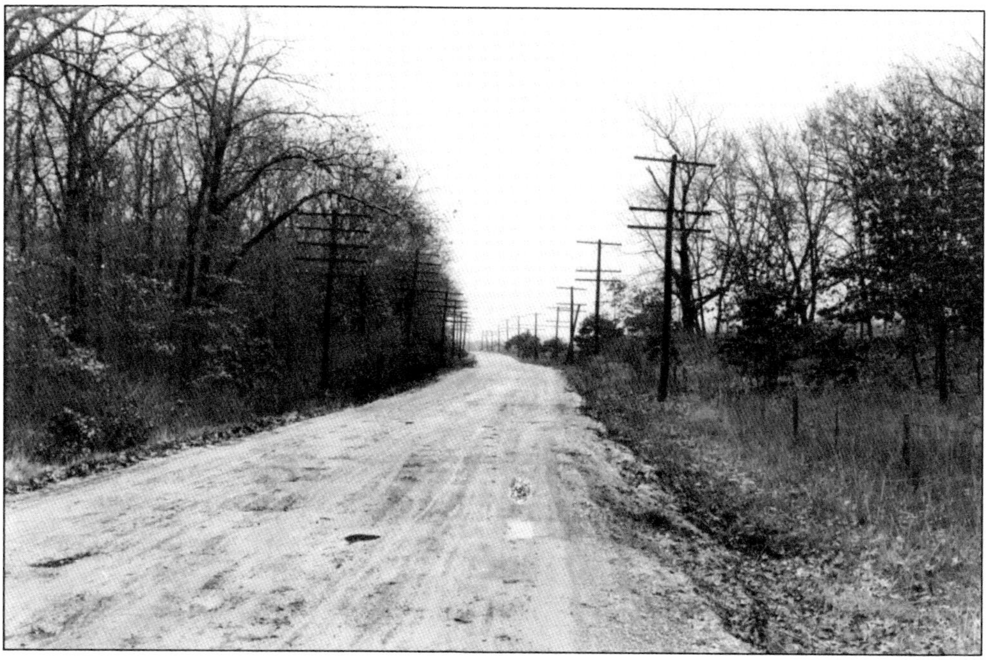

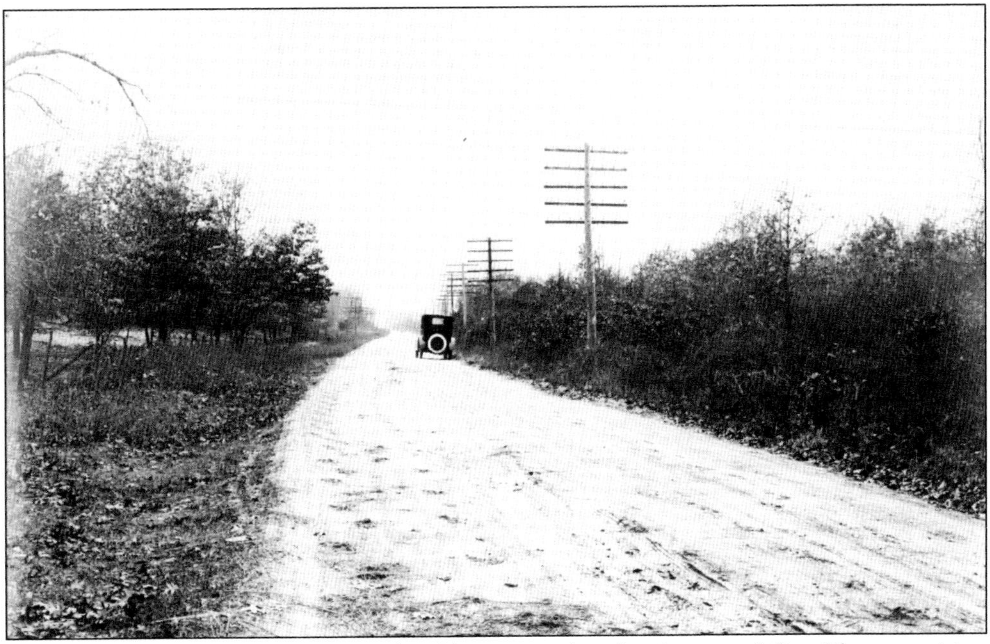

Until the late 1890s, roads were considered by many to be a local responsibility. The supervision of the roads often fell to elected officials, but the basic maintenance was left up to local residents. In some locations, county officials were given more responsibility for the creation and upkeep of the public roads. At the same time, the US government also took a more active role in road development and, in 1893, created the Office of Public Road Inquires to help advise state and local officials on the best methods of improving roads. Within a decade, all levels of local government were beginning to feel pressure to create "good roads." The top and bottom images show typical dirt road sections of the Lincoln Highway near the Illinois and Indiana border. With the passage of federal funding legislation in 1916, unpaved sections of the highway like this would soon be graded and improved to handle increased traffic loads that were common by the 1920s.

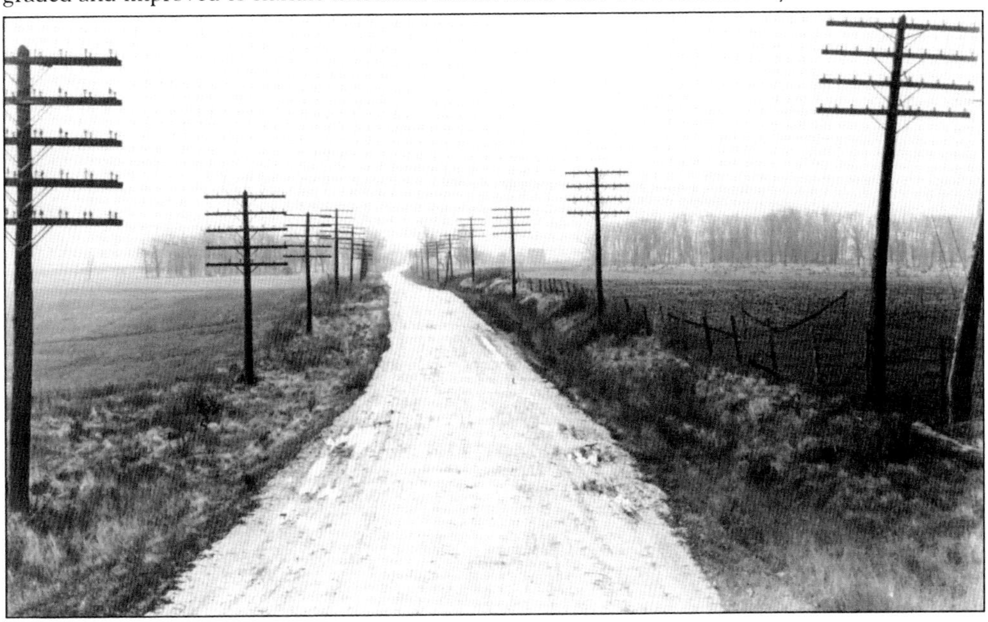

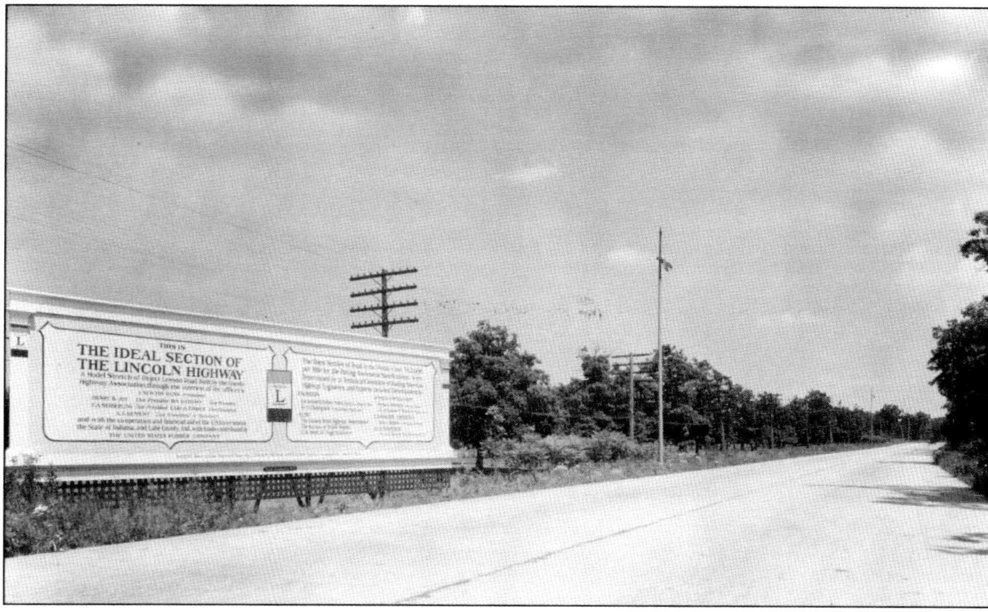

The LHA helped start and refine the nature of road building in the early 20th century. The Seedling Mile program began in 1914 with the construction of the first Seedling Mile west of Malta, Illinois. Using Portland cement, these improved road sections were also constructed in Ohio, Indiana, Iowa, and Nebraska. In 1920, the LHA started work on the ultimate Seedling Mile, a short stretch of road constructed to the highest standards in Dyer, Indiana. A 1.3-mile section of rural road was selected and built as a four-lane, concrete highway bordered by pedestrian walkways and illuminated with electric lights. Opened in 1923, the Ideal Section incorporated many new innovative highway features and was considered a model for highway construction for the future. The Ideal Section handled traffic until 1997, when US 30 was widened in that location. These images show sections of the Ideal Section shortly after construction was completed.

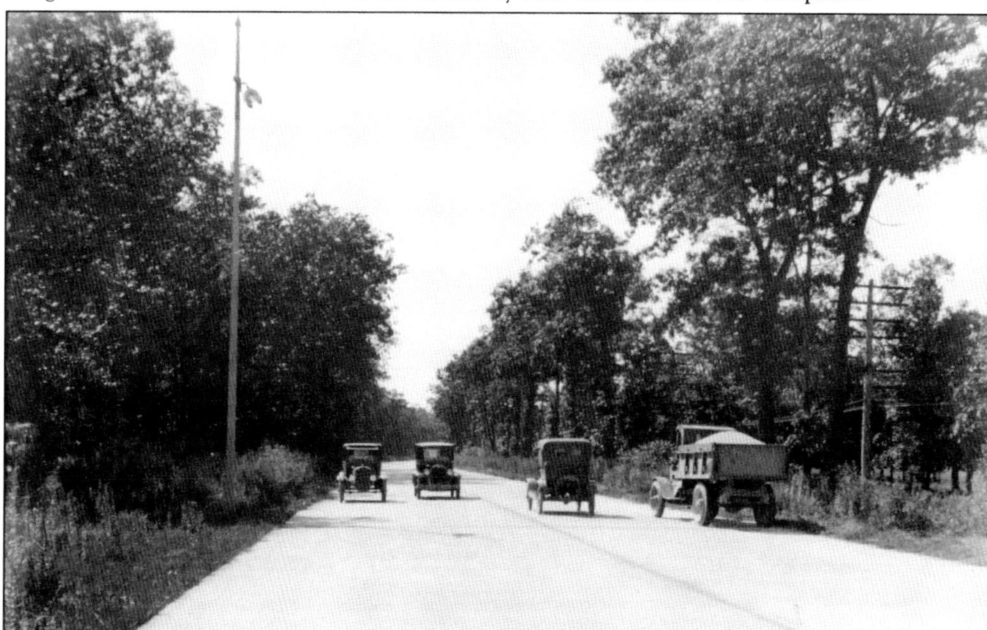

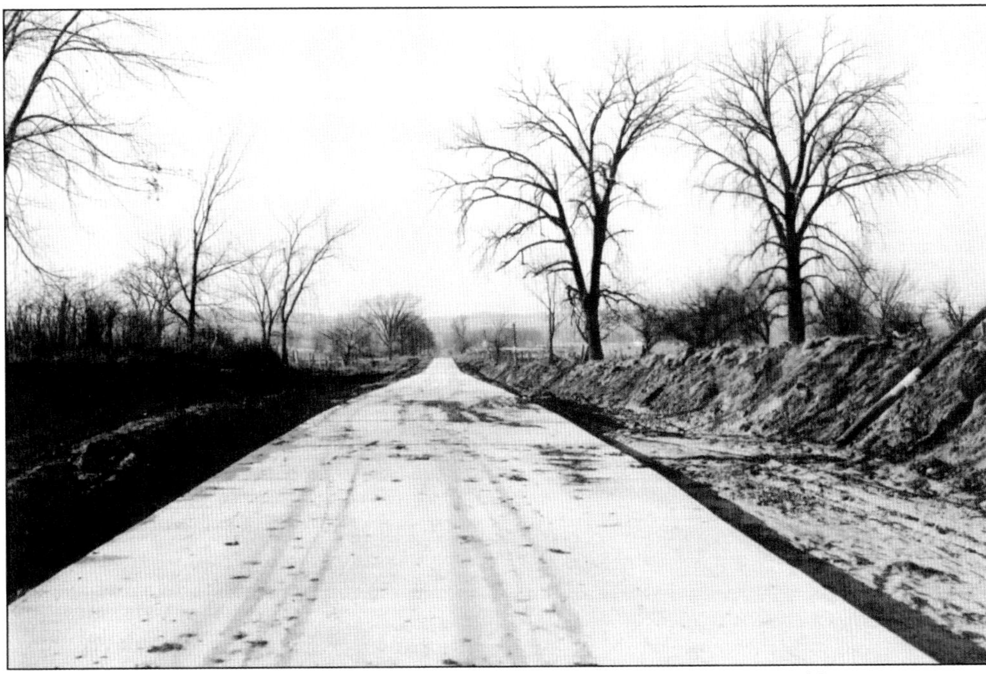

Without government funds or the proper private financing, the LHA was not able to construct an actual new road but could use existing roads that could be properly marked as the official route, regardless of the road's surface—whether it be gravel, dirt, brick, or the like. Soon the LHA's new strategy included not only marking the new route and encouraging towns along the route to rename the road but also enticing local governments to help improve the route by pouring concrete sections to make it a model highway for the public. These new sections were referred to as Seedling Miles. The top image shows a Seedling Mile in Linn County, Iowa. A Seedling Mile near the west edge of Kearney, Nebraska, is shown in the bottom image.

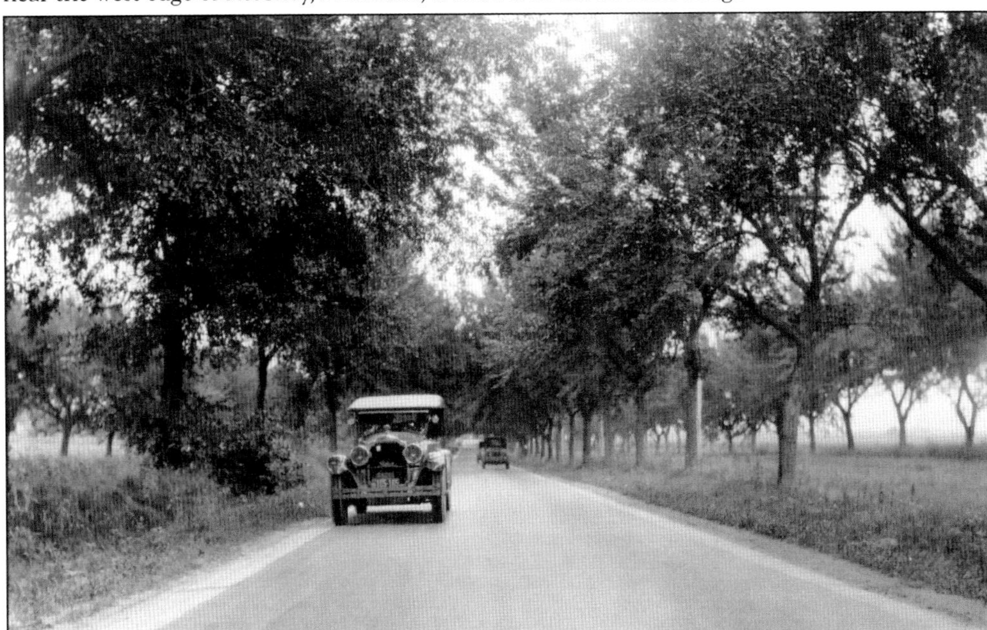

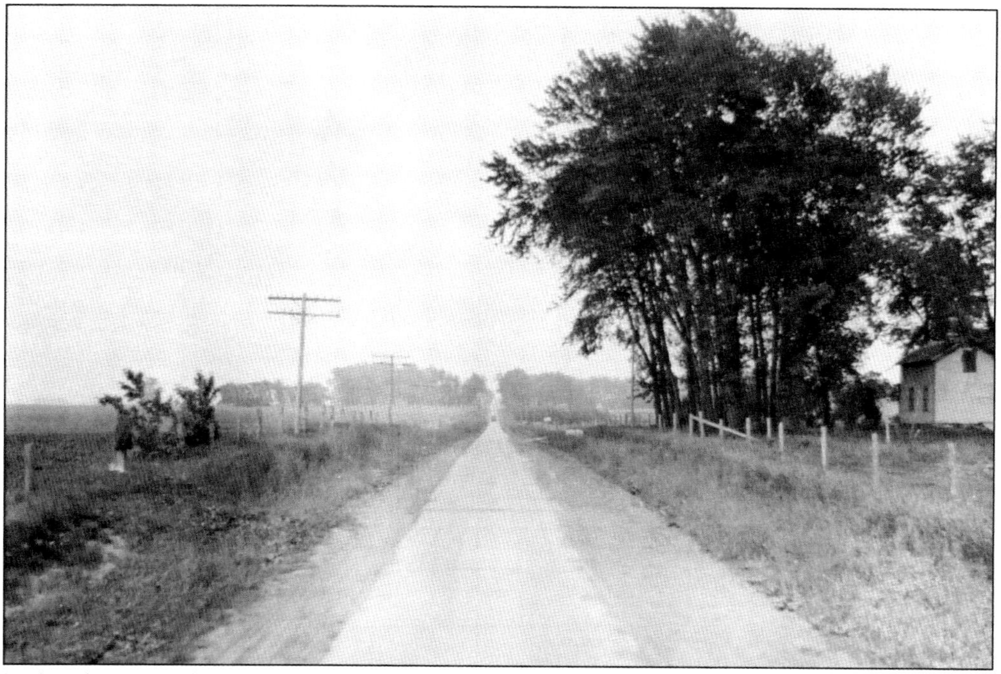

Built at locations that were often considered muddy stretches of dirt road, concrete Seedling Miles would serve as prototypes of what modern engineering could produce to help improve highways across the nation. The first of these Seedling Miles was constructed near Malta, Illinois. The Malta Seedling Mile, a former dirt and gravel road, became one of the first experiments in the use of concrete to create a better hard-surface road. The entire project, funded with private donations, took 14 months to complete and was finished in 1914. The section of road was only 10 feet wide and was engineered to last 20 years. These images show portions of the first Seedling Mile just west of Malta, Illinois.

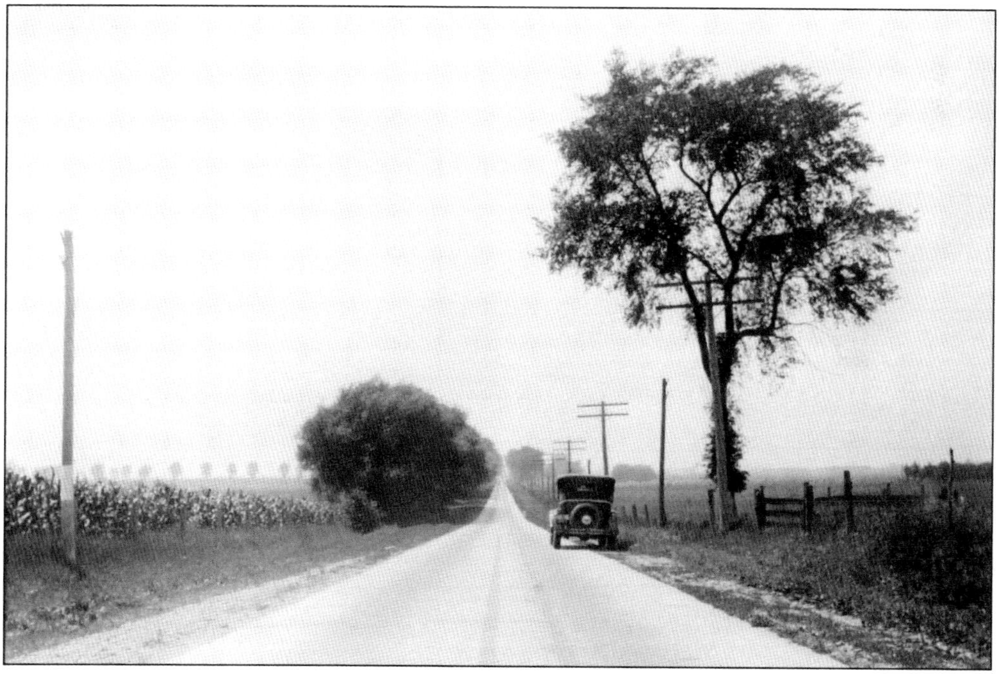

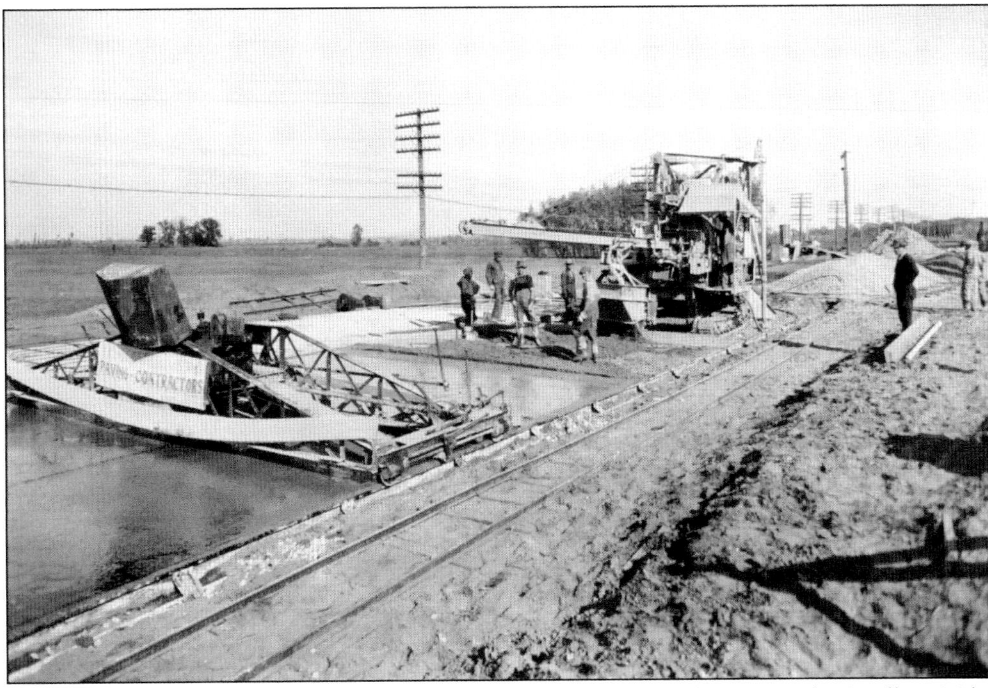

With the assistance of the Portland Cement Company, the LHA also initiated a Seedling Miles program, which consisted of building short sections of concrete highway along poor stretches of country dirt roads. The idea was to illustrate to the public that local tax dollars could help to build good, durable, concrete roadways. The LHA's main objective was to encourage local communities to help fund additional paving projects that would reach the Seedling Miles from either side. The first Seedling Mile along the highway was completed west of Malta, Illinois, in 1914. Iowa's Seedling Mile was constructed in 1918–1919 between Cedar Rapids and Mount Vernon. This stretch of road eventually became part of a continuously paved section of the Lincoln Highway between Chicago and Cedar Rapids, Iowa. The top and bottom images here show the typical paving and mixing machines that were utilized to construct the concrete sections of the highway.

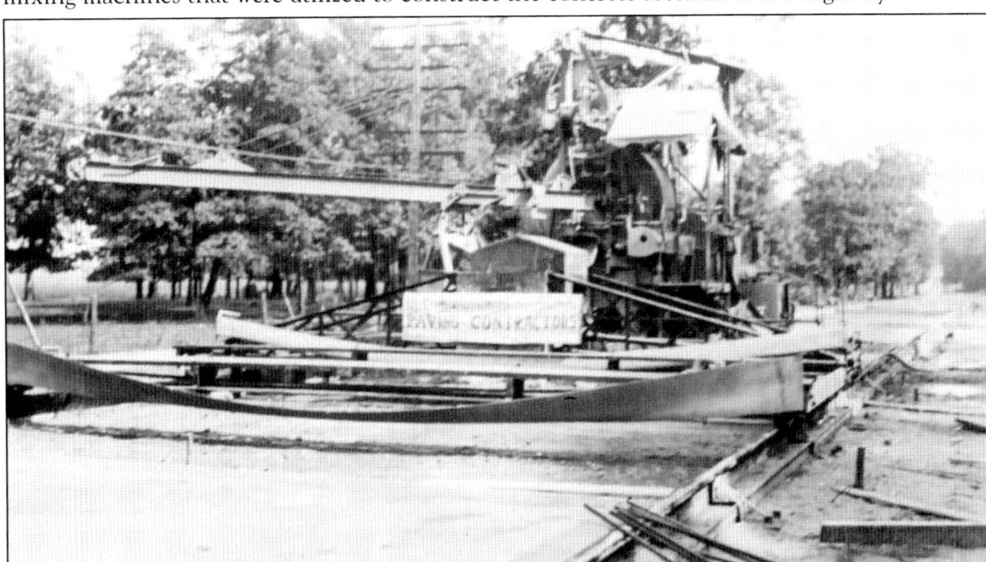

Early in 1919, the Lincoln Highway Association leader, Harry Ostermann, persuaded the US War Department to conduct a transcontinental motor convoy trip from the East Coast to San Francisco on the marked route of the Lincoln Highway. Officially named the Transcontinental Motor Convoy of 1919, the caravan was composed of nearly 300 men and 81 US Army vehicles, including numerous nonmilitary autos and trucks. Although the operation served as a military training exercise and recruiting tool, the true objective of the convoy was to test the feasibility of long-distance movement of military men and supplies by automobile and truck. A young lieutenant colonel named Dwight D. Eisenhower participated in this motor convey, and this early experience influenced his later decisions concerning the building of the interstate highway system during his presidency. The image on the right shows a young Harry Ostermann, and the bottom image shows Dwight Eisenhower during World War II.

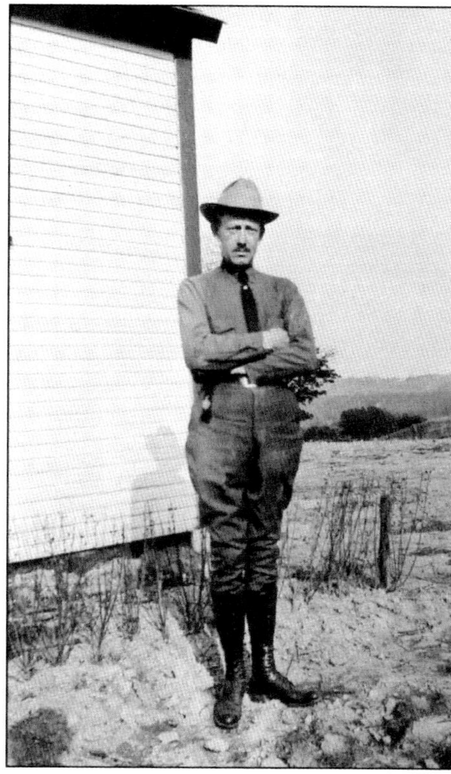

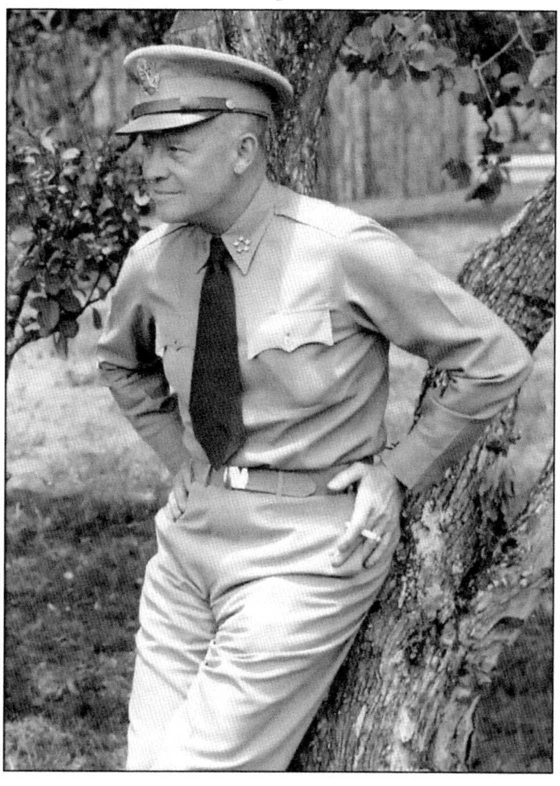

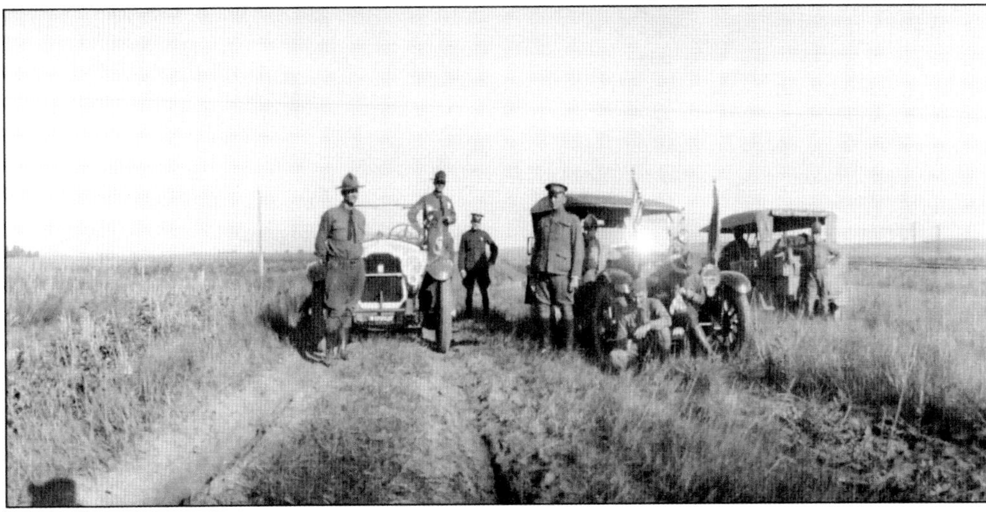

The convoy left Washington, DC, on July 7, 1919; crossed into Illinois on Saturday, July 19; and arrived in Chicago Heights by mid-afternoon. The convoy stayed in Chicago Heights Sunday, as a rest day. The trip resumed on Monday, and the convoy traveled as far as DeKalb, where it camped overnight. On Tuesday, the convoy continued and crossed over the Mississippi River at Fulton. During the two days it spent in Illinois, the convoy covered nearly 172 miles in just over 21 hours on the road. The entire transcontinental trip lasted 62 days and included numerous repairs on military vehicles as well as the rebuilding of bridges that did not support the weight of heavy loads. These images show the Army convoy as it passes through Cheyenne County, Nebraska.

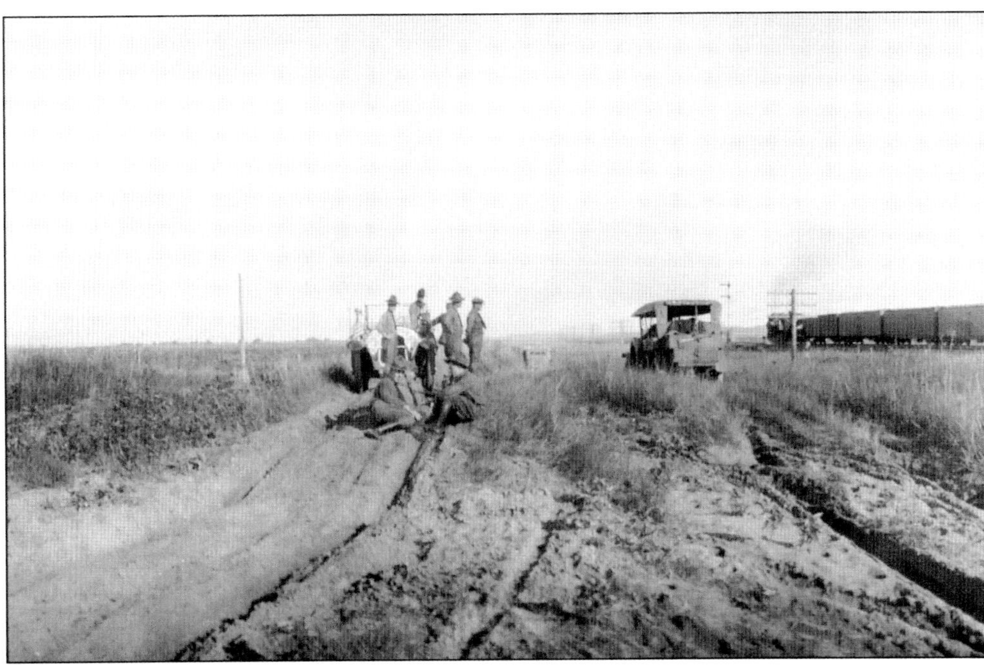

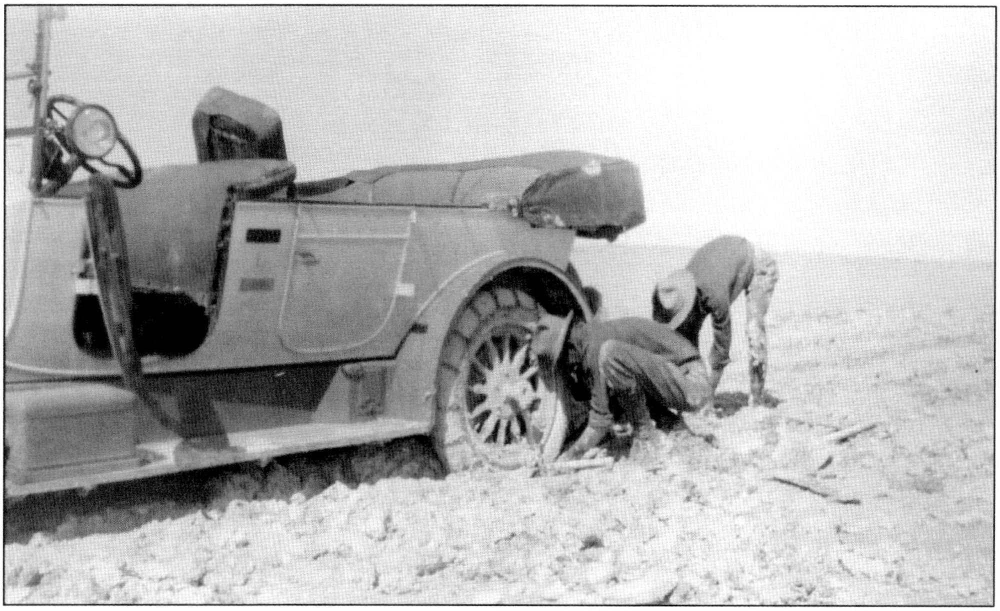

For the motorist trekking across America in the 1920s, automobile travel on the Lincoln Highway could test the patience of even the most seasoned adventurer. Tires went flat, piston rods broke, transmission gears froze, and radiators overheated. While most travelers experienced these dreaded mechanical failures, automobile travel required a bit of planning to assure the trip was a success. Because early radiators were prone to overheating due to their design, most drivers carried a portable canvas "water bag" to keep their engines cool. Originally intended to transport drinking water, these containers were soon used by cross-country drivers as additional insurance for the radiator boil-over. These images show automobiles experiencing mechanical failures in the early 1920s.

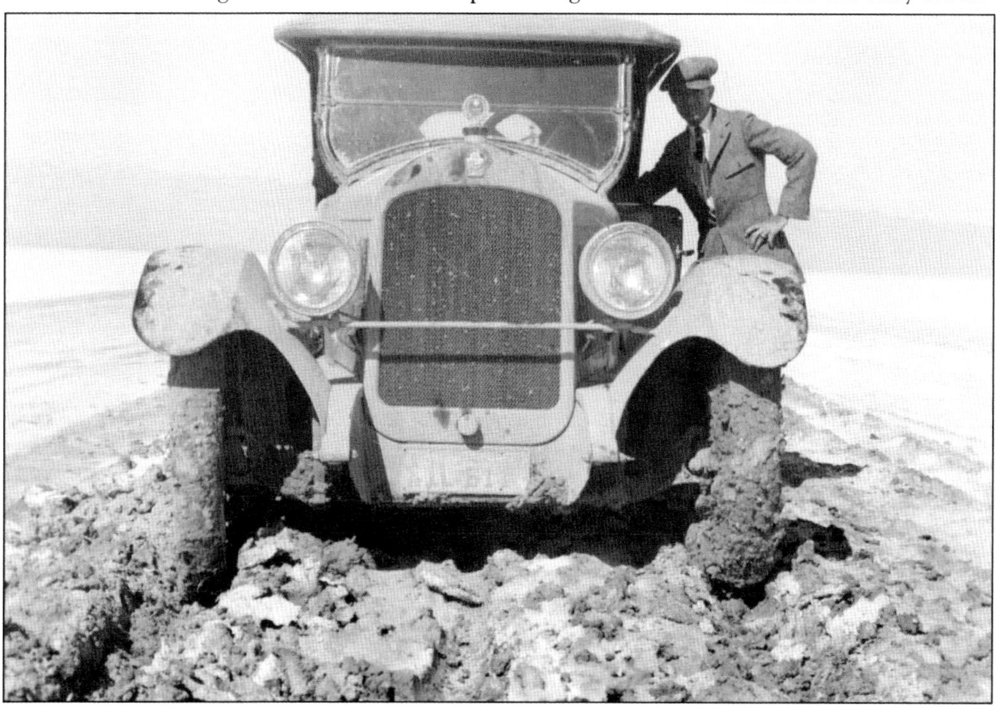

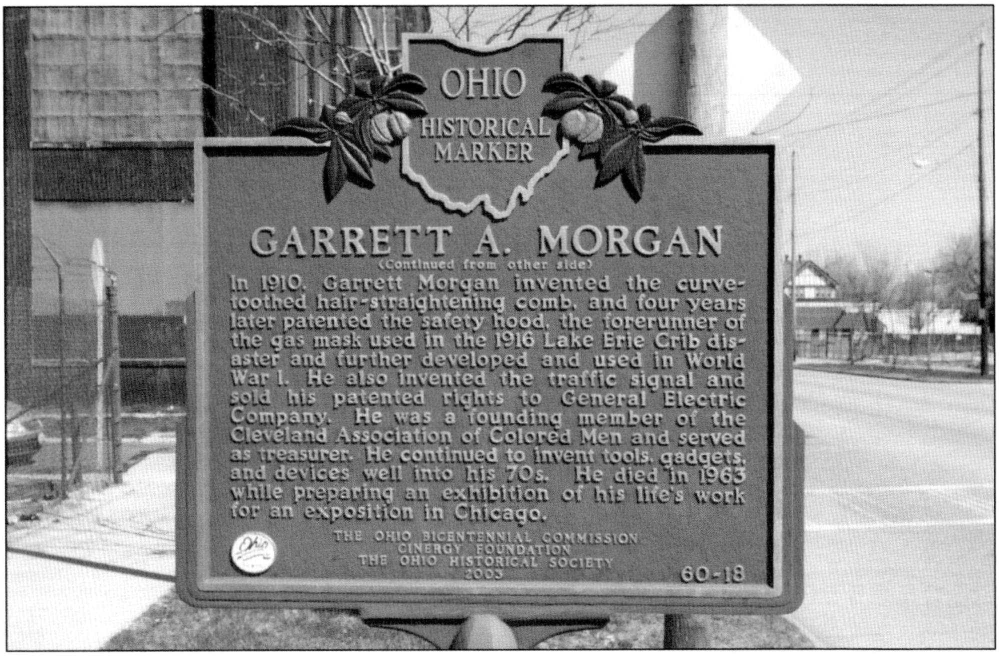

The world's first traffic signal can be traced to a busy street corner in Westminster, England, in 1868. The signaling device was designed to regulate the flow of pushcarts, pedestrians, and wagons along the street as a policeman operated the traffic signal, called a semaphore. This mechanism was mounted on a tall post and included moveable arms or flags and green and red lamps, which were illuminated at night. Most historians credit Garrett A. Morgan, an African American businessman, for inventing the first automatic traffic signal in 1923. His invention was first installed in Cleveland, Ohio, at the corner of Euclid Avenue and East 105th Street. Morgan's invention quickly spread across the United States and Canada. The top image shows a 2003 Ohio Historical Marker honoring Garrett Morgan located on Fifty-Fifth Street just south of Harlem Avenue in Cleveland. The bottom image shows a typical intersection before traffic lights were common. Notice the police officer directing traffic flow from the middle of the street.

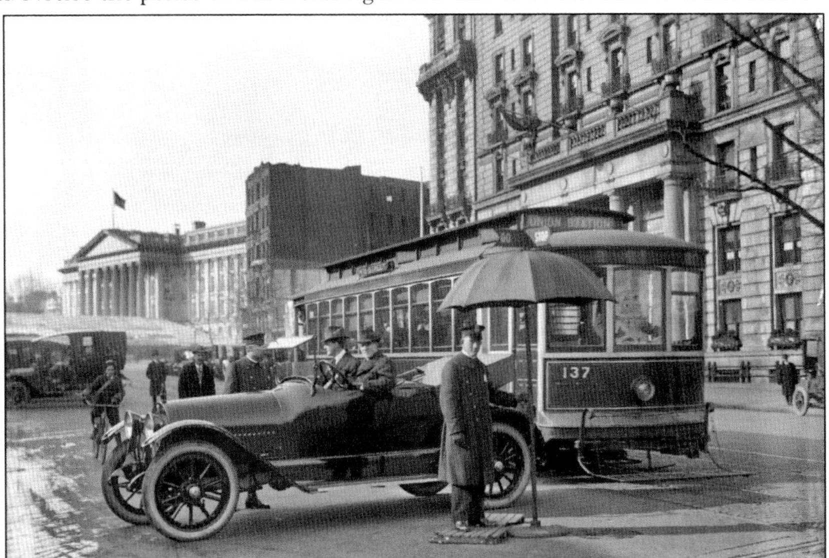

Two

Cook and Will Counties

The 1920s was a period of dramatic economic growth in this country. Prices for cars actually fell during the decade as the assembly-line techniques permitted faster production. Early in the decade, nearly 90 percent of all the world's cars were made in the United States. By 1930, over 20 million cars were registered in the United States, nearly three times the number during the prior decade.

As the interest in car travel grew, so did the number and variety of roadside services available in the United States. It was during the 1920s that many of the modern conveniences for motorists sprang up along highways and major roads. These new roadside businesses catering to the motorist included diners, hamburger stands, and drive-in restaurants.

Many of the earliest suppliers of food on the Lincoln Highway started out selling gas before diversifying into food, snacks, drinks, and other amenities. Other highway caterers, however, became more adventurous and enterprising from the beginning, including many family-run roadside stands, diners, and drive-ins. These small businesses were successful until larger franchises and chains began competing with them for the traveling customer.

In addition to the businesses that catered to the ravenous needs of the traveling public, there were also entrepreneurs who saw the need to help provide shelter for the road-weary motorist. Some provided open-air locations that resembled makeshift campgrounds and offered little to the overnight guest besides a place to park the automobile and pitch a tent. These spartan facilities were soon superseded by sites providing individual huts containing beds. They were, in turn, the forerunners of the typical "tourist court," a semi-circular layout of cabins around a manager's office. Soon, most courts had running water in their rooms, and over the years, air-conditioning, radio, and eventually televisions were introduced. The evolution into the modern motel premises was completed when rooms, offices, and parking spaces were all brought together under the same roof in a single contiguous structure.

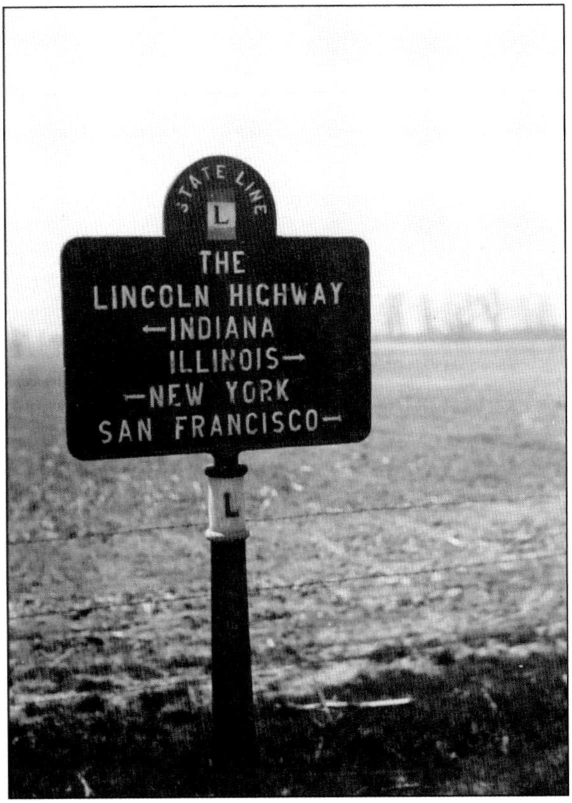

The eastern portion of the Lincoln Highway enters Illinois on US Route 30 and continues west through Chicago Heights, where it crosses the historic Dixie Highway. The highway continues west through New Lenox to Joliet, where it crosses the original alignment of historic Route 66. Lincoln Highway continues northwest through Plainfield as it heads toward Aurora. From Aurora, the highway takes Illinois State Route 31 toward Geneva, where it turns west and follows Illinois Route 38. The highway continues west through the towns of Rochelle, Franklin Grove, and Dixon. West of the town of Sterling, Lincoln Highway rejoins US 30 and travels through Morrison and then joins Illinois Route 136 into Fulton, where the road crosses the Mississippi River into Iowa. These photographs show the official Illinois and Indiana state line sign located in Lake County, Indiana. The Portland Cement Company took both images shown here in 1923.

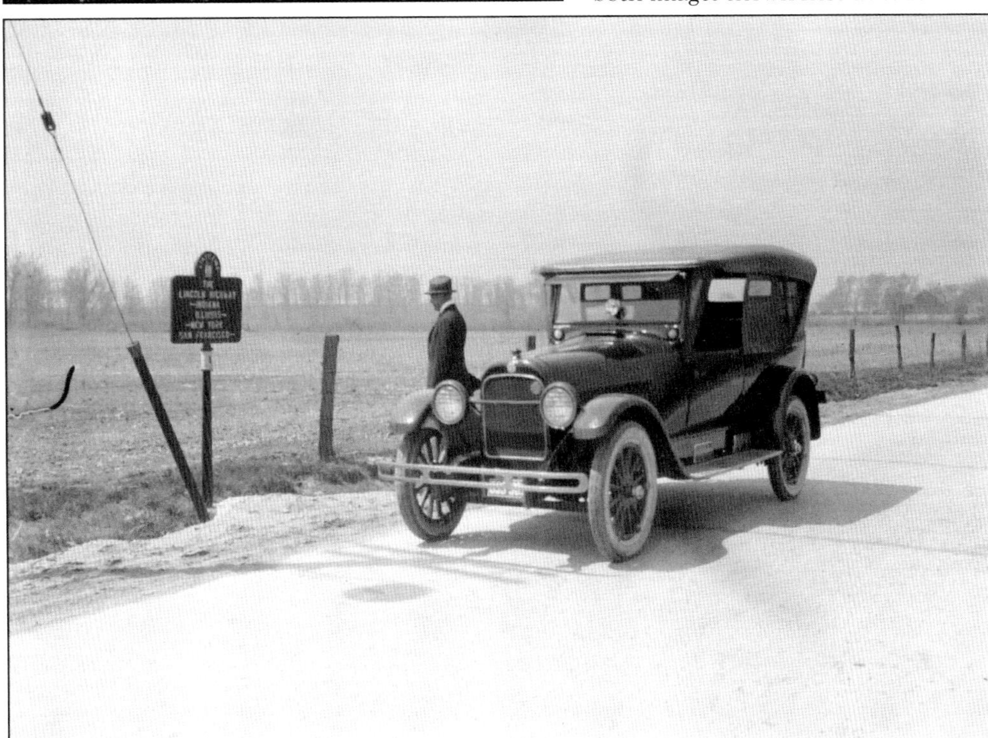

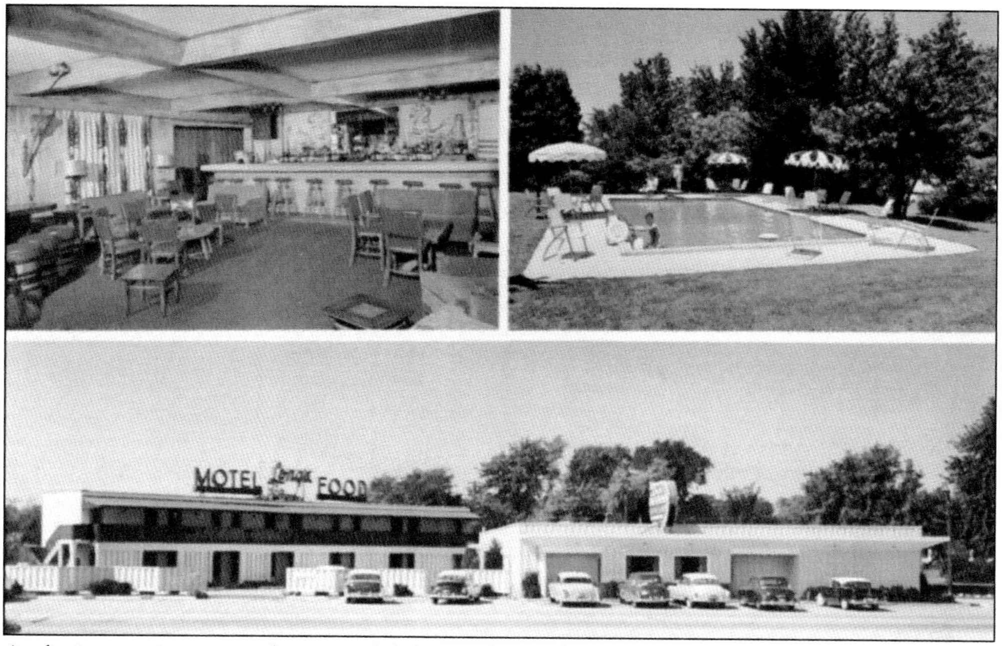

As the interest in car travel grew, so did the number and variety of roadside services available along Lincoln Highway. It was during the 1920s and 1930s that many of the modern conveniences for motorists sprang up along highways and major roads. These new businesses catering to motorists included motor courts, gas stations, diners, hamburger stands, and drive-in restaurants. These postcard images show Long's Motor Court, located near the Illinois State Line in Chicago Heights. Long's specialized in fine food and modern, restful tourist court accommodations for the motoring public. Notice the Sinclair service station located on the left in the bottom image. The sign above the entrance reminds travelers that Long's is the "Last Stop" on the Illinois side of the state line along the Lincoln Highway. (Both, courtesy of Russell Rein.)

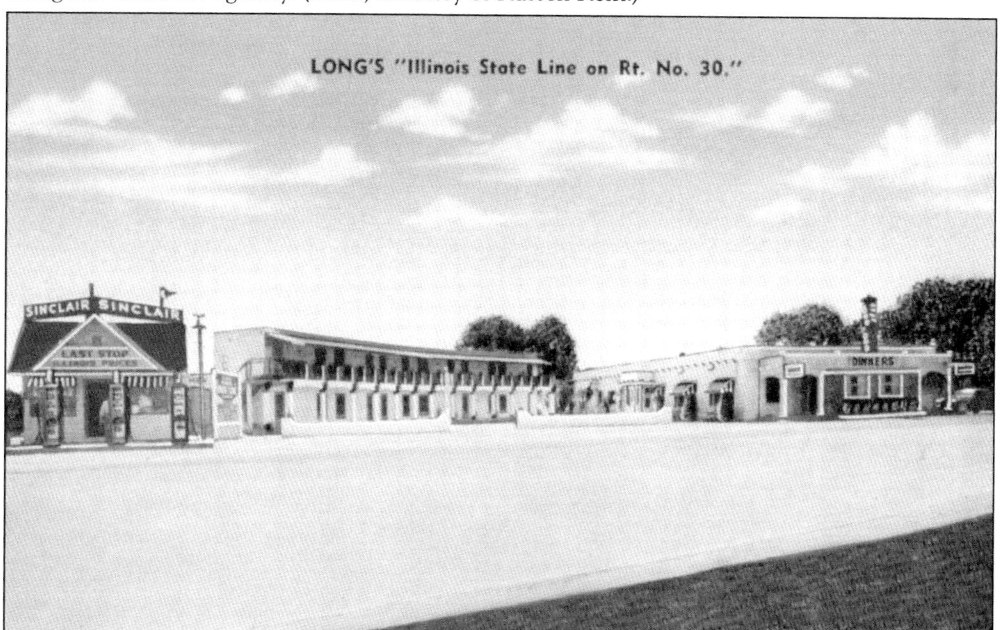

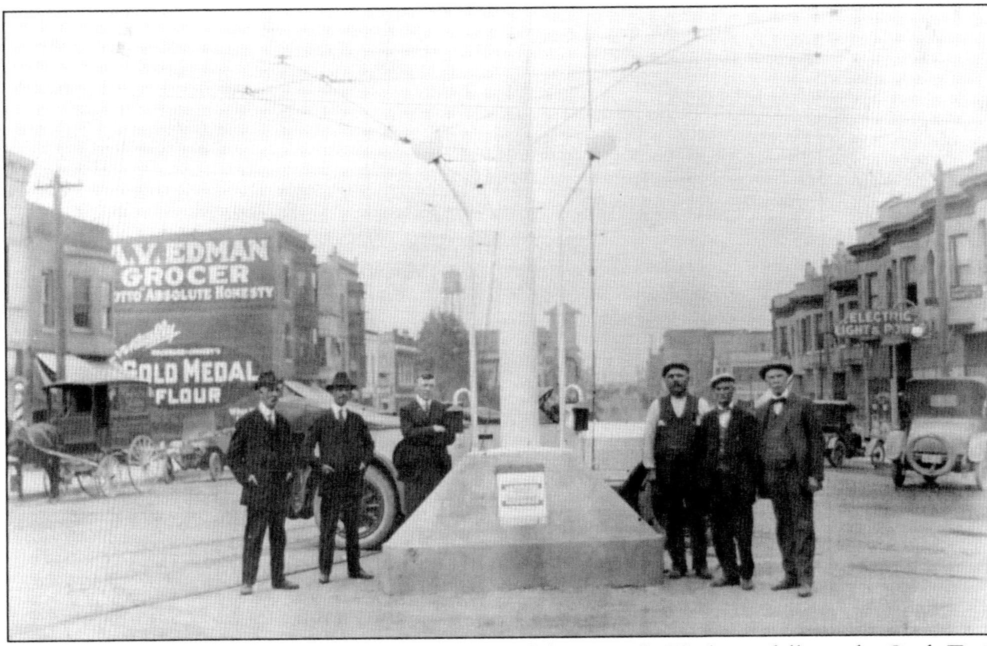

In the town of Lynwood, the original alignment of the Lincoln Highway follows the Sauk Trail through Sauk Village until it meets Chicago Road. The intended route of the road would follow the Sauk Trail into Frankfort; however, plans changed when LHA officials suggested moving the alignment north through Chicago Heights and Matteson. By 1913, the Lincoln Highway was rerouted north from the Sauk Trail along Chicago Road and then west along Fourteenth Street in Chicago Heights. When Chicago Road became the official route of the Dixie Highway in 1915, the two roads ran concurrently for two miles through Chicago Heights. The top photograph, taken at the intersection of Illinois Street and Chicago Road looking east, shows a flag pole erected to commemorate the historic alignment of the roads. Henry C. Ostermann (left) and Benjamin H. Vannatta (right) are shown standing in this photograph. The bottom photograph shows a closer view of the base of the flagpole.

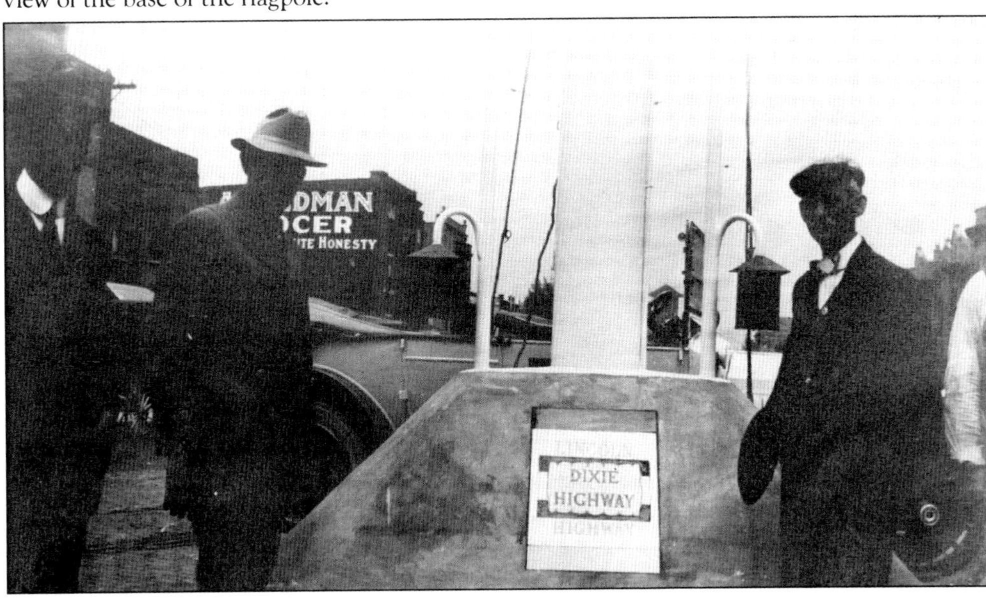

Chicago Heights is considered by many to be the "crossroads of the nation," as the town is situated near the intersection of the Lincoln and Dixie Highways. At the junction of these thoroughfares, travelers will find a number of historic markers, including the Arche Fountain, the Mound, and the *Road to Greatness* statue, which help to celebrate and commemorate the importance of this community and location. In 1916, members of the Arche Club of Chicago decided to commemorate the 50th anniversary of Abraham Lincoln's assassination by erecting a monument. Dedicated on October 13, 1916, the Arche Fountain was sculpted by George Etienne Ganiere and erected on the southwest corner of the Lincoln and Dixie Highways. The image on the right shows a view of the Arche Fountain, and the bottom image shows the *Road to Greatness* statue. This statute, located on the northeast corner, was sculpted by John Bucci in 2003 and depicts Abraham Lincoln receiving flowers from two girls.

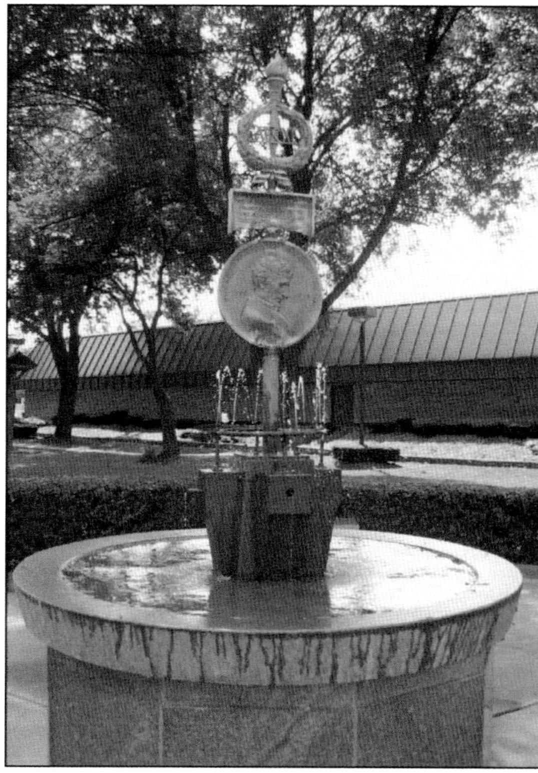

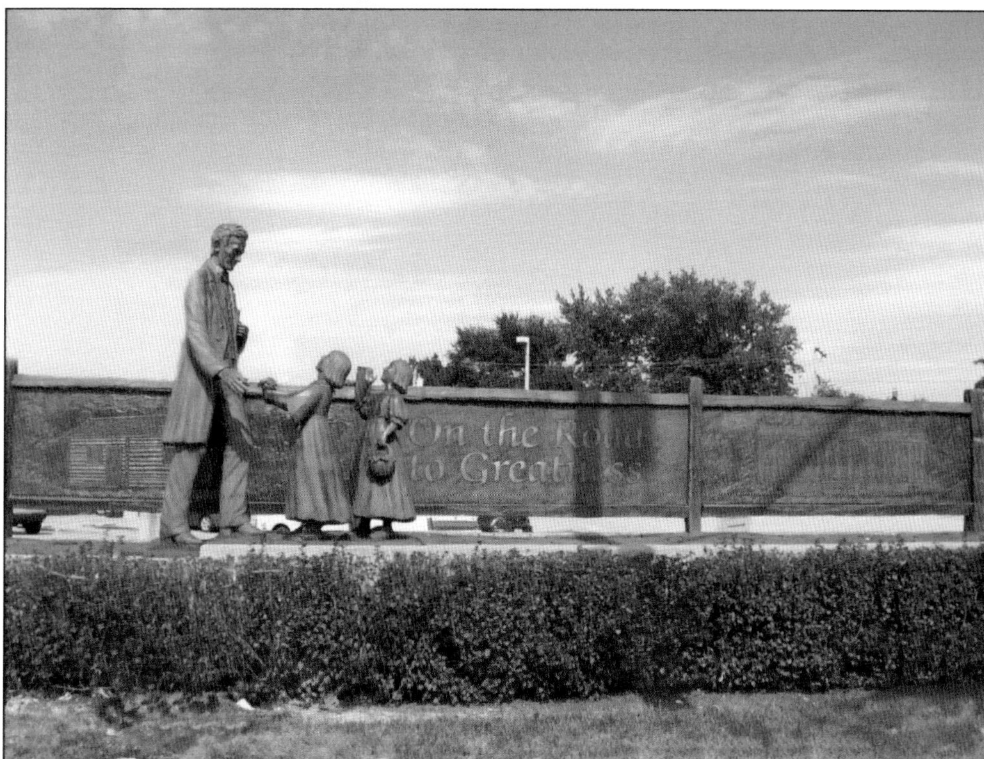

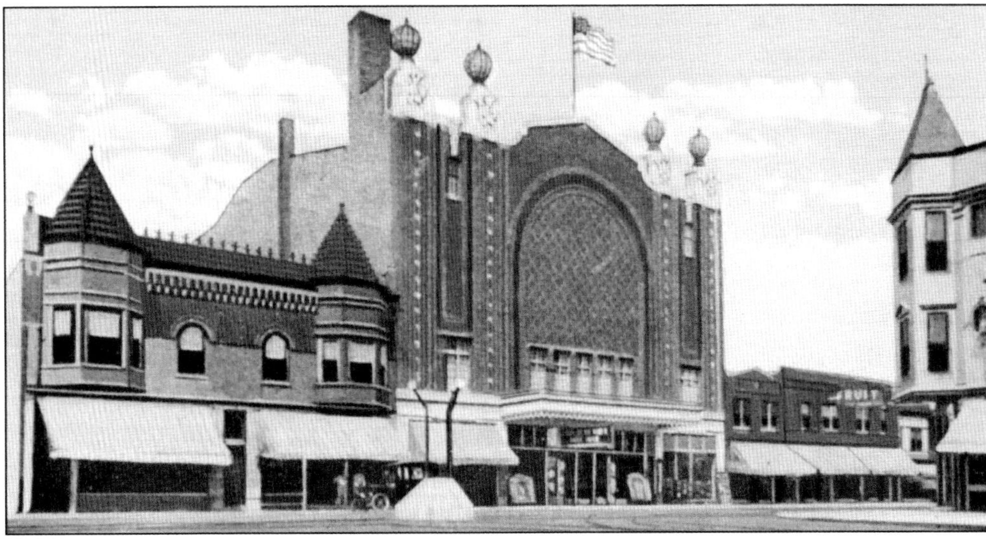

Located along the original alignment of the Lincoln Highway in Chicago Heights, the Lincoln-Dixie Theatre opened to the public on June 23, 1921. Considered one of the finest theaters in the Chicago area, the over-2,000-seat theater was once the center of cultural entertainment for the residents of the area. Known locally for its grand, classic facade, long decorative torrents, grade proscenium stage, and fashionable box seats, the theater eventually succumbed to financial difficulties in later years and was demolished in 1972. (Courtesy of Russell Rein.)

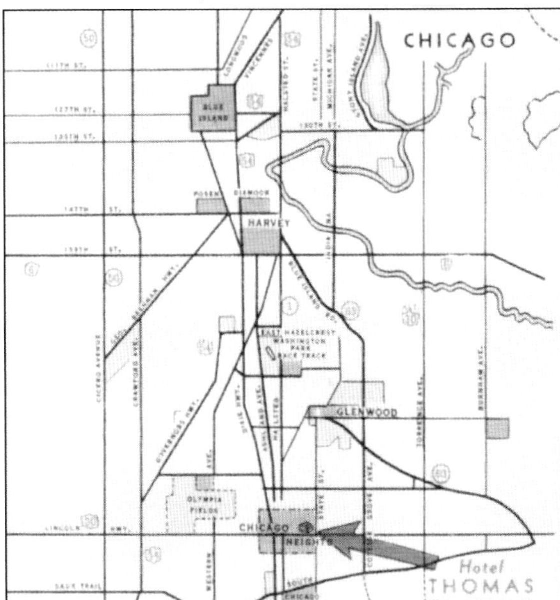

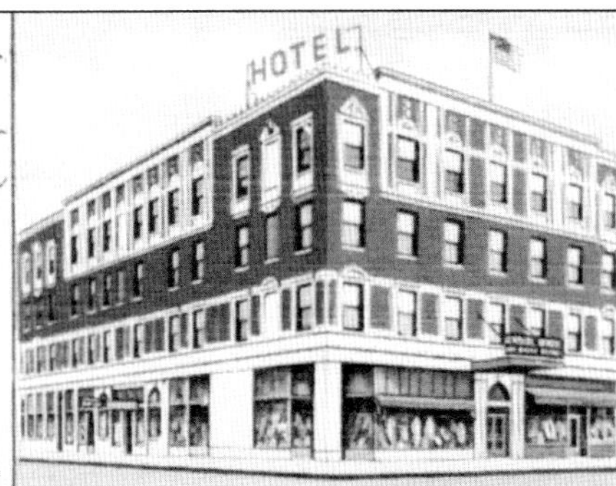

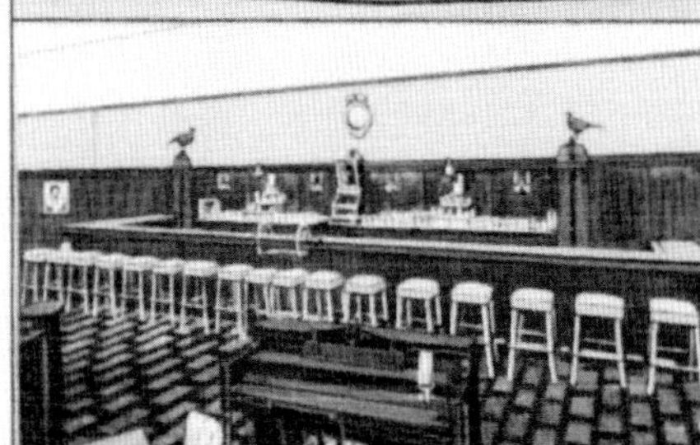

In the 1920s, the town of Chicago Heights saw a building boom as department stores, theaters, and hotels began to spring up in the area. Located on the southeast corner of Seventeenth and Halsted Streets, Lincoln Highway tourists often used the Thomas Hotel on their way to Chicago. Constructed in 1923, the upscale hotel opened a year later and was known locally for its many modern conveniences and luxurious accommodations, especially the crystal ballroom. The hotel later became the Albert Hotel and was destroyed by fire in 1979. (Courtesy of Russell Rein.)

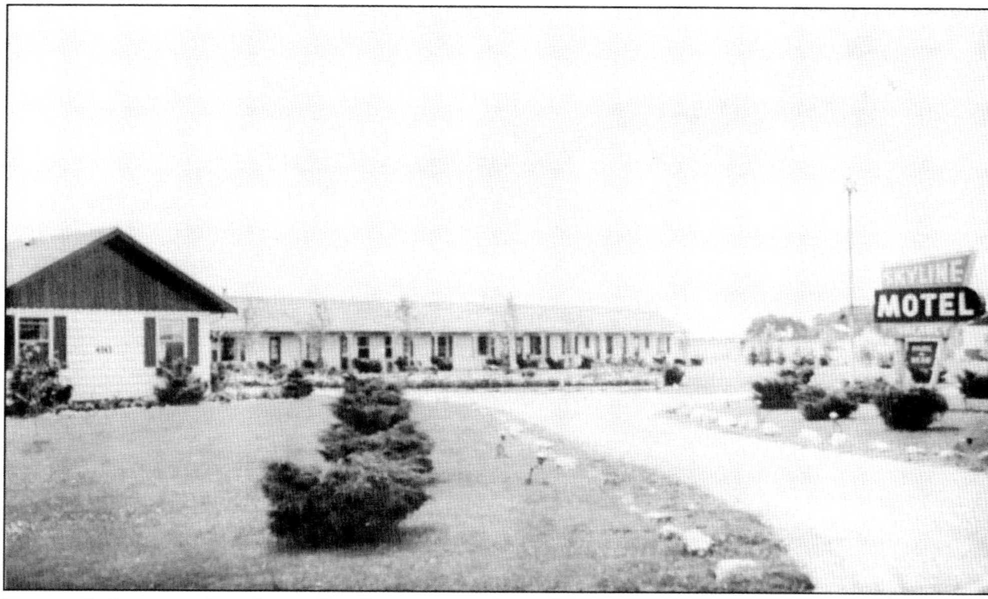

Postcard photographs of motels often centered on the essential architectural elements of the structure, and any highway, road, or driveway are often missing traffic or congestion in the image. Automobiles arriving or departing are seldom seen in the views, and this is unusual, as the mobility offered by vehicles was the life-blood of the motel industry. Nonetheless, the automobiles shown in some images are thought to belong to the people staying at the motels and are invariably shown at rest, parked presumably in front of the driver's motel room. The images shown in these postcard photographs follow the photograph format that was common for motels along the Lincoln Highway. The top postcard shows the Skyline Motel, located along the Lincoln Highway in Matteson. The bottom image shows the Twilight Motel, located near the Indiana State Line in Chicago Heights. (Both, courtesy of Russell Rein.)

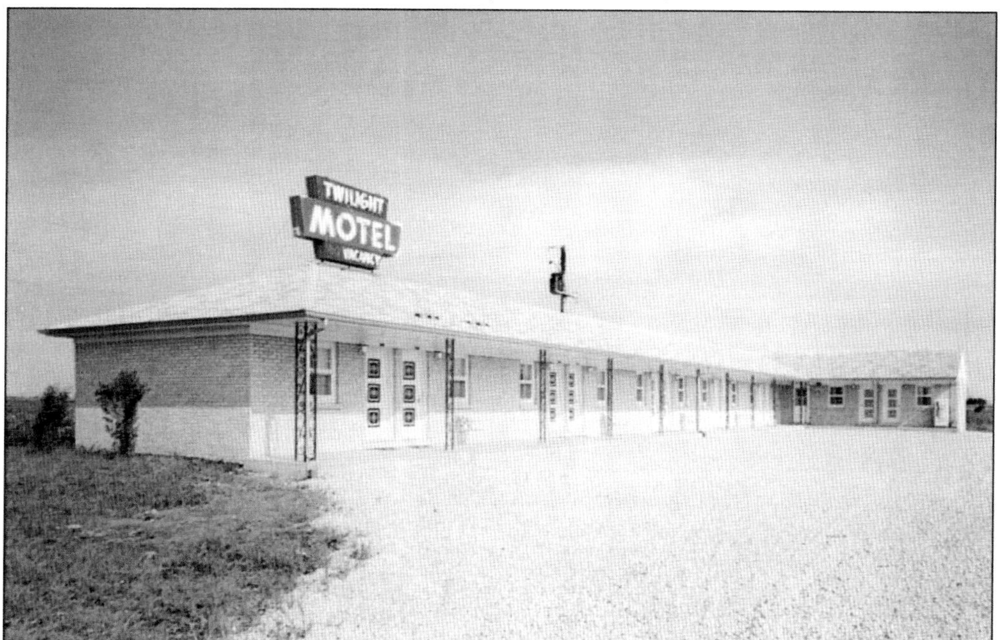

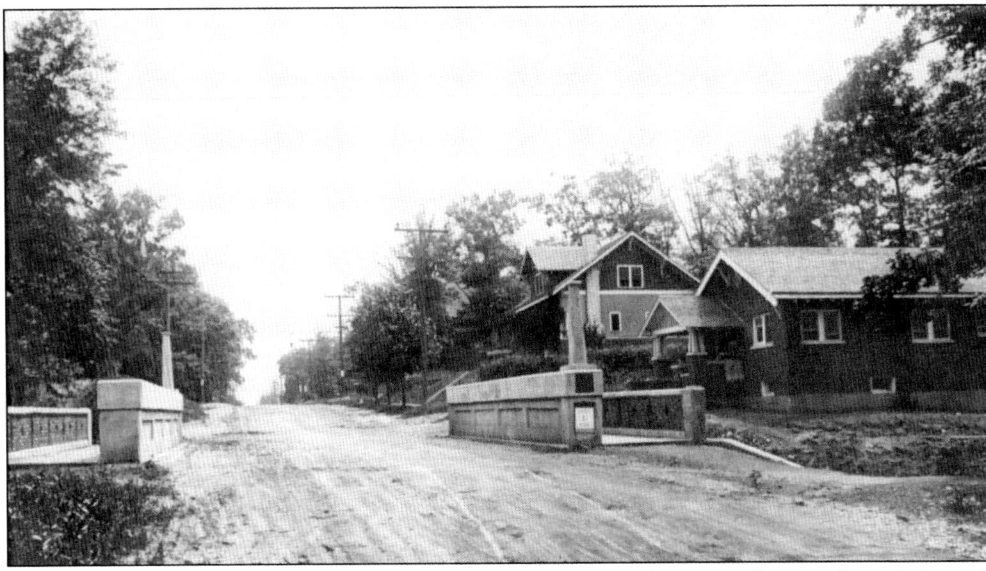

Thorn Creek is a small tributary of the Little Calumet River that meanders northward through Cook and Will Counties. The nearly-20-mile-long river has its origin in eastern Will County near Monee and ends with its confluence with the Little Calumet River in southern Cook County. The river runs through a number of towns, including Chicago Heights. This photograph shows the old Lincoln Highway Bridge over Thorn Creek just west of town. Note the official Lincoln Highway emblem embedded on the bridge deck below the column.

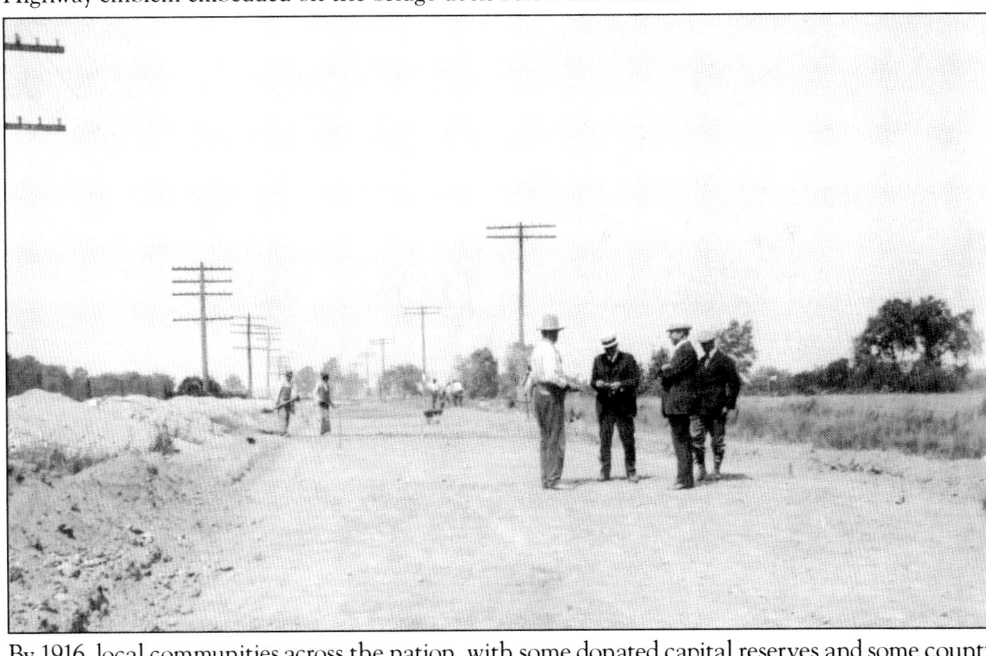

By 1916, local communities across the nation, with some donated capital reserves and some county and state money, were working to make road improvements along the Lincoln Highway. In some areas, culverts were constructed, bridges were reinforced, and some embankments and intersections were improved. On July 11, 1916, Pres. Woodrow Wilson signed into law the Federal Aid Road Act, which allowed for the highways of America to be built by government funds. This photograph shows road construction engineers in 1918 preparing for a concrete sub-grade near Chicago Heights.

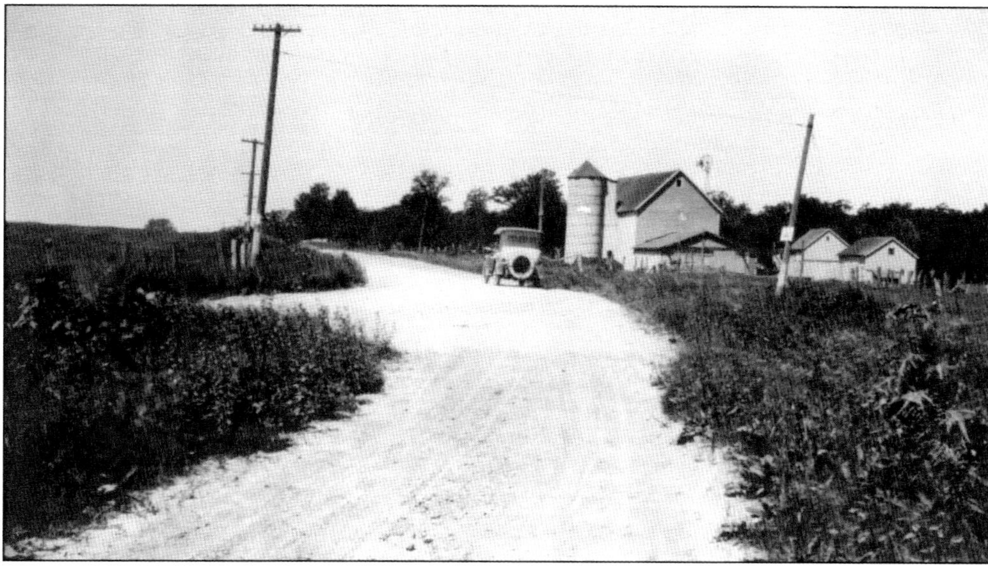

While the automobile was well established by 1912, good roads to travel on were hard to find. In many parts, motorists were able to use roads and streets in good weather, but during the winter or raining season, automobiles remained idle. Throughout America, there were hundreds of miles of brick roads, but that was the extent of hard paving. Not until the experimental Seedling Miles program took off was concrete used as a road-building material. Most roads across the nation, especially in the rural areas, were just basic dirt roads used by farmers to bring goods into town to access the rail centers. These two images show typical road conditions that early motorists would encounter as they traveled sections of the Lincoln Highway near Frankfort. The bottom image is typically called a "natural" road, indicating that nothing had ever been done to improve that section of the roadway.

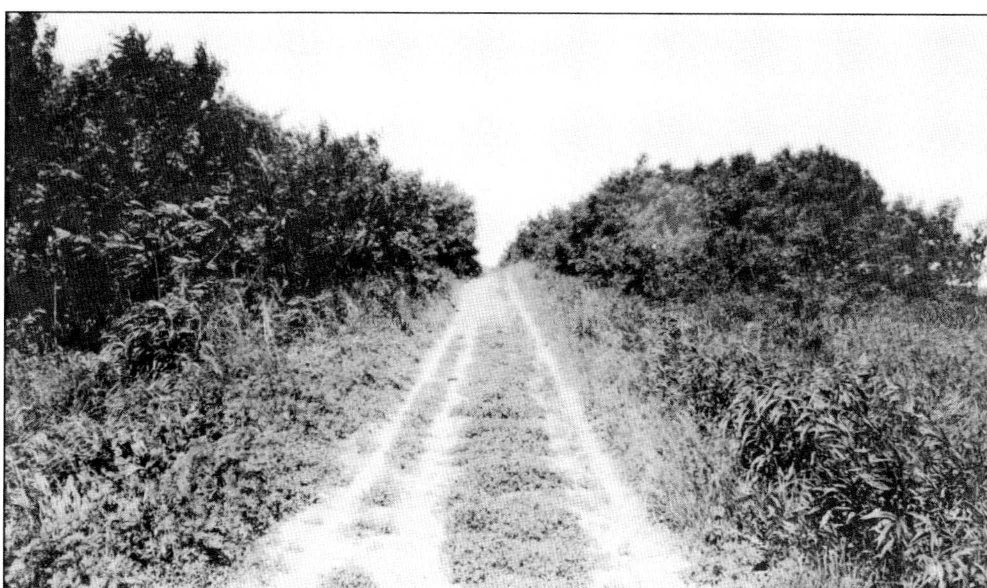

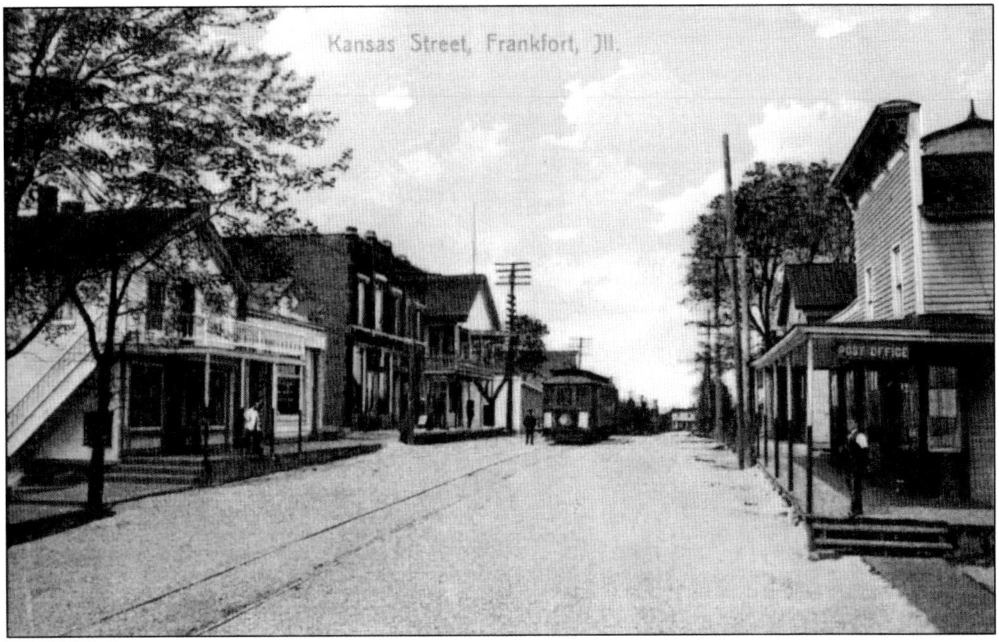

The Joliet & Southern Traction Company, a sister company to the Aurora, Plainfield & Joliet Railroad Company, operated rail service from Joliet beginning in 1905. The line ran east, parallel to the Michigan Central Railroad tracks, and connected the southern communities of Joliet, New Lenox, Frankfort, and Matteson before ending in Chicago Heights. The first interurban cars to run on these tracks were architecturally little more than long streetcars but in later years had a unique arch-shaped roof and windows, which became a traditional interurban styling. These picture postcards show the interurban trolley running past the Folkers Hotel, an interurban station in Frankfort. Notice the conductor helping travelers load their luggage in the bottom photograph. By the early 1920s, automobiles and the paving of the Lincoln Highway made Aurora–Joliet–Chicago Heights interurban service unnecessary.

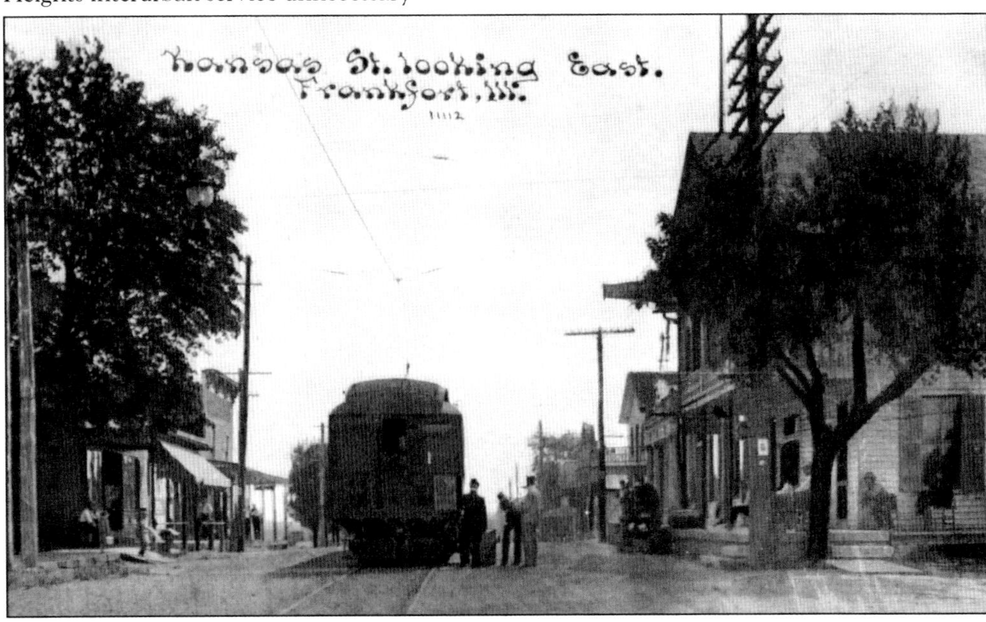

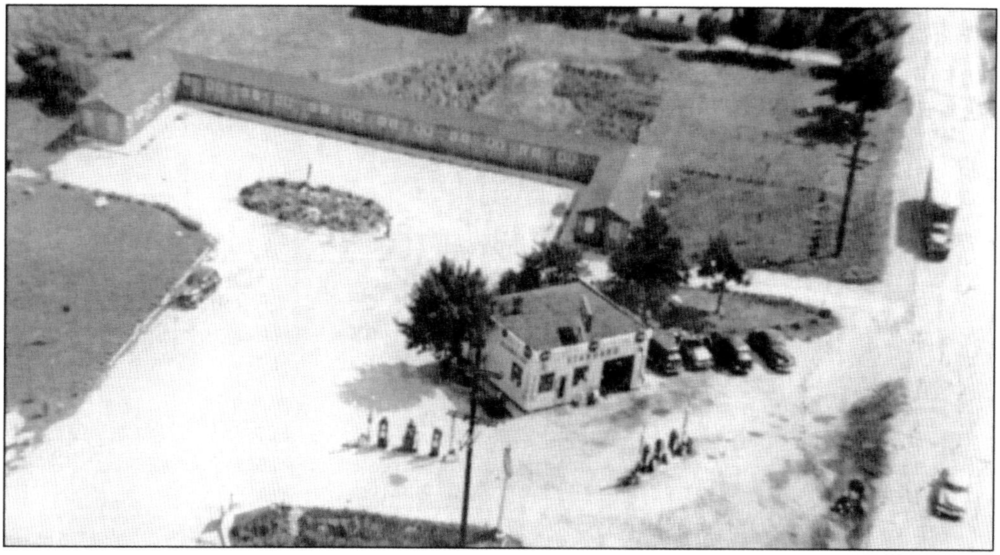

A Lincoln Highway roadside haven, designed to be automobile friendly, was the Pilgrims Rest Standard Service Station and Motor Court Motel. Located on the corner of Route 45 and Lincoln Highway in Frankfort, the Pilgrims Rest offered the travel-weary motorist a fine roadside motel and filling station with 24-hour service daily. The top photograph shows an aerial image of the entire complex. The Standard station can be seen in the foreground, and the *U*-shaped motor court, which is a typical design layout seen in the 1940s, is visible in the background. The bottom photograph shows a view looking north from Route 45. Today, a Walgreens business occupies the space of the old Pilgrims Rest Service Station. (Below, courtesy of Russell Rein.)

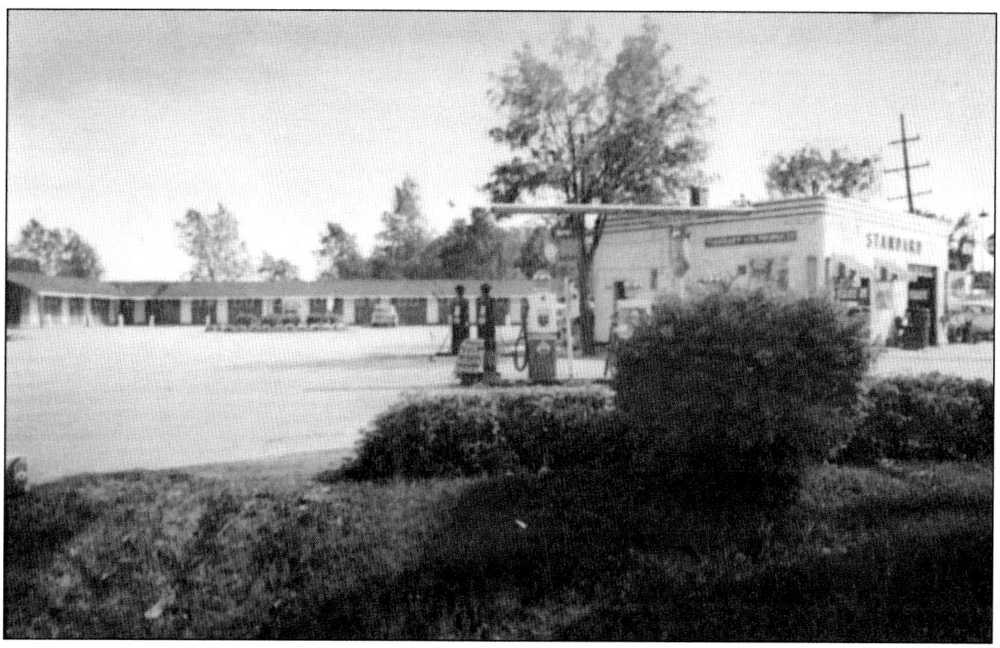

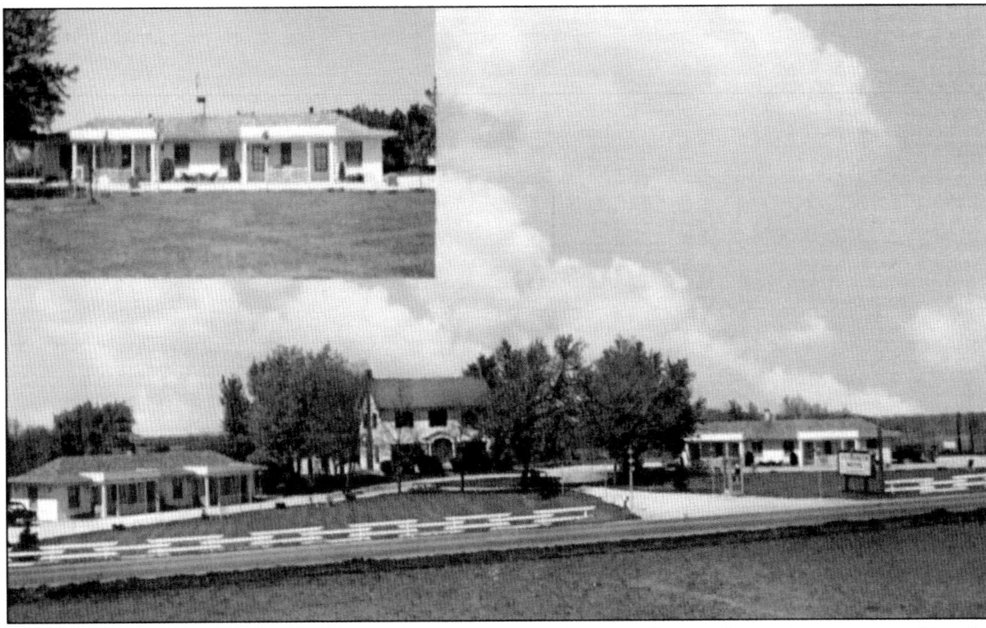

It was not until the 1920s that cheap, basic accommodations for road travelers appeared in the form of "motor camps," open-air camping grounds with communal laundries and washrooms. These facilities were gradually superseded by sites providing individual huts containing beds, and thousands were built across the country between 1929 and 1933. These establishments were the forerunners of the typical "tourist court," a semi-circular layout of cabins around a manager's office. Soon, most courts had running water in their rooms, and in years to come, air-conditioning, radio, and, eventually, television were introduced. These picture postcards show two such establishments in Frankfort on the old Lincoln Highway. The top postcard shows the Evergreen Motel, which included 10 acres of rolling country with an orchard and shade trees, playground equipment, and picnic tables. The c. 1960 postcard below shows the Valley View Motel, which included 14 modern units, a restaurant, a cocktail lounge, and a swimming pool.

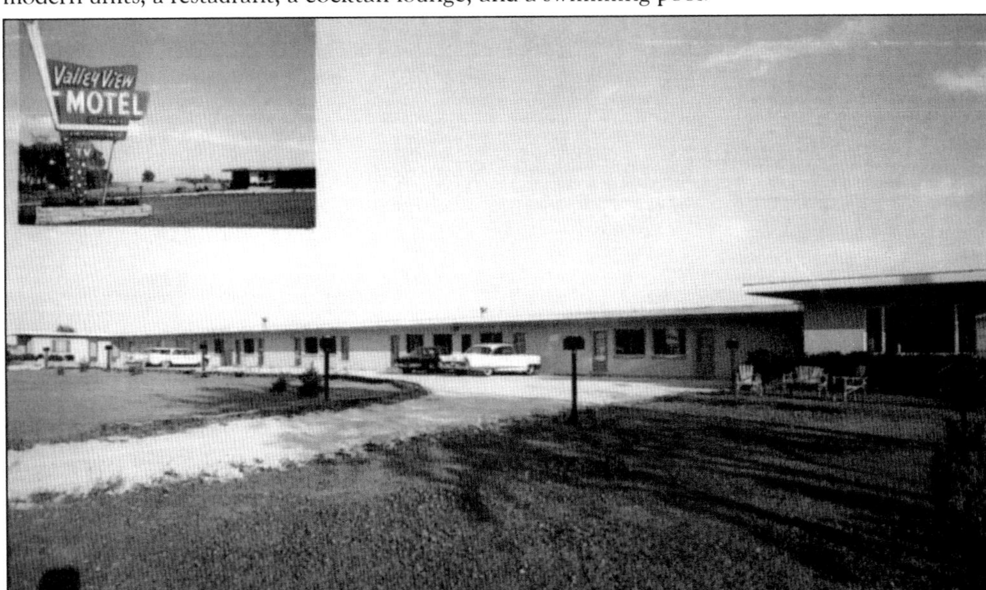

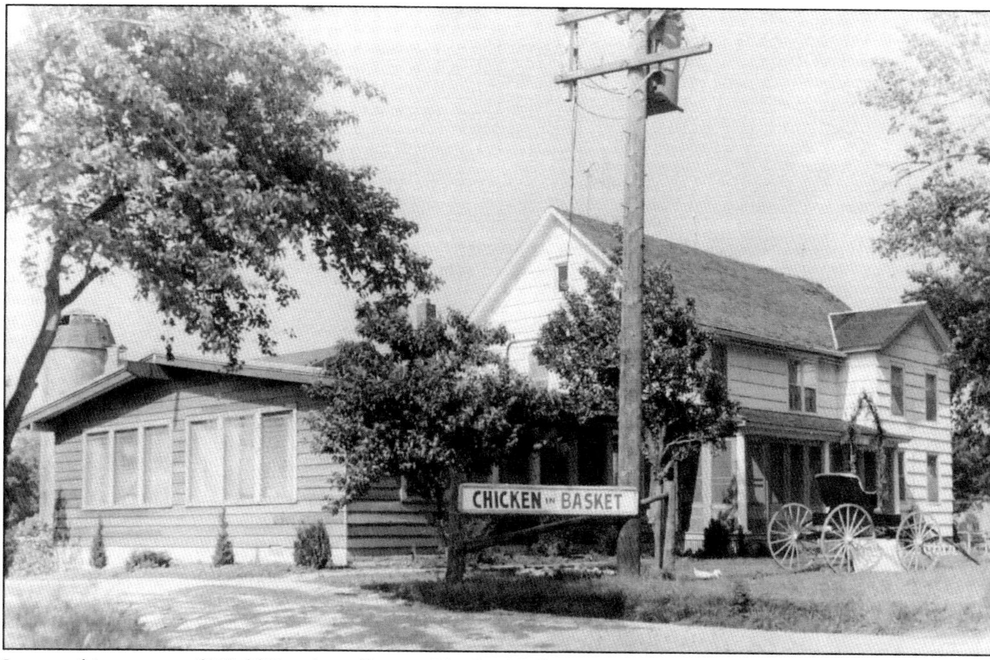

Located just east of Wolf Road on Route 30, the Valley View Farm and Restaurant in Frankfort, shown in the top image, was a favorite spot for locals or Lincoln Highway tourists who wanted good food and a relaxing environment. Although the majority of food served in the restaurant was raised on the farm, Valley View Farm was best remembered for its numerous dining rooms, including the Sun-Air Room and the Lean-To Lounge with its piano bar. Tourists who needed to stay the evening could find accommodations in the Vacation Center, which included a motel and swimming pool. The bottom postcard shows a c. 1960 view of the motel swimming pool. Today, the Frankfort Township offices are located on the old farm complex, and the swimming pool, which for many years offered area residents a place to cool off in the summertime, was closed in 2005, and a new township building was constructed in its place.

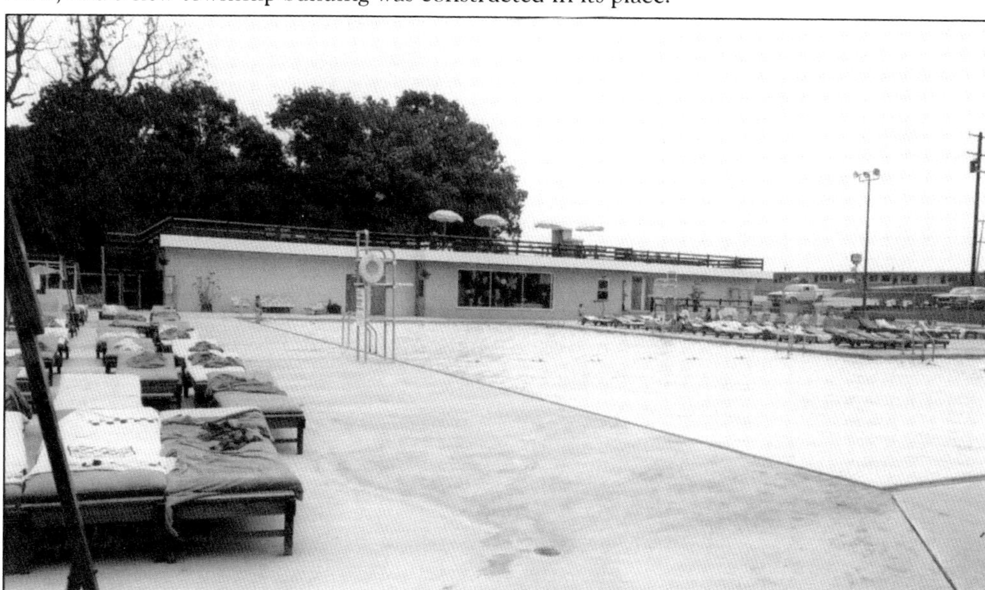

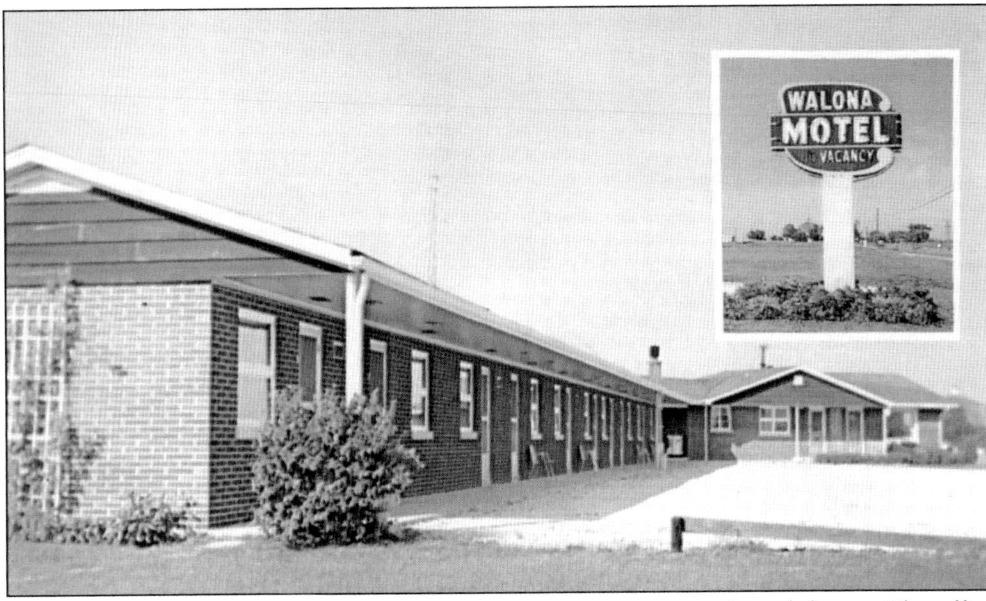

By the late 1940s, most motels were arranged in an open *U-* or *L*-shaped design. The office was no longer front and center but located to the left or right of the architectural layout. This allowed for increased space for the sign, which was located on its own, away from the motel and near the street. The Abe Lincoln Motel near Frankfort, built in the late 1950s, is an example of an *L*-shaped design and still operates in its original location today. The bottom image shows a postcard advertisement for the Walona Motel in New Lenox. Notice that the artist uses an insert feature to highlight the motel sign. The irregular shape of the Walona Motel sign represents a shift away from the traditional vertical or box format design that was common in the late 1950s. Still in operation today, the Walona Motel is an example of a theme motel that provided temporary shelter for Lincoln Highway tourists.

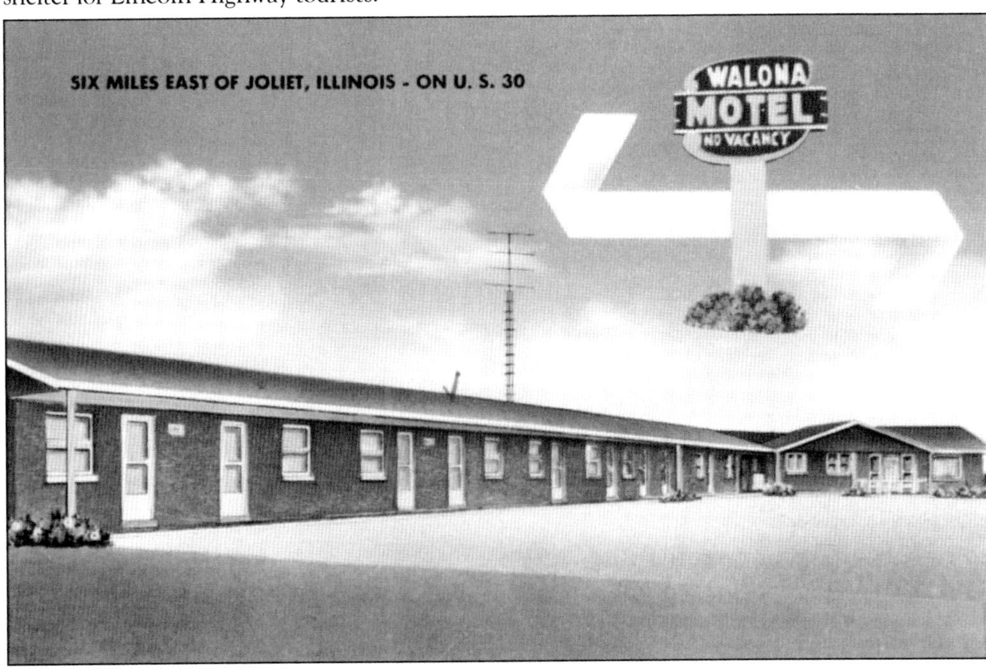

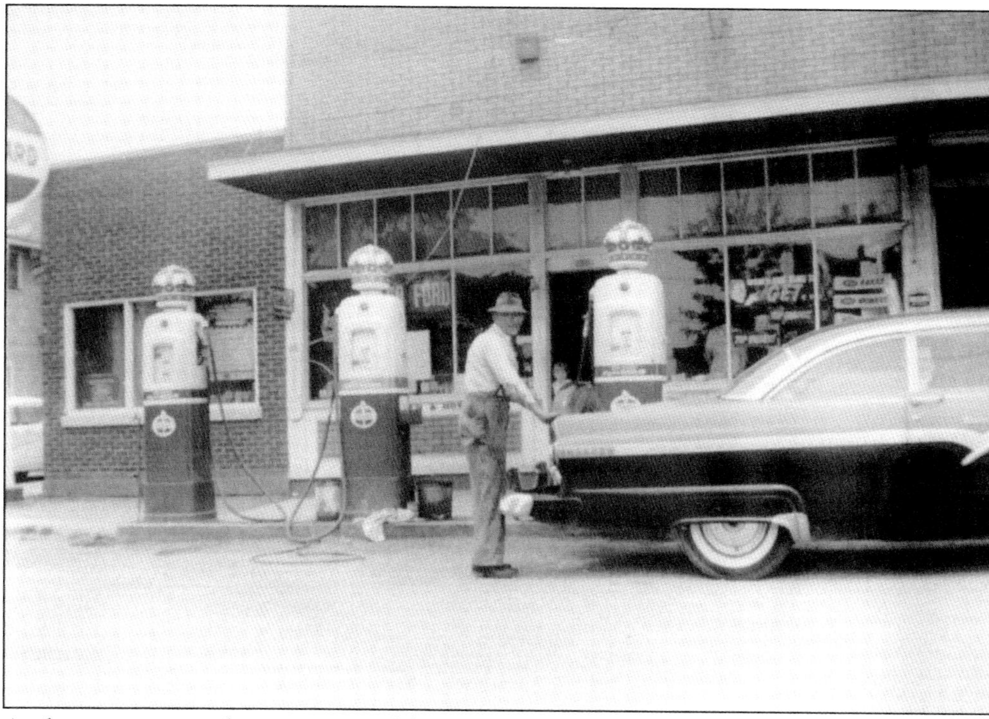

As the promotion and construction of the Lincoln Highway drew new automobile enthusiasts to take to the road, this new sense of traveling freedom created a demand for vehicle service and auto dealers. In the rural town of Mokena, the first auto garage in the area opened for business in 1916. Located along the north side of Front Street, just east of Mokena Street, the Cooper and Hostert Garage was the area's first Ford dealership and was part of Mokena's business community for more than 50 years. Cooper and Hostert sold cars, trucks, and tractors as well as offering excellent repair work to the rural farming town until the business closed in the early 1970s. In 2013, the Illinois Lincoln Highway Coalition erected a mural near the original location of Cooper and Hostert. The top image shows the Cooper and Hostert Garage in the 1950s, and the bottom image shows the newly installed Mokena mural. (Above, courtesy of Robert Horras.)

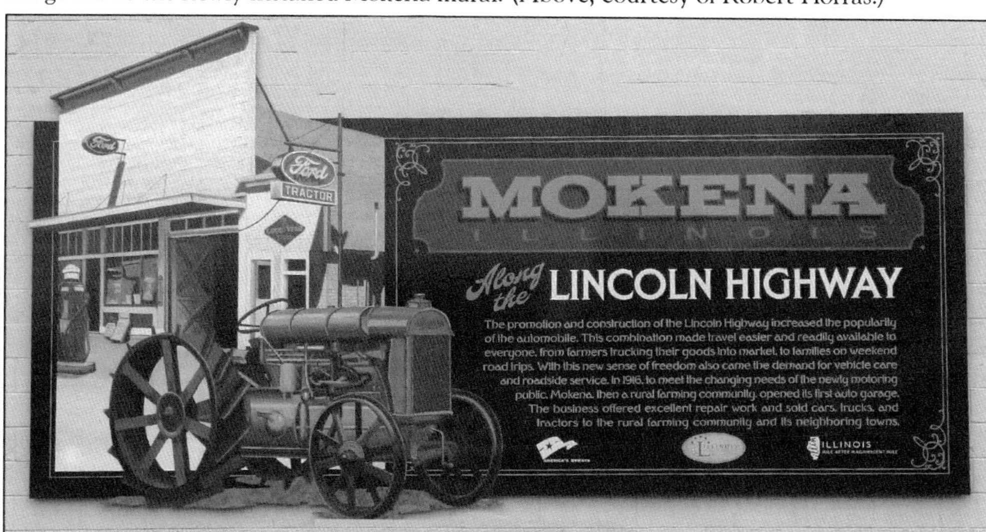

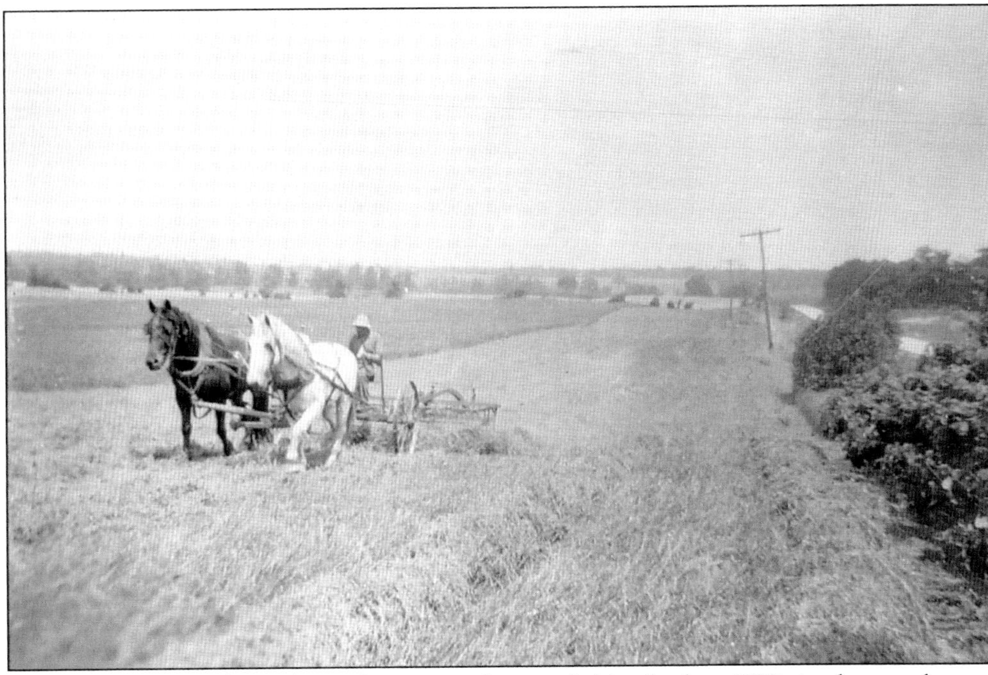

What is now the village of New Lenox was first settled in the late 1820s in the area known as Gouger Crossing (Route 30 and Gouger Road). New Lenox Township was established in 1852 when Will County was created. The village was laid out by George Gaylord of Lockport and was surveyed by A.J. Matthewson. Originally, the town was named Tracy in honor of the general superintendent of the Rock Island Railroad. John F. Tracy later requested that the name be changed to New Lenox after the township. J. Van Duser, a supervisor who had come from Lenox, New York, had named the township. Like many rural towns in Illinois, New Lenox was established and grew with the building of the Rock Island Railroad between Chicago and Rock Island. These images show sections of the Lincoln Highway near the town of New Lenox. (Above, courtesy of Robert Horras.)

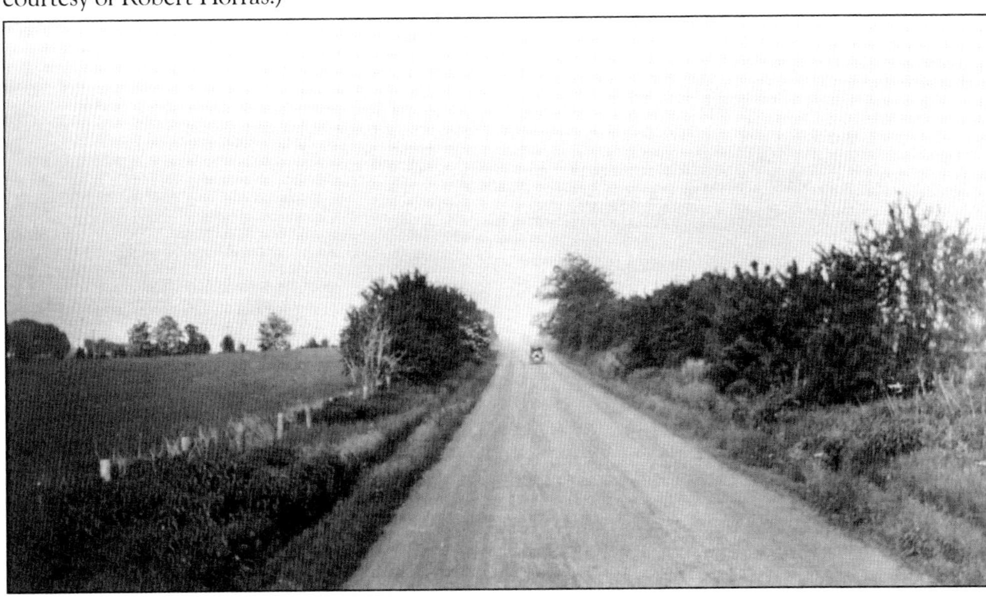

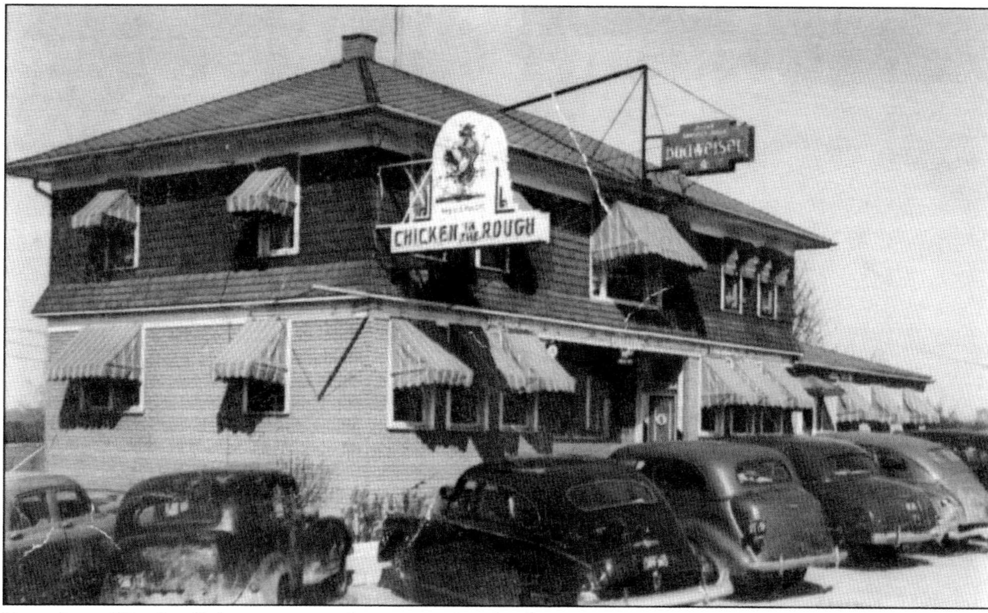

Beverly and Rudye Osborne created a unique fast food operation that served fried chicken, shoestring potatoes, hot biscuits, and honey during the late 1930s. By the 1950s, this delectable meal was known to many as Chicken in the Rough and sold in nearly 250 franchised outlets around the country. One outlet along the Lincoln Highway serving Chicken in the Rough was Brun's Tavern and Restaurant in New Lenox. This c. 1950 photograph shows a view of the popular tavern and restaurant owned by Herbert and Alma Brun. (Courtesy of Russell Rein.)

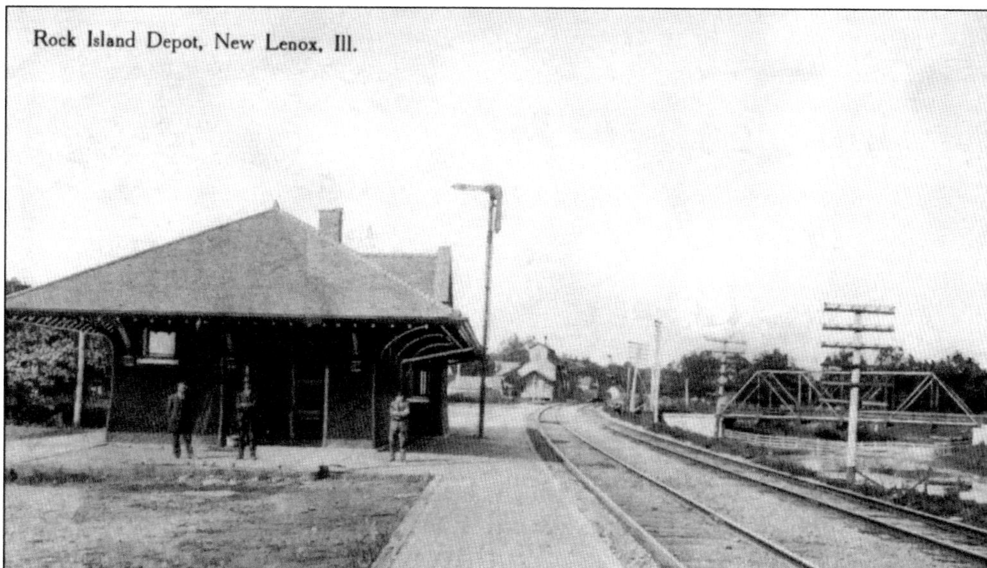

Hickory Creek flows southwestward through the heart of New Lenox Township, feeding into the Des Plaines River at Joliet. Following Route 30 much of the way through its 21-mile journey, the creek flows through many southern communities, including Mokena, Frankfort, New Lenox, and Joliet. This postcard photograph, looking west from the Rock Island Railroad tracks, shows a view of the old steel bridge at Cedar Road, which crosses Hickory Creek just west of the Rock Island depot and just north of the Lincoln Highway.

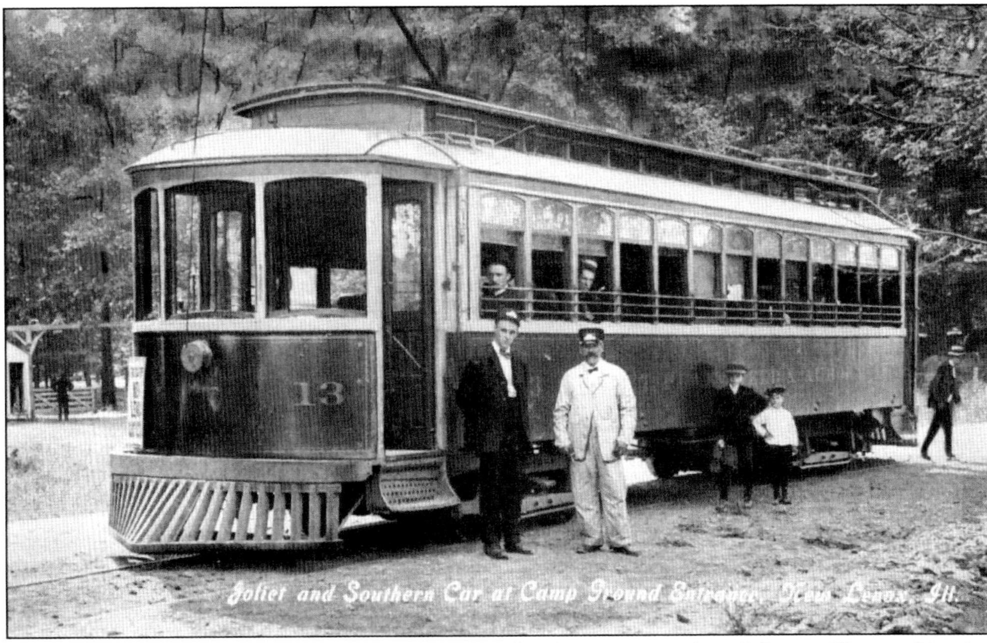

The Joliet & Southern Traction Company operated rail service east from Joliet to Chicago Heights beginning in 1905. The line ran parallel to the Michigan Central Railroad tracks and connected the southern communities of Joliet, New Lenox, Frankfort, and Matteson before ending in Chicago Heights. The first interurban cars to run on these tracks were architecturally little more than long streetcars, but in later years, the streetcars look more like small trolleys. The top picture postcard shows the interurban trolley stopping at the entrance to the campground in New Lenox. The bottom postcard shows a group of area residents standing on Maple Street near the Cedar Road intersection, next to the first streetcar to arrive in New Lenox from Joliet in December 1907. Notice the early Ford Model T in the center of the photograph. By the early 1920s, automobiles and the paving of the Lincoln Highway made Aurora–Joliet–Chicago Heights interurban service unnecessary.

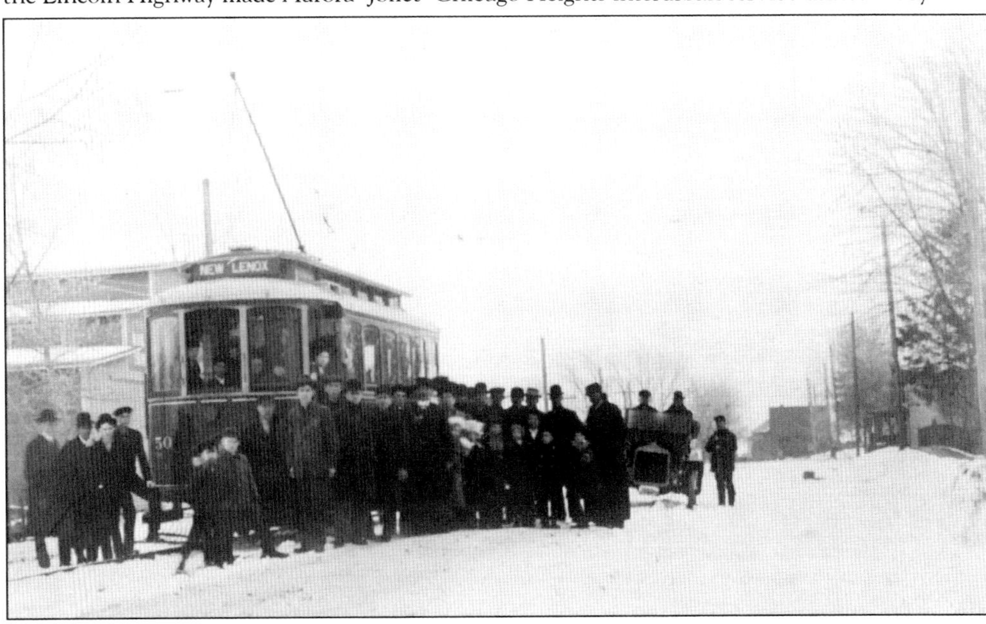

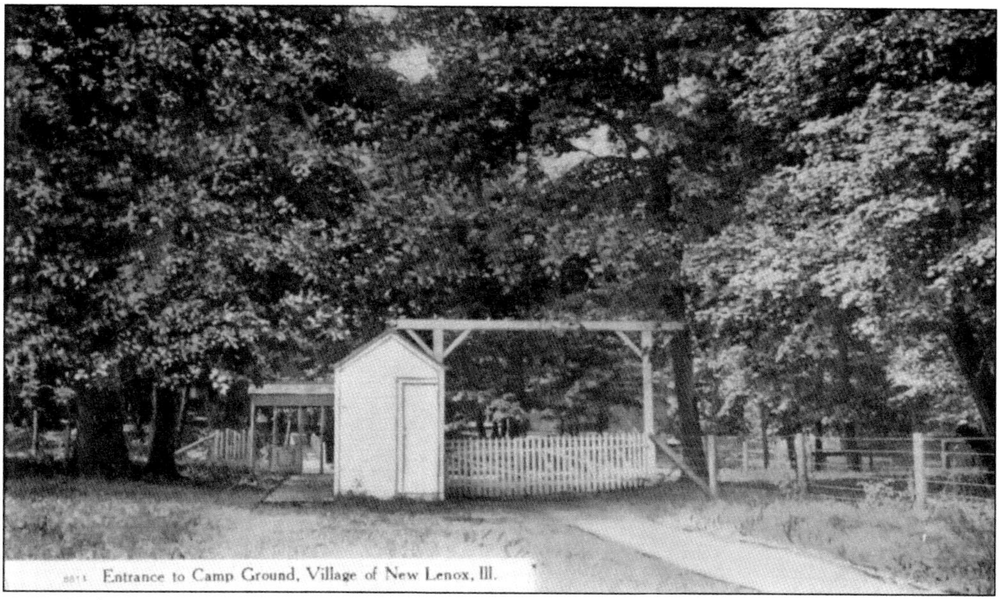

In 1867, the 21-acre campgrounds on the west edge of the village were purchased by the Centenary Campground Association of the Methodist Conference for annual summer camp meetings of the church. Organized by four Methodist church leaders, George Barr, Charles Francis, Fred Haven, and Cal Nicholas, the first meeting was held in 1868. This picture postcard shows a view of the campground entrance just off Maple Street and the Lincoln Highway in New Lenox.

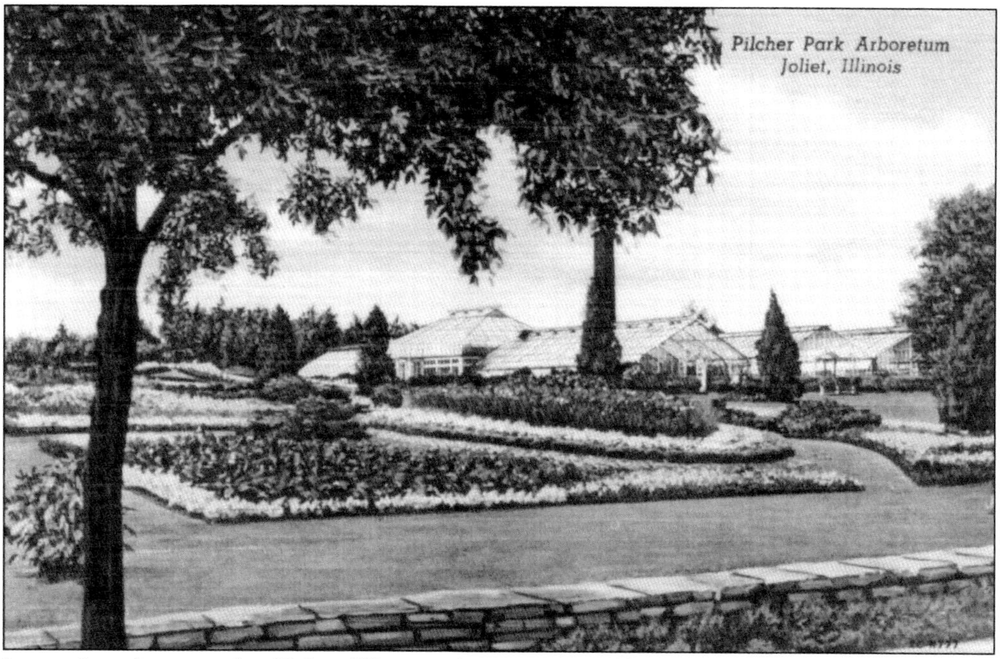

Located on the east side of Joliet, Winston Avenue is a small street that runs parallel to Hickory Creek from East Fourth Avenue to Elmwood Avenue. Hickory Creek flows southwestward for nearly 21 miles, feeding into the Des Plaines River at Joliet. The creek flows through many of Will County's beautiful parks, including Higginbotham Woods, Pilcher Park, and the Hickory Creek Preserve. In the early years, Lincoln Highway travelers used Pilcher Park as a tourist camp.

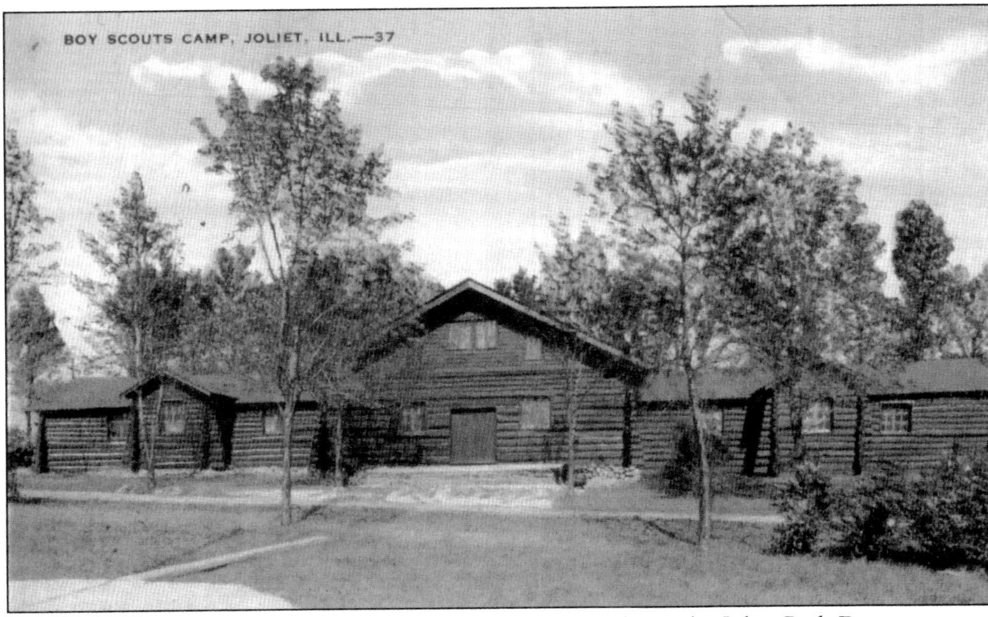

Pilcher Park and Highland Park are considered the first parks in the Joliet Park District system. Located east of downtown Joliet along the Lincoln Highway, the parks provided visitors throughout the years with such amenities as tennis courts, a dance pavilion, boating, swimming, ice-skating, and picnic areas. A large log cabin, pictured in the top photograph, was located in the far northwest corner of Highland Park, near the baseball diamonds, and was used by various organizations, including the Boy Scouts, for meetings and gatherings. As auto camping became the rage in the early 1920s, parks and greenways along the highway were used by the automobile vagabond as a way to experience the independence and excitement of traveling. In 1923, an estimated 9,000 travelers stopped in Pilcher Park, which was used as at the tourist camp located along scenic Hickory Creek. Pilcher Park can be seen in the bottom image.

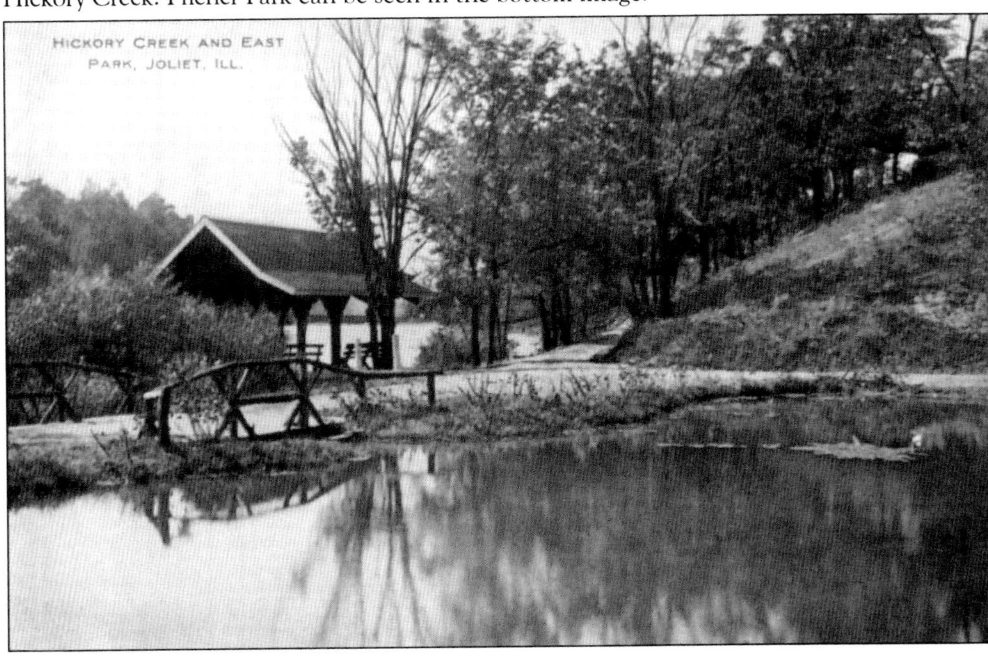

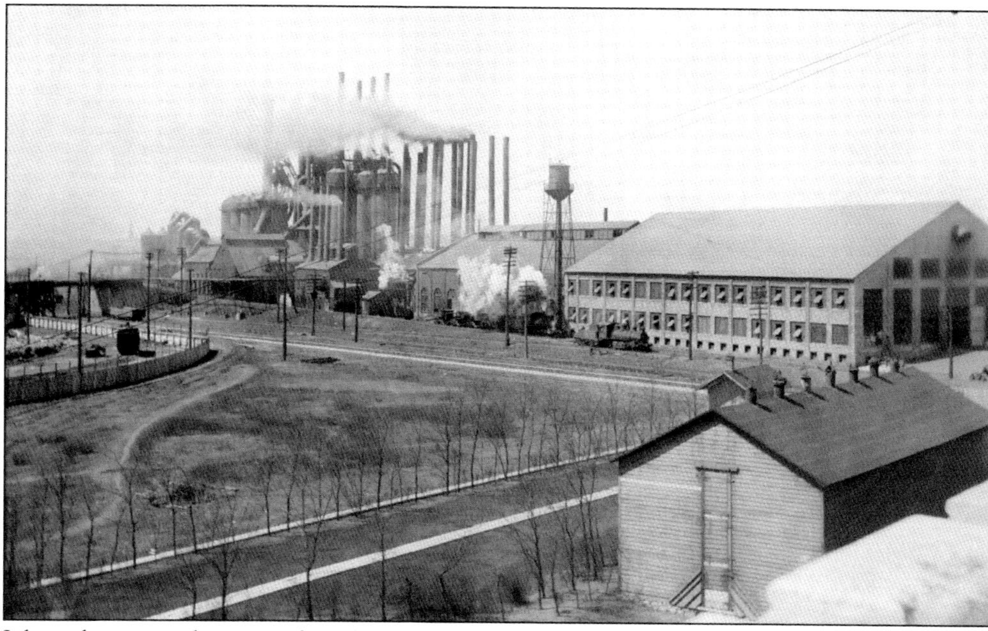

Joliet is known as the "City of Steel" because the town was a major steel-producing center for many years. Located on the city's north side stood one of the largest iron and steel manufacturing facilities in the nation. Between 1869 and 1930, the Joliet Iron and Steel Works employed thousands of Joliet-area residents—most of them emigrants from Poland, Sweden, and Slovenia—who produced iron and steel products, including rails for the nation's growing railroad system. The plant assumed new ownership numerous times and eventually became part of the Illinois Steel Company, which would eventually become part of US Steel Corporation. By the 1930s, the operations became unprofitable, and the plant's six major blast furnaces were demolished, leaving only foundations. In 1998, the Forest Preserve District of Will County opened an interpretive walking trail through the remains of the old structures.

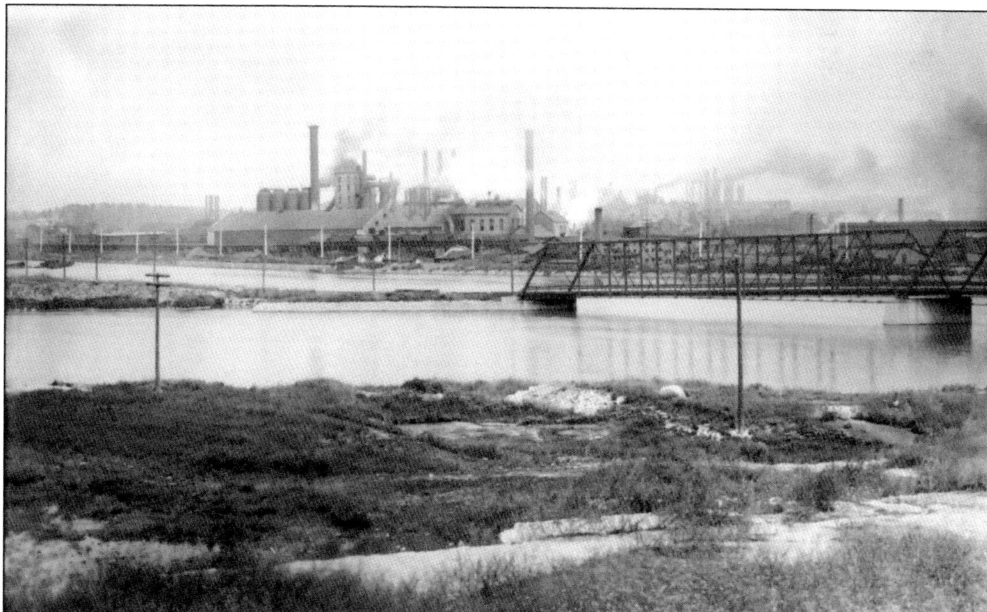

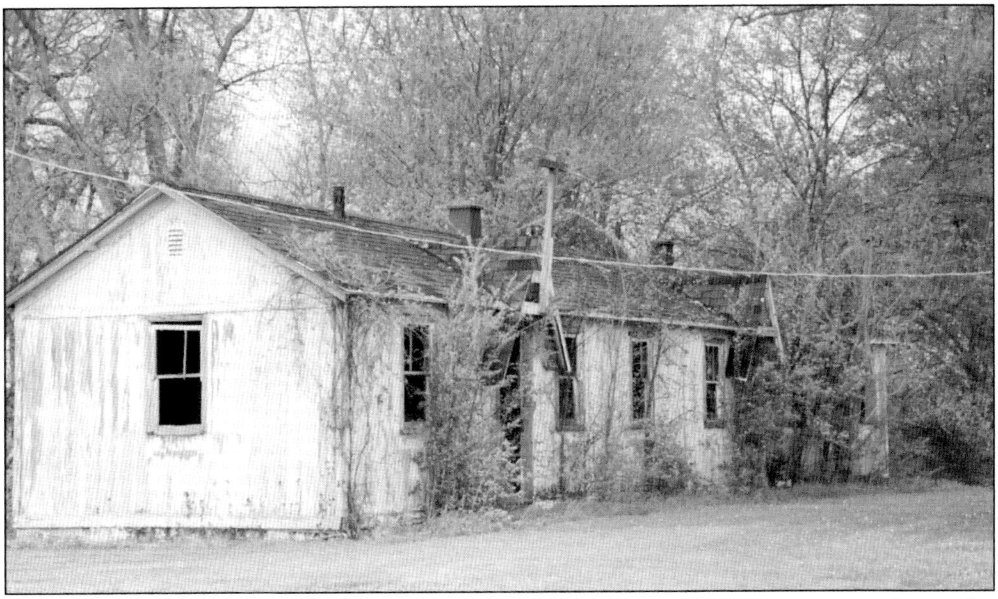

Convenience and location are the two ingredients that made cabin camps so popular in the 1930s. These roadside courts gave automobile riders more privacy, easy check in, less traffic and noise, economy, housekeeping facilities, no lobbies to pass through, and a home-like atmosphere. Arriving guests could also rent or purchase additional amenities, such as blankets, sheets, pillows, and snacks. For all that they offered the traveling motorist, cabin camps were often flimsily constructed and not winterized. Because of their makeshift construction techniques, these early cabins deteriorated quickly and were soon replaced by more solidly constructed motels. These images show examples of early auto cabins located along the east side of Route 53 near Laraway Road in Joliet that are still visible today. This site was located along old Route 66 and included at least two sets of motor court buildings. Currently, only one of these rare buildings, with three separate units, and the office structure still stand.

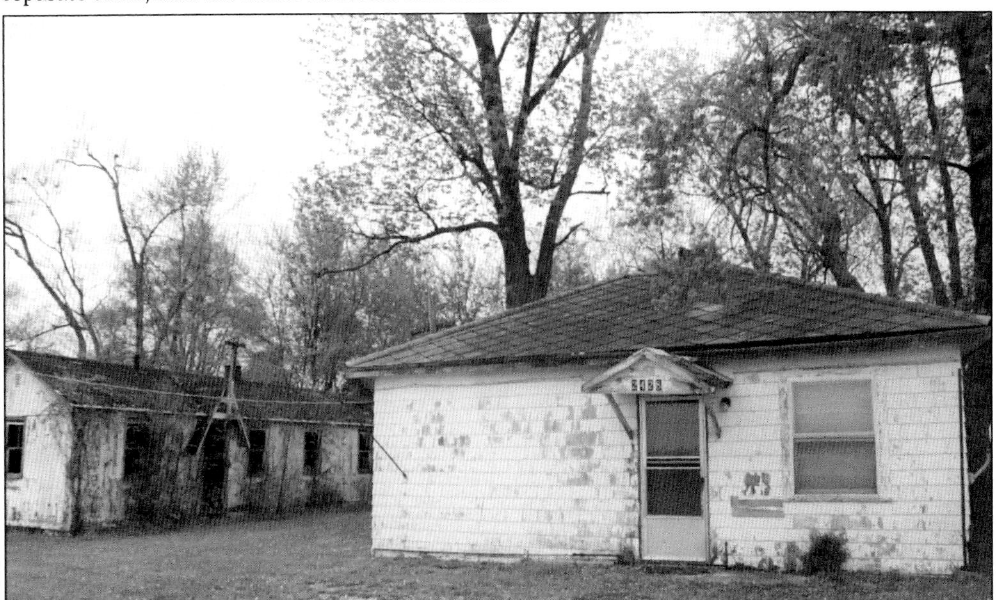

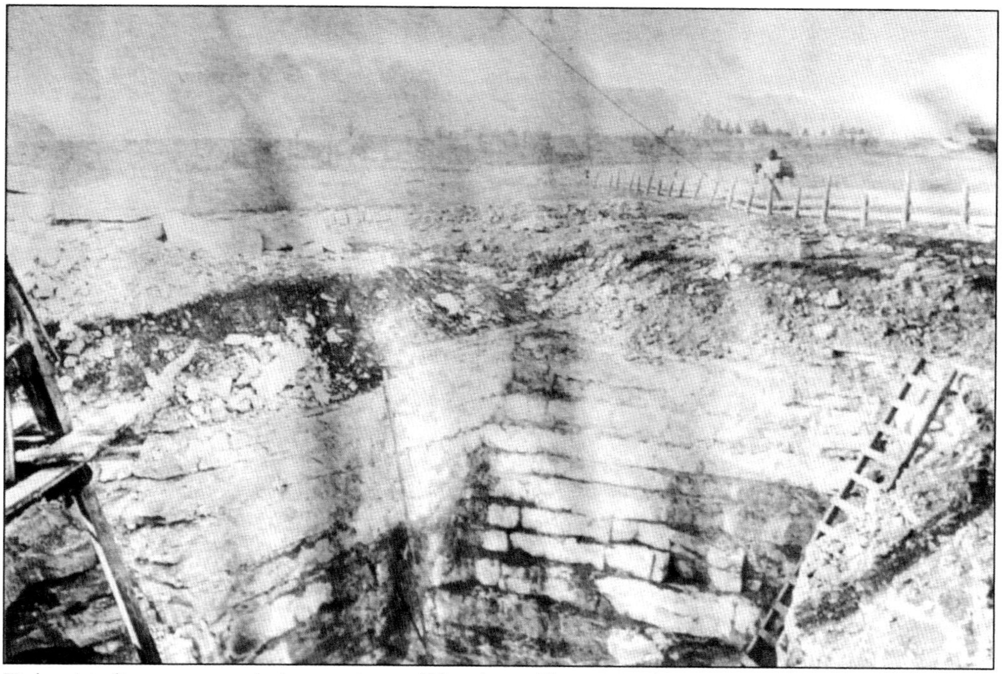

Dolomitic limestone underlay sections of Northern Illinois, and quarries are often located where thick stone deposits occur near the surface. Stone quarrying in the Joliet area began during the 1830s, and limestone was used locally and regionally for a variety of structures. The towns of Joliet, Lockport, and Lemont all became the centers of 19th-century quarrying activity. Limestone blocks were used for building foundations, bridge abutments, canal aqueduct piers, and lock walls. Most stone used along the canal was quarried just north of Joliet, but two other tracts in Aux Sable and Ottawa were also utilized. The top c. 1891 photograph shows a 19th-century quarry hole near the Des Plaines River in Lockport. The bottom c. 1897 photograph shows quarry workers cutting and cracking the stone.

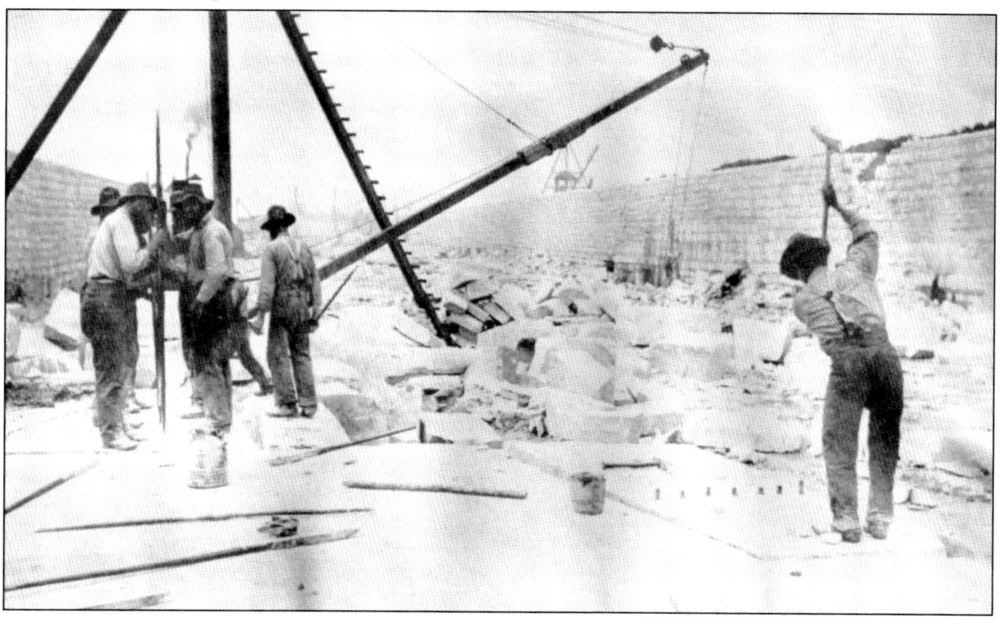

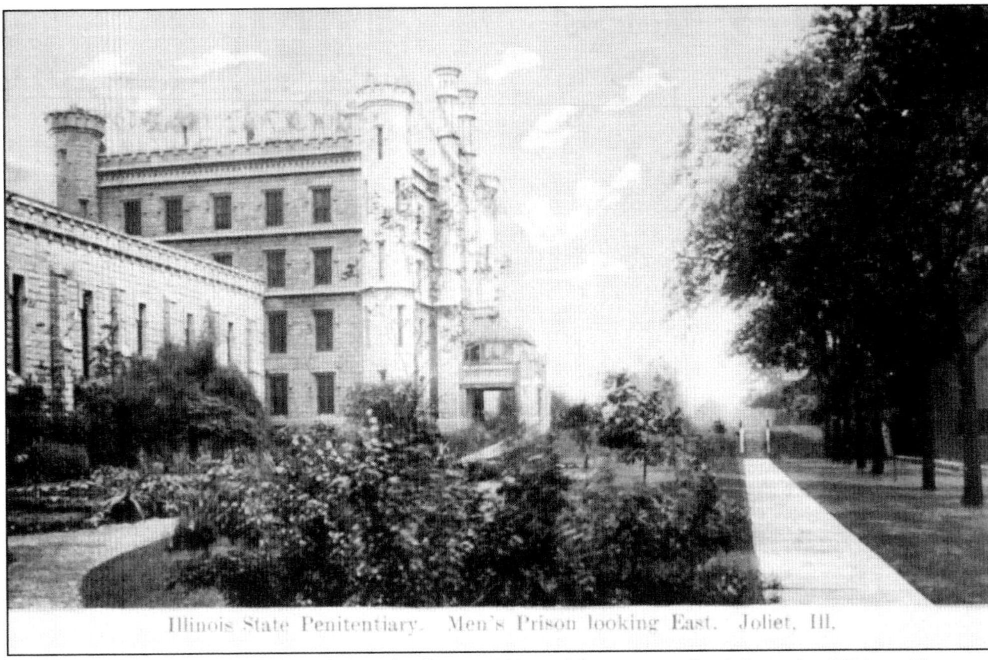

The first penitentiary in Illinois was built in 1831 at Alton near the Mississippi River. Because of overcrowding, in February 1857, the general assembly authorized the building of a new state prison in the northern part of the state and appropriated $300,000 to begin construction. Built with convict labor, the architectural design of the new prison is described as castellated Gothic. This postcard shows the front of the Illinois Penitentiary in Joliet. Located on Collins Street, this is the entrance to the men's prison looking east.

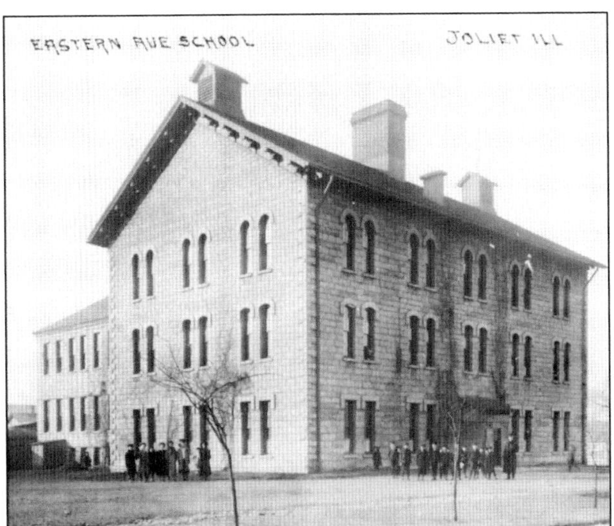

The three-story Eastern Avenue School was built in 1863 and located on the southeast corner of Eastern Avenue and Cass Street (Lincoln Highway), just west of Herkimer Street. In December 1915, the superintendent of schools declared the building a firetrap and said the building should be rebuilt or abandoned. The old Eastern Avenue School was razed, and in 1916, a new school was constructed on the same site and was named the F.E. Marsh Elementary School. Marsh was a Joliet native who served on the first school board and ran a grain business in Plainfield and a bootery in downtown Joliet.

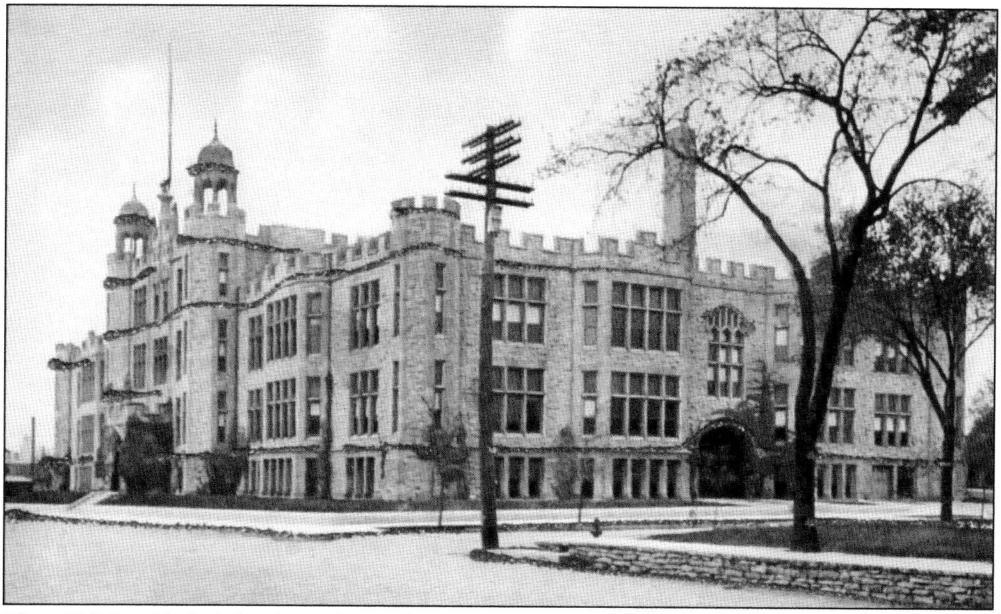

The old Joliet High School was located on the corner of Chicago and Webster Streets. By 1899, overcrowded conditions prompted voters to establish a new township high school and approve the purchase of a site for the construction of a new school. In 1901, the Joliet Township High School was opened to the 600 students enrolled that year. Designed by F.S. Allen and built in the collegiate Gothic style, the building was constructed primarily of Joliet limestone, and for decorative detailing, Bedford stone was used on the exterior. Over 100 years later, the building still operates as a school and is commonly known as Joliet Central High School. The top photograph is a view from the corner of Eastern Avenue and Jefferson Street. The bottom photograph is a view looking east near the corner of Van Buren Street and Eastern Avenue.

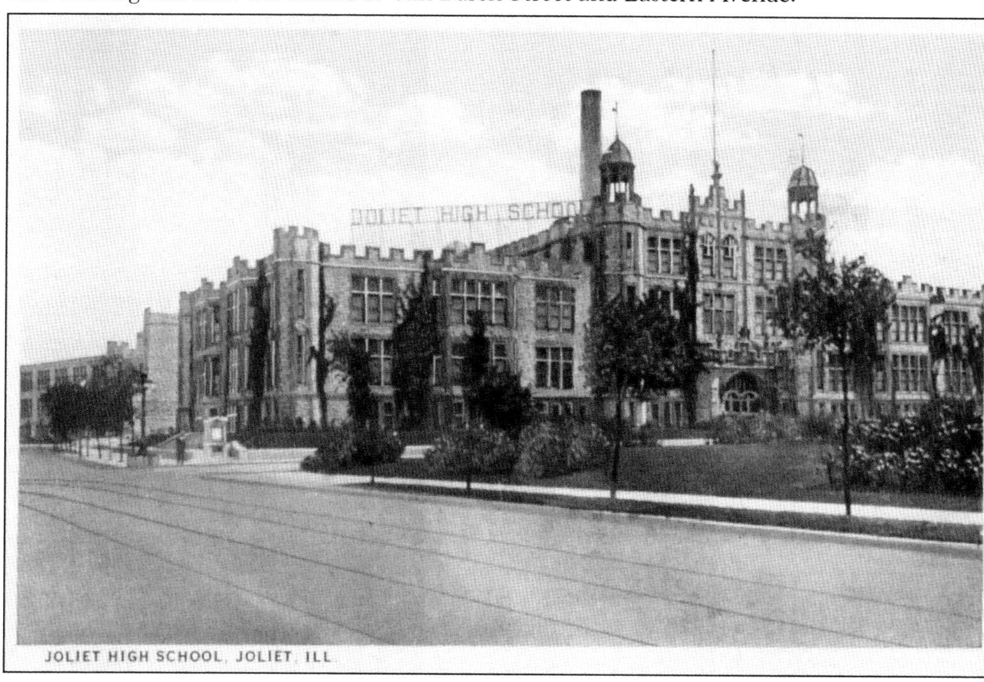

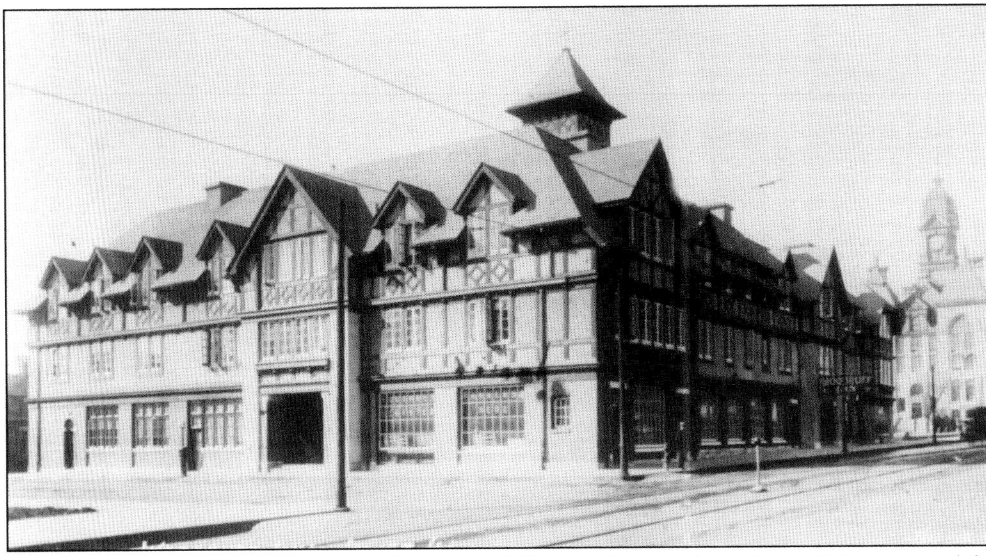

Located on the southwest corner of Scott and Jefferson Streets, the Woodruff Inn opened for business on November 1, 1915, with 102 guest rooms, a large inviting lobby, an inner courtyard that provided guests with a tranquil setting, and fine cuisine prepared by chef Marcel A. Pfister. The English-style architecture of the Woodruff Inn made guests, including Lincoln Highway travelers, comfortable during their stay in Joliet. The hotel was razed on December 21, 1971, ending an era as a distinctive downtown landmark.

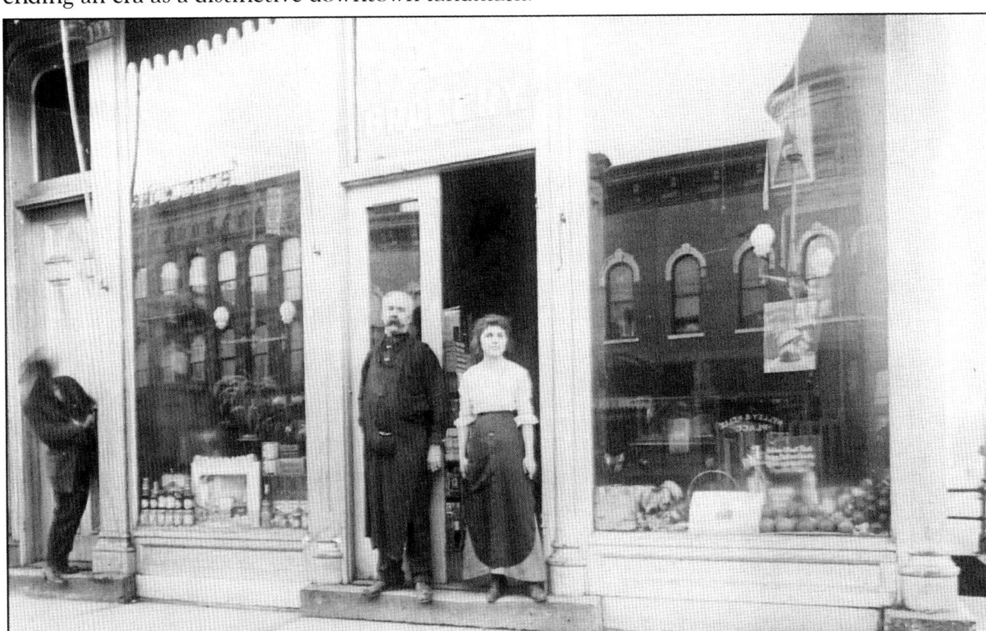

The intersection of Cass (Lincoln Highway) and Chicago Streets has always been a busy location for businesses and their customers. The Mahoney Grocery Store, located on the southwest corner of Chicago and Cass Streets, was established in 1867 and featured fresh fruits, vegetables, eggs, and other staples. The Mahoney family lived above the grocery store and owned five horses and a cow that were housed in the barn behind the store. Jeremiah Mahoney II and his granddaughter, Evelyn Mahoney, are pictured here in front of the store in 1914.

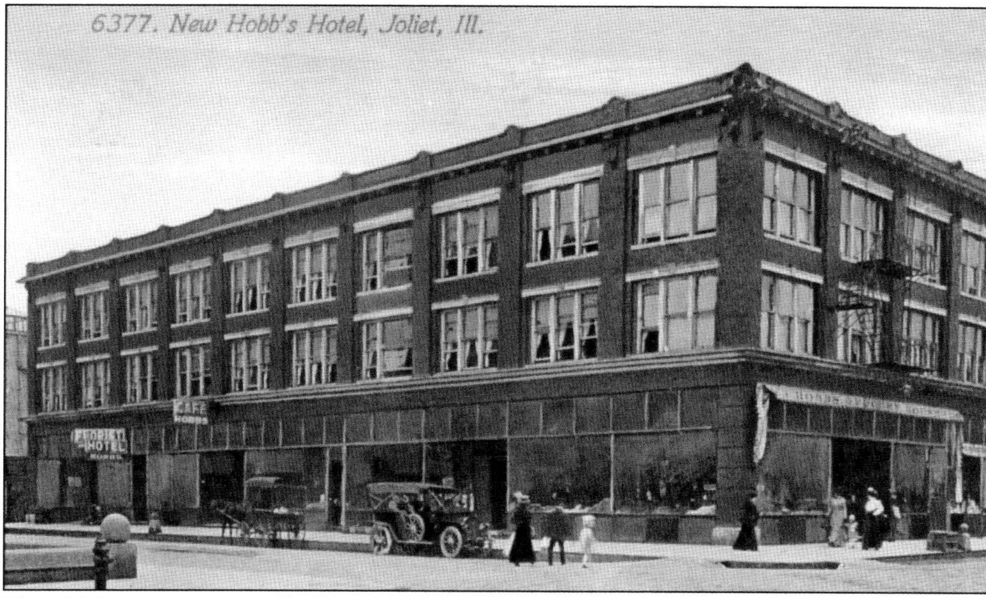

The old Ottawa Street Methodist Church occupied the southeast corner of Ottawa and Clinton Streets for many years. In 1909, the congregation sold the property to James R. Hobbs and built a new church on the northeast corner of Ottawa and Cass Streets. Hobbs soon replaced the old church with a three-story building that operated a variety of businesses over the years, including a hotel, a grocery store, a café, and a florist shop. This postcard photograph shows the Hobbs building in the early 20th century.

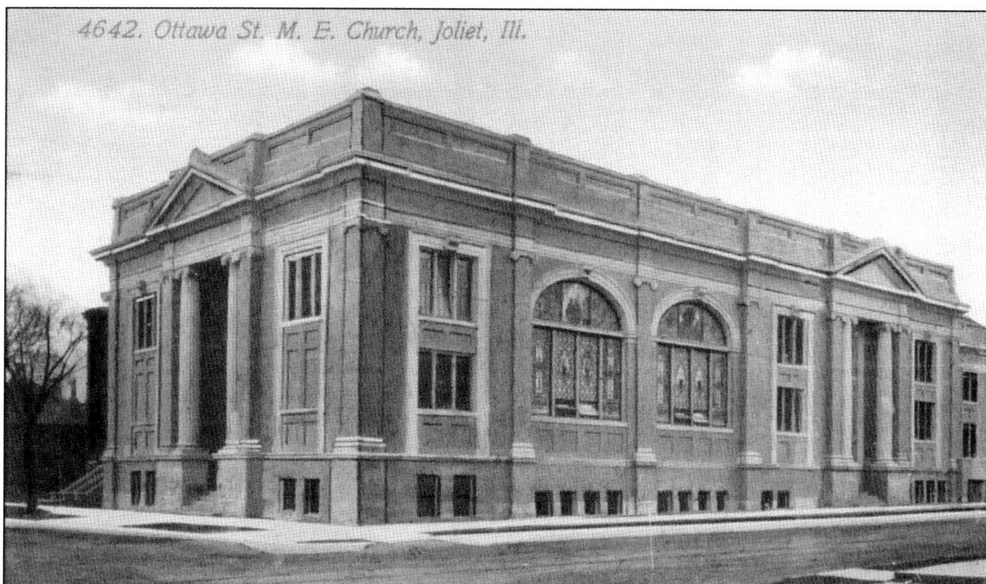

Located on the northeast corner of Ottawa and Cass Streets, the two-story Ottawa Street Methodist Church was completed in 1910. The congregation worshiped in the church until 1996, when it merged with Grace United Methodist Church on Avalon and Larkin Avenues. In 2002, the Ottawa Street building became part of the new Joliet Area Historical Museum complex. The corner of Ottawa and Cass Streets in downtown Joliet is significant, as this intersection marks the crossing of Route 66 and the Lincoln Highway.

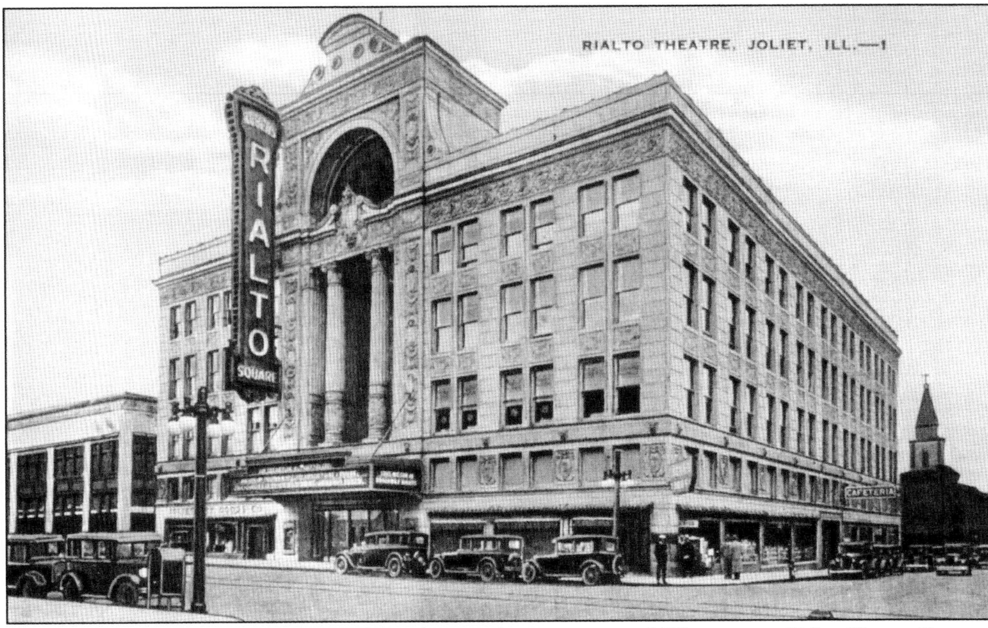

The Rialto Square Theatre, located on the northeast corner of Chicago and Van Buren Streets, stands as a familiar site in the downtown Joliet district. On May 24, 1926, the Rialto Theatre was officially opened to patrons. Considered to be one of the most beautiful theaters in the nation, the stage has been graced with thousands of entertainers over the years, including Bob Hope, Lawrence Welk, and the Marx Brothers. In 1980, a $6-million restoration program began to restore the theater to its original splendor. The grand reopening of the theater took place in November 1981.

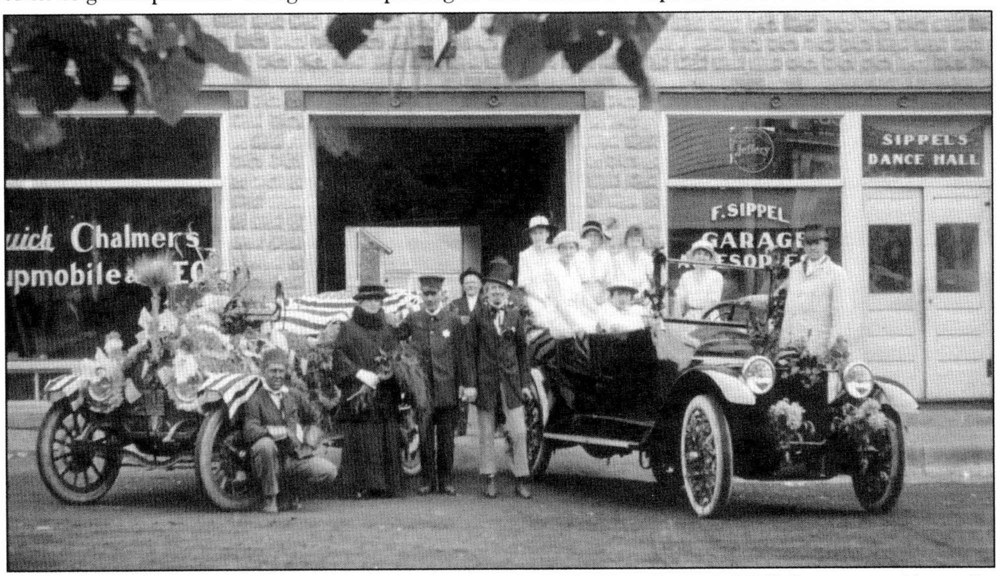

For many years, the Lincoln Highway was a well-traveled route through Will County and brought thousands of travelers through Joliet. As a result, many local businesses devoted to automobiles were started in town, particularly dealerships and repair shops. The Fred Sippel Auto Company, located at 100 North Scott Street near the northeast corner of Scott and Jefferson Streets, was both a Studebaker distributor and a repair garage. Advertised as the "largest and best garage in Will County," the Sippel showroom had a capacity for 60 automobiles.

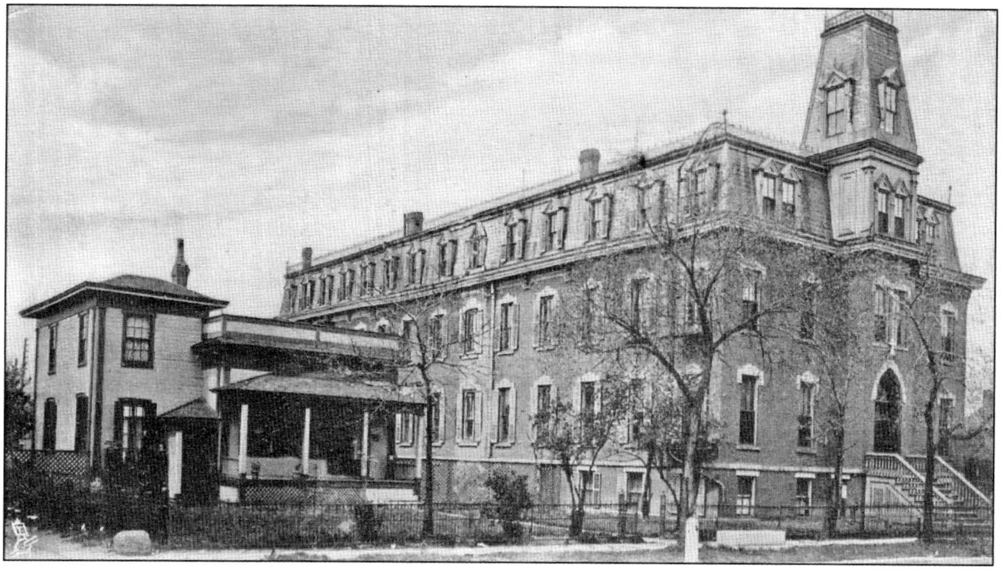

Built in 1883 and located on the southwest corner of Ottawa and Cass Streets, the Sisters of Loretto established a school for young children that provided the proper mental and physical training to students that would give them a solid and refined education. Music, drawing, painting, Latin, French, German, and English were all given particular attention in the school curriculum. Providence High School had its beginning in this building in 1918 before moving to its present campus in New Lenox.

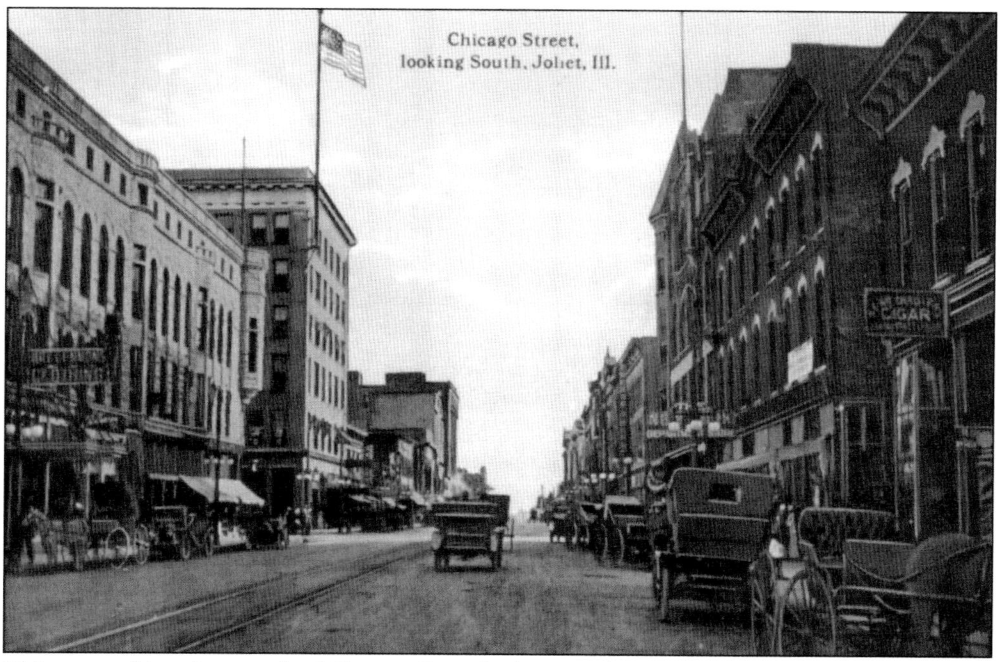

This postcard is a photograph of Chicago Street looking south near Cass Street. The long limestone building on the left is the Auditorium Building, which housed the city's first civic auditorium and functioned throughout the years as a cultural arts center for the community. Farther down the block, the six-floor building flying the American flag was home to Ford Hopkins Drugs and Lewis Brothers' Shoes. Across the street, the Joliet Opera House, with its cone-shaped tower, can be seen.

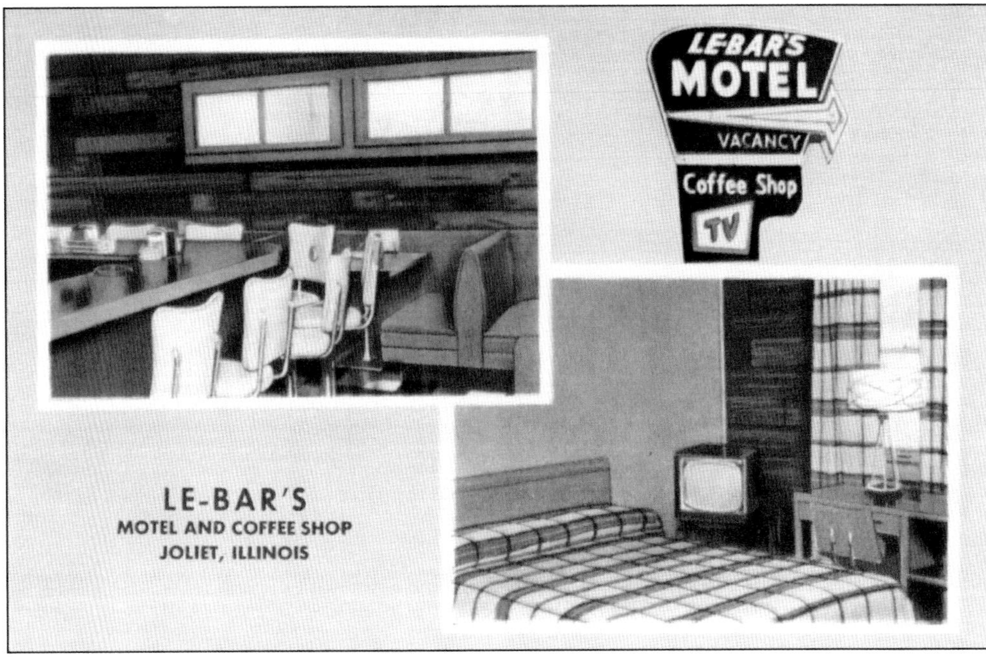

The economic boom of the postwar era spawned many new motels along the Lincoln Highway, causing owners to differentiate their new businesses from the competition down the road. The era also saw the emergence of personal expression and abstraction, which caused many motel owners to design fresh new signs that would stand out and attract attention from the passing tourist. The leaning or slant form design of Le-Bar's Motel in Joliet, together with its dramatic flashing arrow, certainly attracted customers along the busy Lincoln Highway strip in Joliet. Le-Bar's Motel and Coffee Shop was located at 928 Plainfield Road, about three-fourths of a mile northwest of downtown Joliet. The bottom image shows the former location of Le-Bar's Motel and Coffee Shop. (Above, courtesy of Russell Rein.)

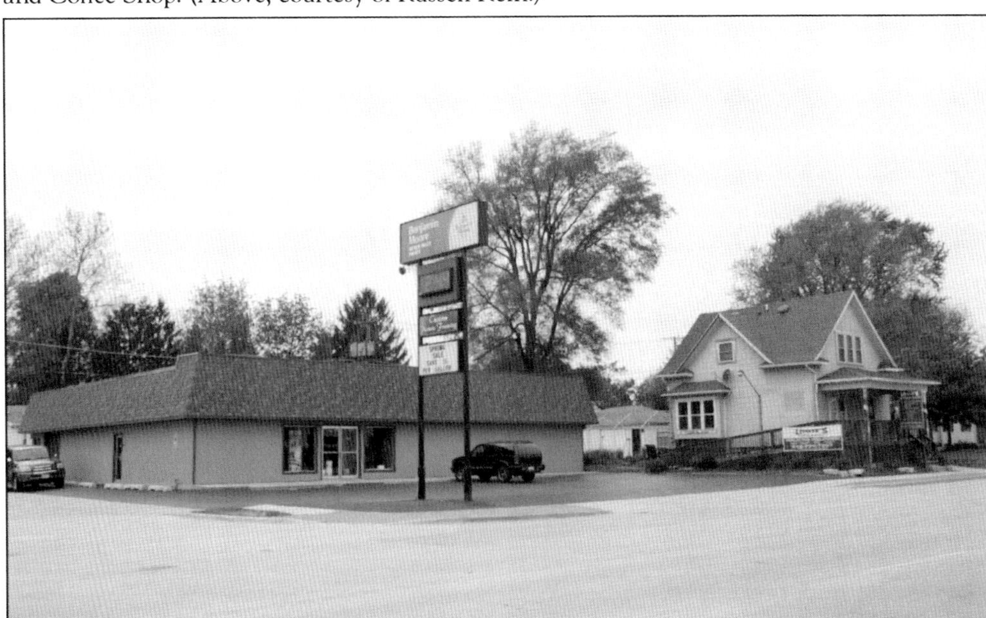

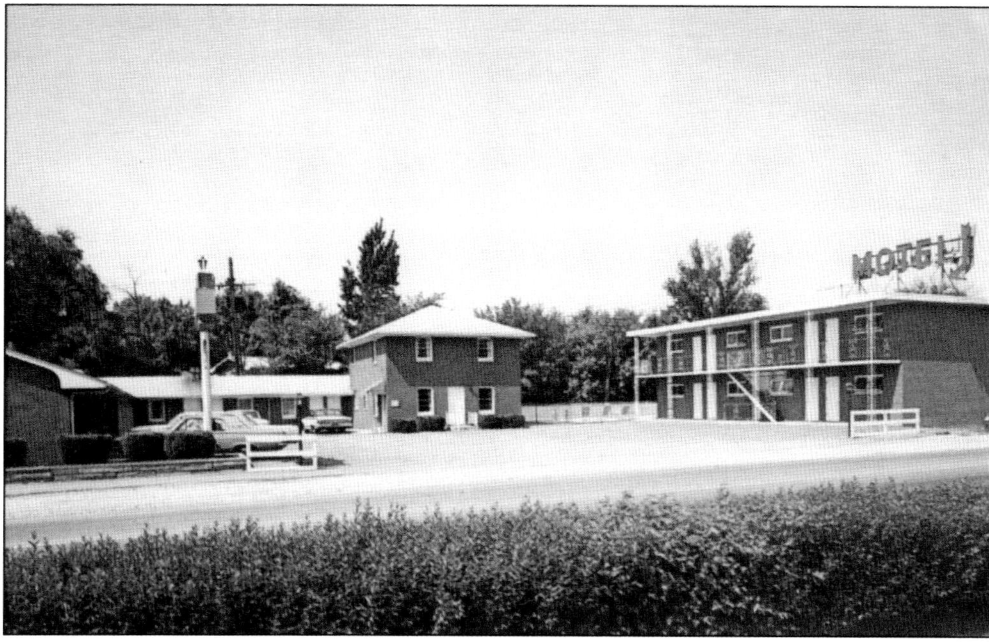

By the 1950s, many motels had cleared away native plants and trees and replaced them with non-native or exotic varieties applied in neat arrangements surrounding the buildings. During the same decade, large arrows were popular additions to signs, as they served both to direct customers to the motel from a distance and to provide a decorative element to the sign itself. In the postcard photograph above, the Town House Motel, located along the Lincoln Highway in Joliet, uses two signs to attract customers from the road. On the left is the traditional, un-themed *L*-shaped rectangular sign. The neon roof sign with the directional arrow seen on the right was added later to provide differentiation along the increasingly crowded highway as competition and traffic patterns in the area grew. The bottom image shows a similar view of the hotel today. (Above, courtesy of Russell Rein.)

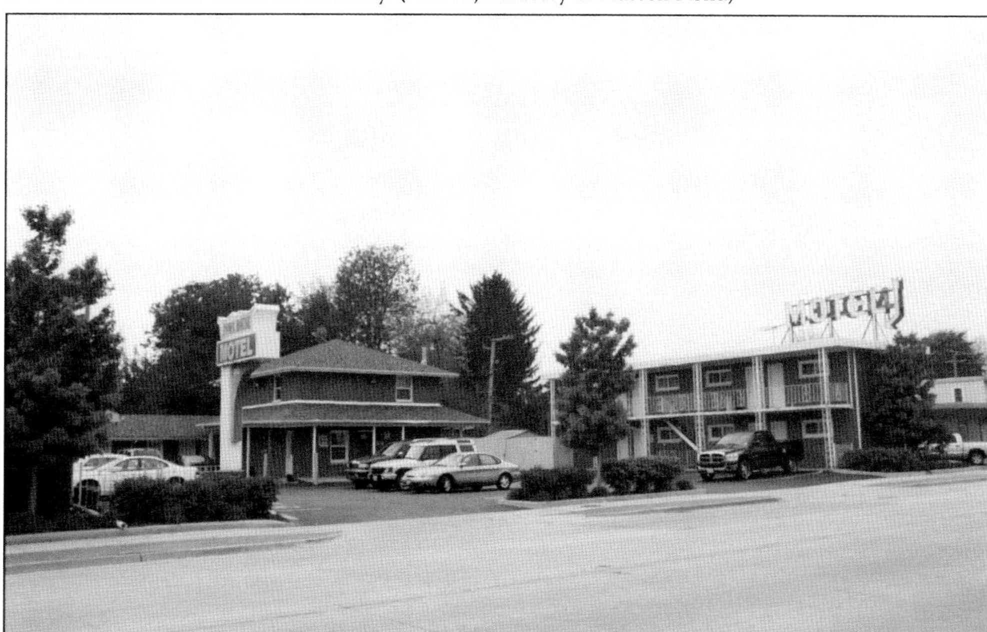

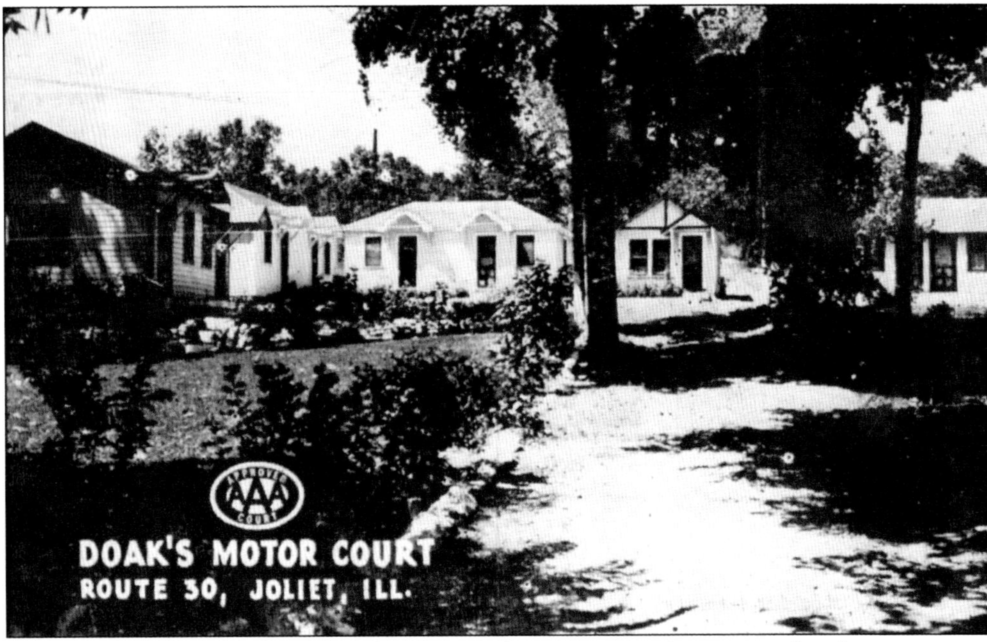

Postcards from the 1930s and 1940s often convey the importance that owners placed on integrating the motel business into a natural context. Trees, shrubs, vegetation, and other scenic vistas were featured in the image that was taken from the road or entrance. In early motor court images, the abundance of vegetation provided the traveling customer with the idea of privacy and seclusion from other guests, as the cabins were nestled among the tress and away from other public structures. Doak's Motor Court, located along the Lincoln Highway in Joliet, is a good example of an image using the natural context to convey a peaceful message.

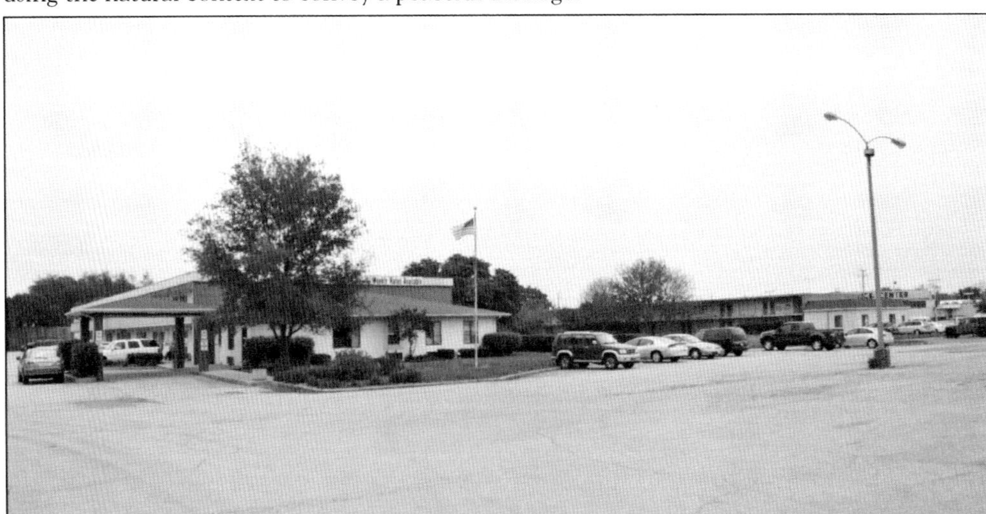

The evolution of 20th-century tourist accommodations can be seen along stretches of the Lincoln Highway through Joliet. From early tourist camps, to homeowners who established "tourist homes" and rented out spare rooms, to "tourist courts" with individual cabins for rent, to more modern multiunit motels with rooms under a single roof, all of these local businesses were eventually eclipsed by larger franchises, such as the Holiday Inn complex that opened west of the city in 1963. Today, the location still functions as a hotel complex and is known as the Joliet Inn.

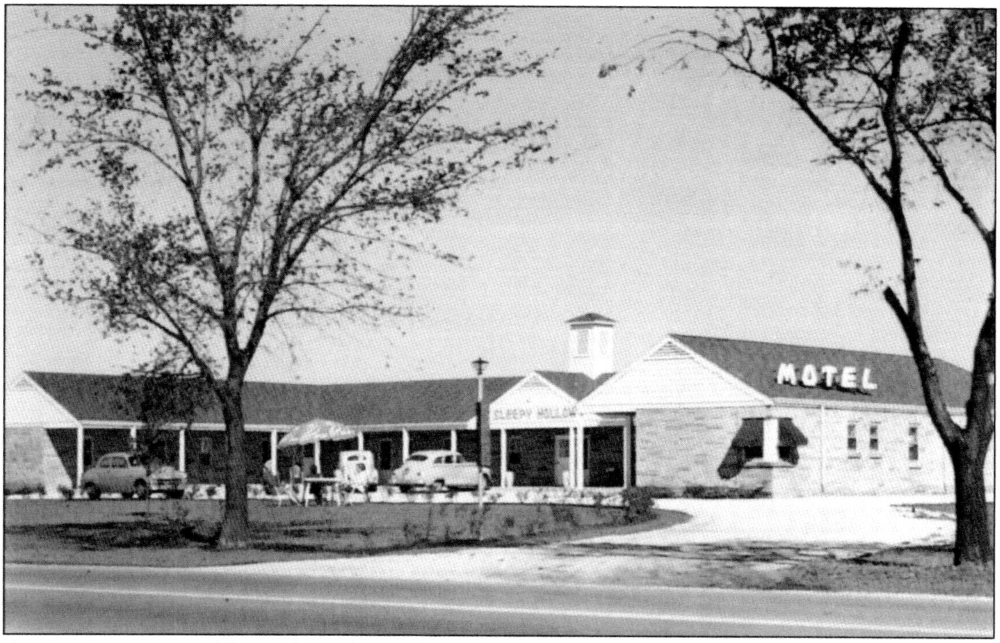

As the American public took to the road, motor courts, inns, and highway motels appeared and catered to the traveling public. In 1921, Plainfield built the portion of the highway through its main street (Lockport Street) and connected neighboring towns on what is now Route 30. Southeast of Plainfield, two motels existed for the traveling public as they traversed the transcontinental highway through Will County. One was the Sleepy Hollow Motel, located for years near today's Louis Joliet Mall. The other was the Lakeview Motel, across from tranquil Lake Renwick. The nearly 60-year-old Lakeview Motel caught fire in September 2010 and was razed in early 2011. The only structure still standing is a house which doubled as the main office.

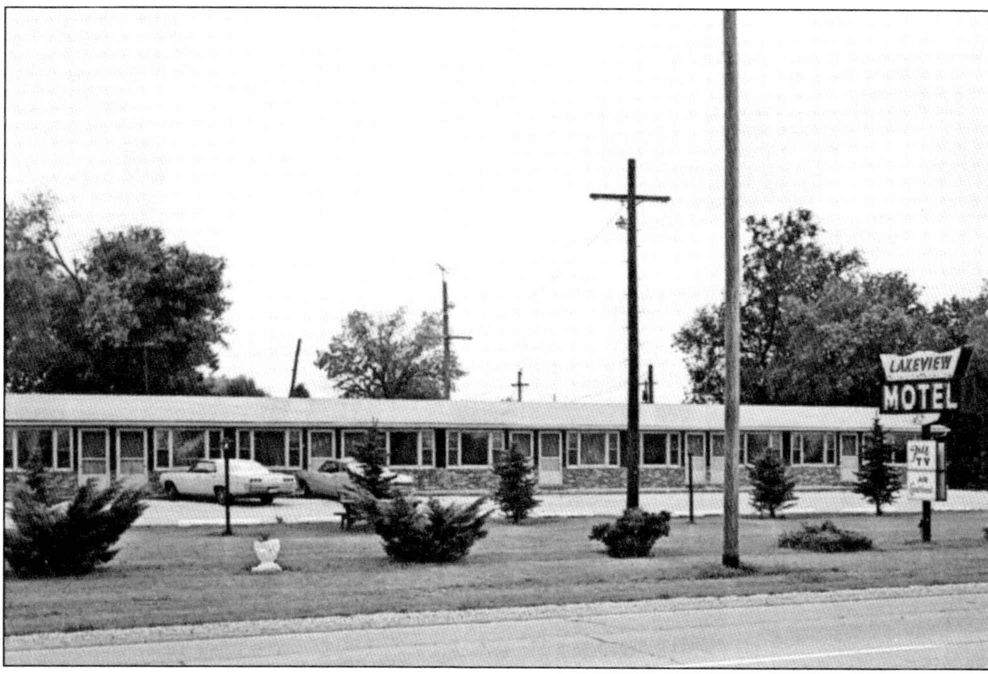

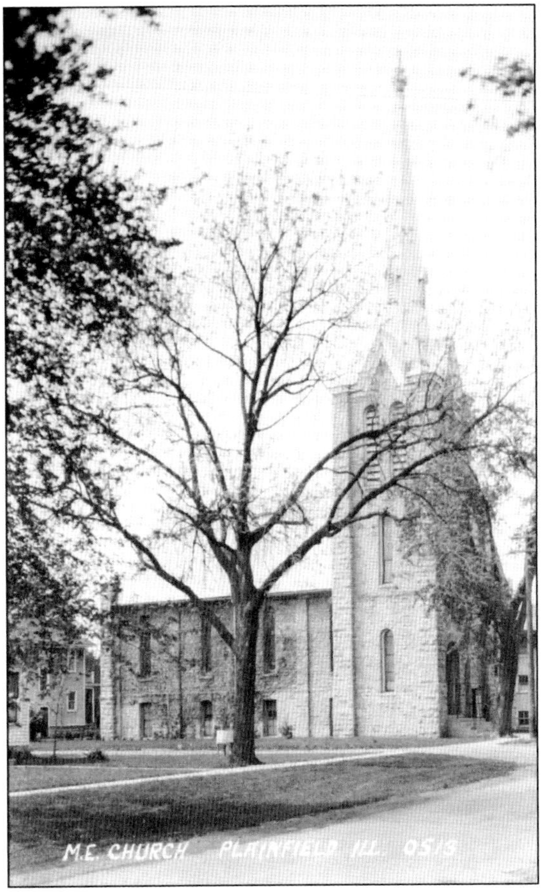

In 1829, Rev. Jesse Walker and 10 other settlers met together in Walker's Grove and formed the first Methodist church in the area. The first meetings were held in a log cabin near the intersection of Joliet Road and Route 59. In 1866, a stone church was constructed on the northwest corner of Illinois and Chicago Streets. Built using locally quarried limestone, the construction cost was nearly $20,000. This postcard shows a view of the church looking northwest from Illinois Street.

Between 1834 and 1835, the southern, eastern, and northern portions of Plainfield were platted and the new town was given its name. It was during this time that an inn and tavern was constructed on Main Street, and today it is the oldest documented building in town. Commonly called the "Plainfield House," the building is otherwise known as Halfway House. The Plainfield Halfway House was added to the National Register of Historic Places in 1980.

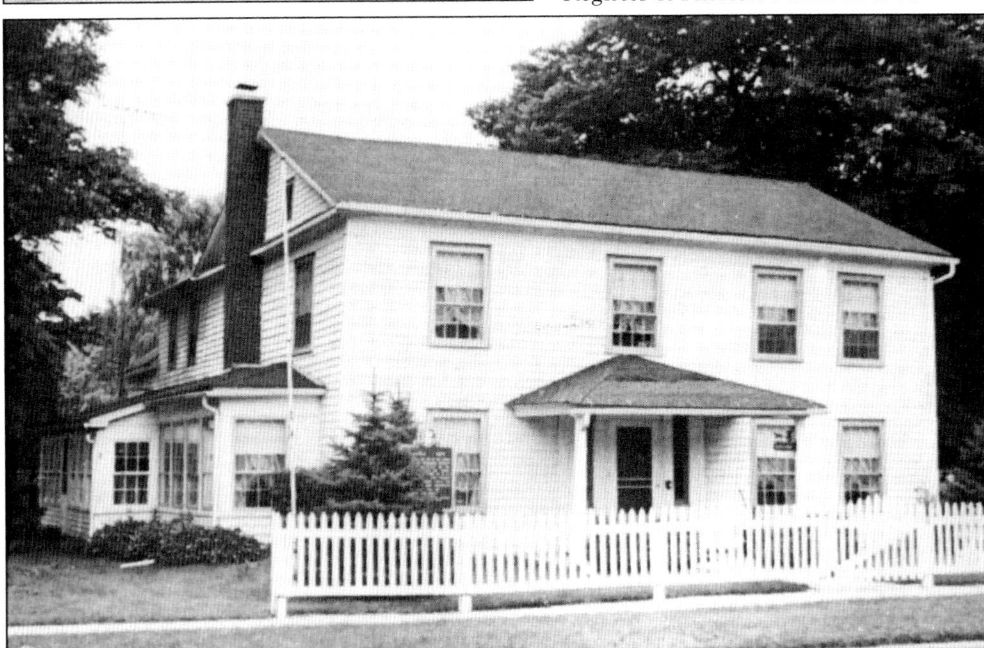

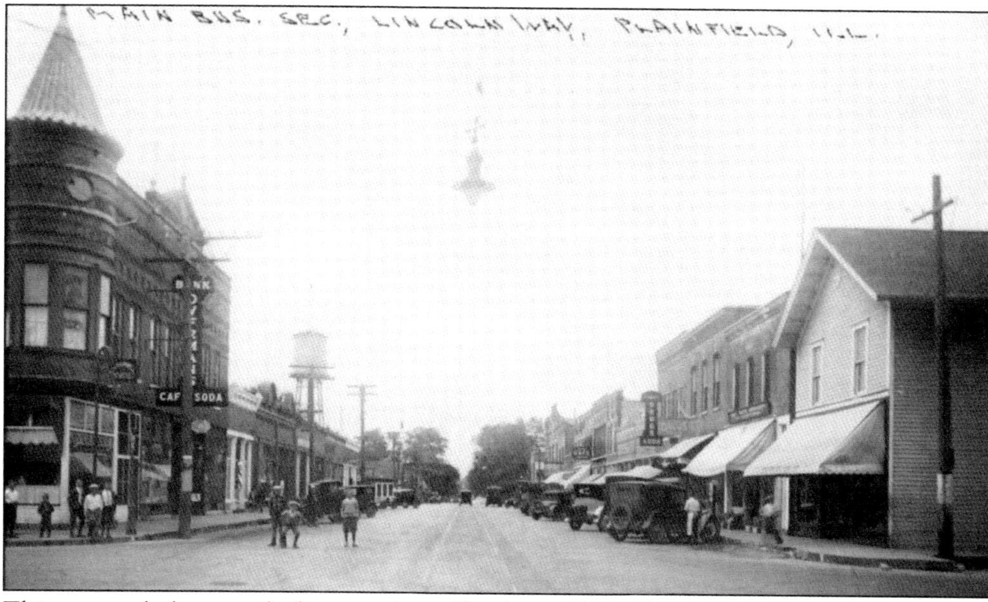

This postcard photograph shows a view of Lockport Street (Lincoln Highway) in downtown Plainfield looking west from the intersection of Illinois Street. One notable feature in this early-1920s photograph is the opera house building to the left with its unique alcove windows, cone tower, and a clock mounted above the windows. The small crowd on the corner is standing in front of Overman's Restaurant and Soda Shop. In the center of the photograph, the interurban railroad tracks running down Lockport Street can been seen.

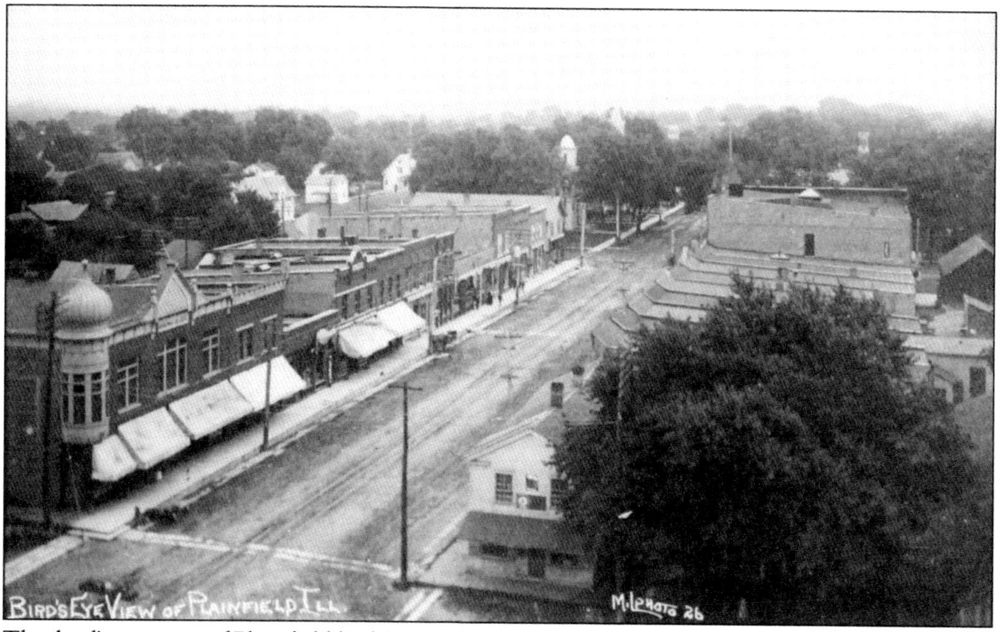

This bird's-eye view of Plainfield looking northeast down Lockport Street (Lincoln Highway) was taken from the top of the old water tower. On the north side of Lockport Street, the Masonic Block Building can be seen on the left, and the spire of Plymouth Congregation Church is visible in the distance. On the south side of the block, the old Central Hotel can be seen on the southeast corner of Lockport and Des Plaines Streets.

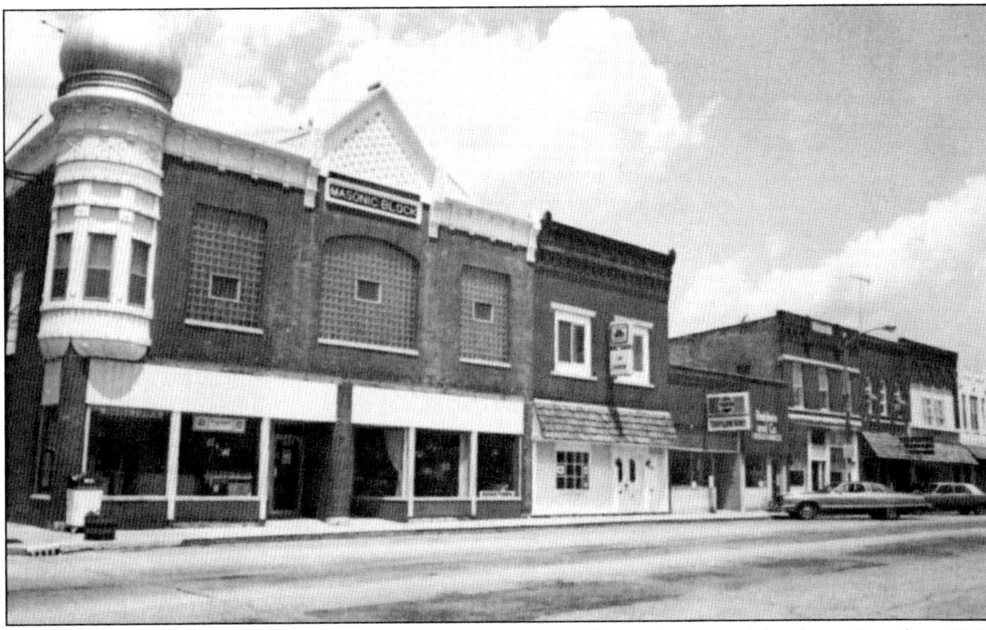

The history of the Masonic fraternal lodge in Plainfield can be traced back to October 1867 when it was chartered. In 1891, the Masonic building burned, and this left the Masons without a meeting place. Immediately, plans were made to construct a new building, and two lots were purchased on the northeast corner of Lockport and Des Plaines Streets. The new building, with its unique, onion-shaped corner dome, was officially dedicated in February 1896 and has been an important part of Plainfield's downtown history for over 100 years.

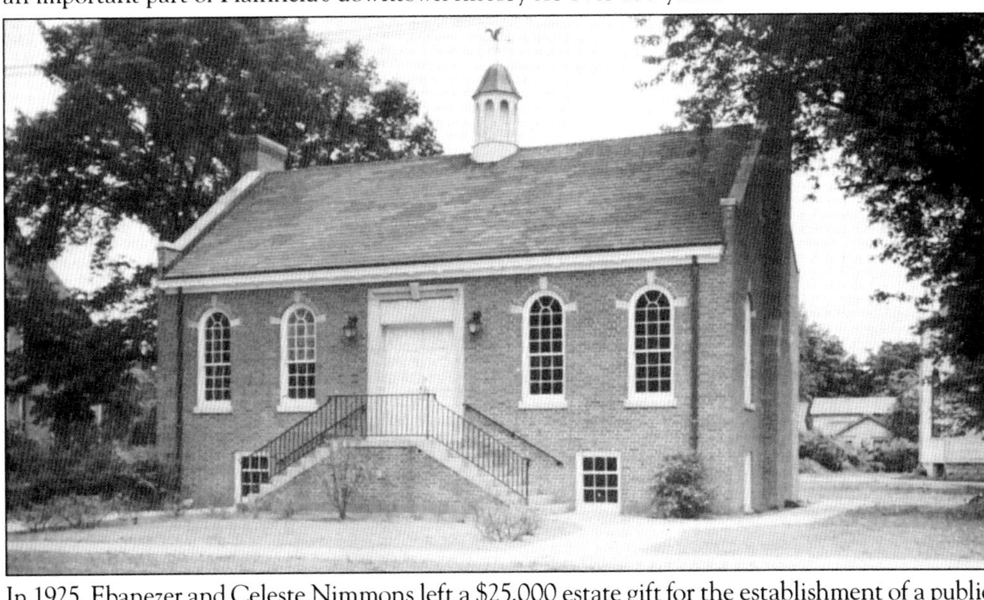

In 1925, Ebanezer and Celeste Nimmons left a $25,000 estate gift for the establishment of a public library. In April 1926, the first library, located in a small frame building on a lot on the south side of Lockport Street, opened its doors. In 1940, the library board decided to build a larger facility and purchased a lot from the Plainfield Congregational Church. On June 1, 1941, the new library was opened to the public and the McClester and Nimmons names were carved in stone above the front entrance.

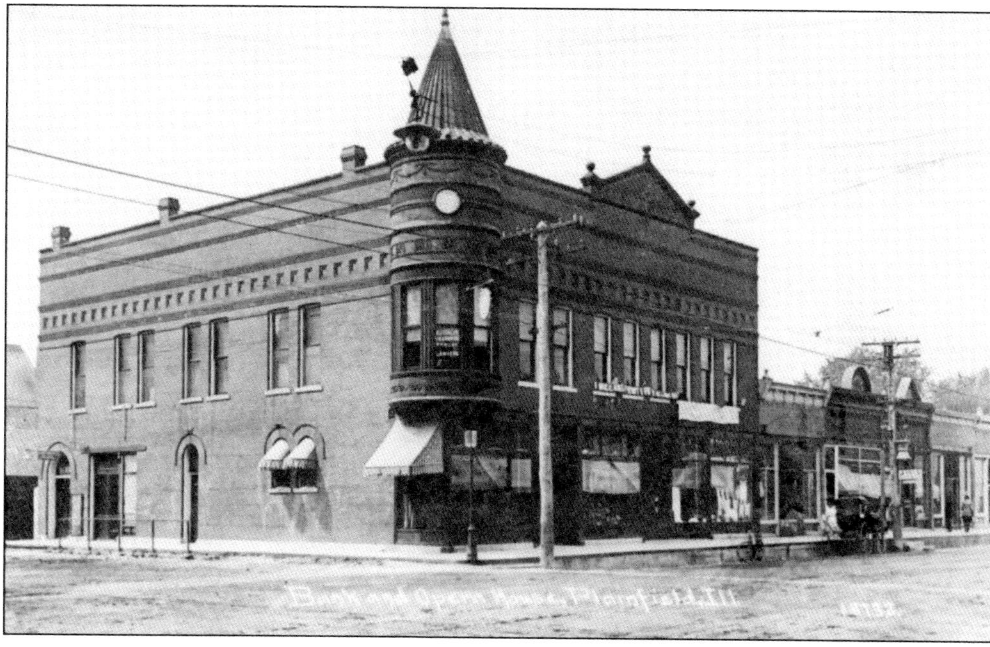

In 1889, the first opera house in Plainfield was built on the southwest corner of Lockport and Illinois Streets. The first floor housed a bank and hardware store. The second floor had a theater and stage. In February 1898, a fire broke out on the south side of the block and destroyed a number of buildings, including the post office and opera house. Shortly after, a new, redbrick opera house building was constructed on the old foundation. The top picture postcard shows the new building with corner tower and clock mounted over the alcove windows. The bottom c. 1930 postcard shows a view of Lockport Street looking west, and the opera house, without its cone tower roof, can be seen on the left.

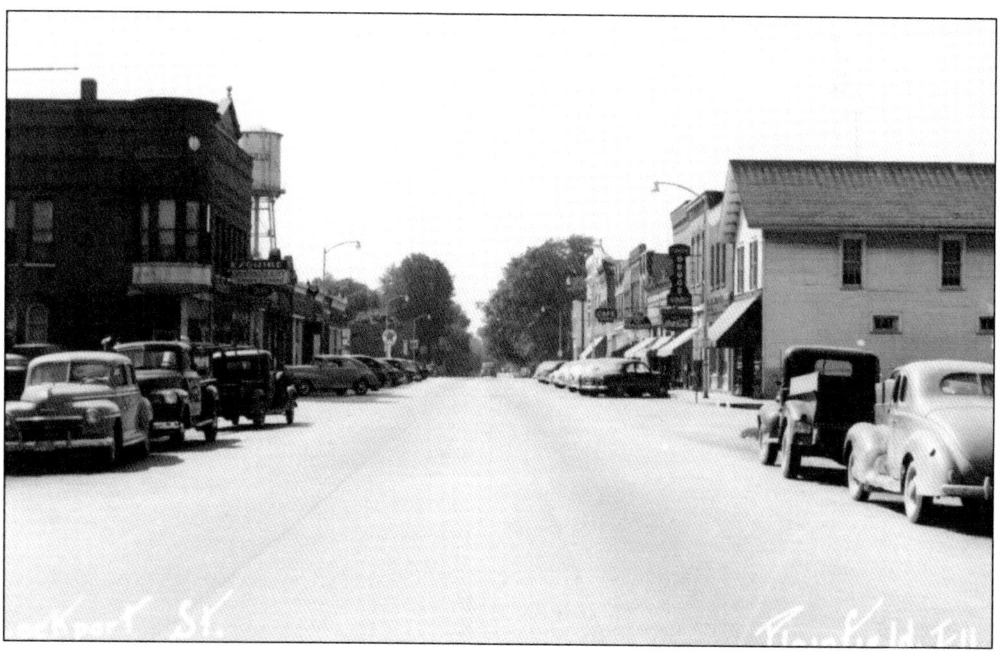

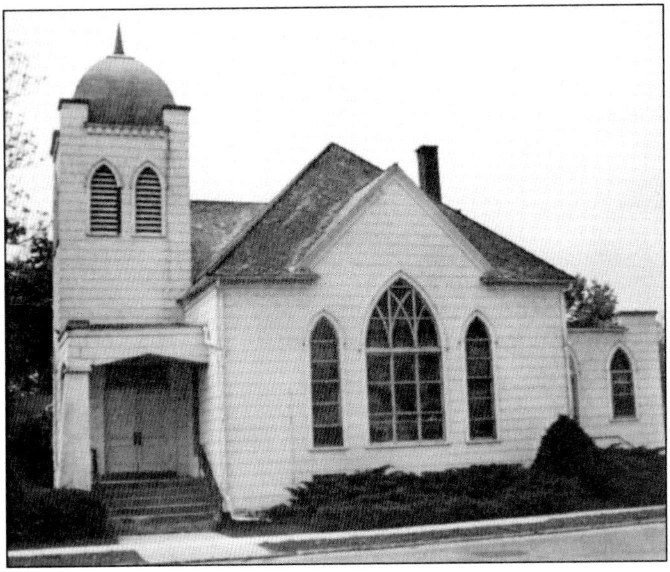

In August 1834, Rev. J.E. Amborse arrived in Plainfield and helped arrange for the formation of the First Baptist Church. The first meetinghouse was occupied until 1857, when a new and larger house was built on the same site. In December 1914, a fire broke out and destroyed the old church. Within a year, a new church was constructed, and it was dedicated in November 1915. On September 4, 2004, the historic landmark church, located on the corner of Route 59 and Lockport Street (Lincoln Highway), was razed.

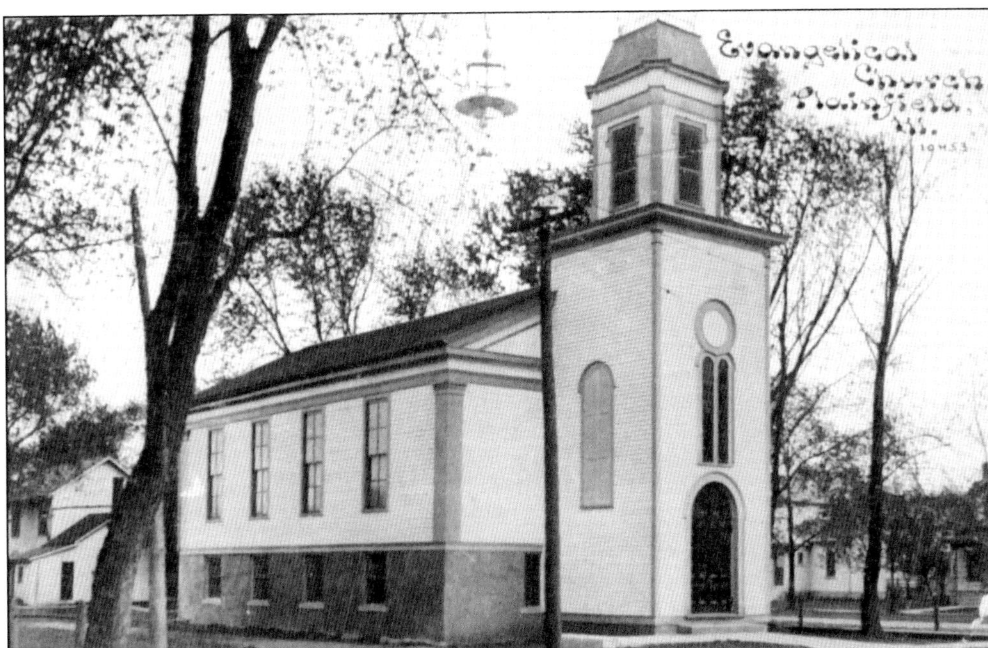

In 1847, Daniel Shreffler and his family migrated to the area from Pennsylvania. About the same time, Rev. George Mottinger arrived from Ohio, and together both men were responsible for the beginning of the Evangelical Class. As one of the oldest houses of worship in Will County, the Rose of Sharon Church was constructed in 1855 on the southeast corner of Dillman and Lockport Streets. After the Civil War, the front facade of the Greek Revival church was modified with the addition of the present bell tower, which was constructed in the Romanesque style.

Located on the north side of Lockport Street, between Illinois and Division Streets, the old Universalist church was built in 1868. In August 1907, Fr. William McNamee, pastor of St. Mary's Church in Joliet, purchased the old framed church. For the first few years, the church was known as a mission church and was under the direction of St. Mary's of Joliet. This postcard shows a view looking north from Lockport Street of the old Universal (St. Mary's) church. For many years, the Baci Italian Ristorante operated in the old parish building.

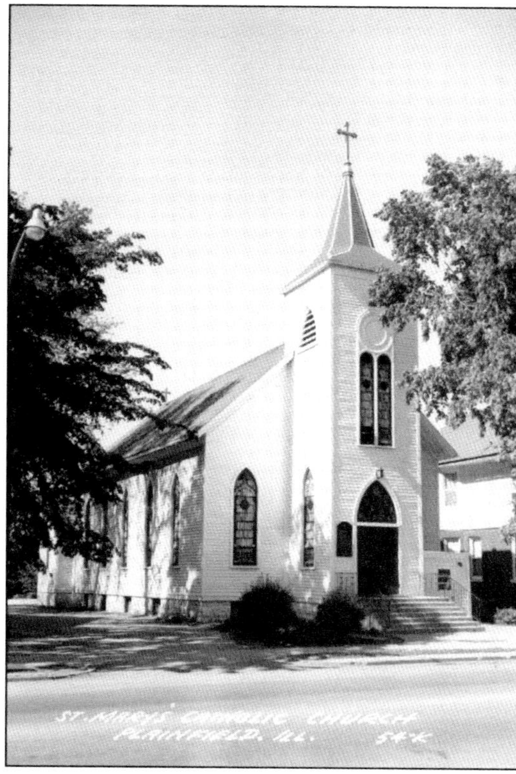

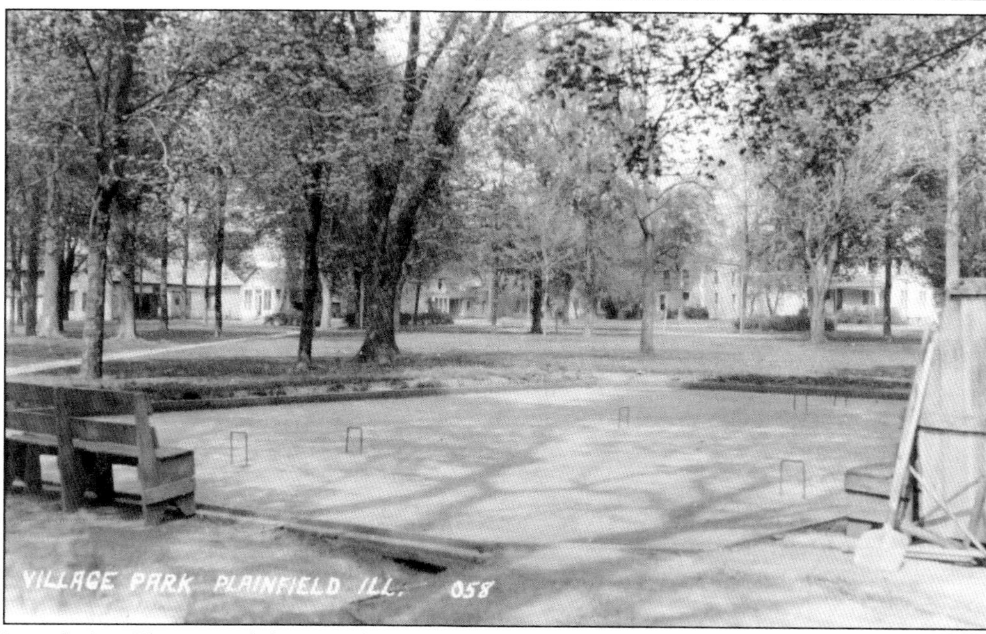

Long before Electric Park became the gathering place for summertime enjoyment, Village Green Park was a beautiful place to visit and relax. Located south of Lockport Street and bordered by Chicago, Des Plaines, Ottawa, and Fox River Streets, Village Green Park was part of the original 1834 plat of the village by Chester Ingersoll. This picture postcard shows a view of the croquet courts installed in the park in the early 1930s.

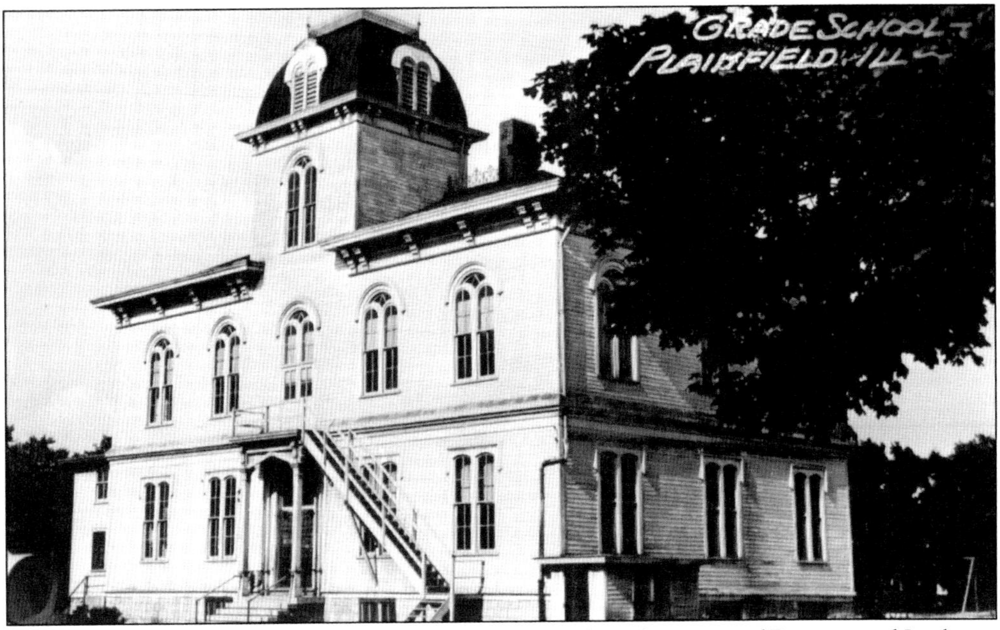

In 1861, a three-story, wooden-framed building was erected on the corner of Division and Lockport Streets to be used for a high school. In 1872, the building became the Plainfield Academy, and within a year, a mysterious fire broke out and the school burned to the ground. In 1882, a new school building was completed upon the old stone foundation of the college and looked similar in design. Over the years, the school was known as the White School and housed elementary and secondary school children. As the population in the village increased, new school buildings were erected on the same corner, including the 1915 redbrick Plainfield High School building and the 1951 elementary school. The top postcard shows the old White School building, and the bottom postcard shows a view of the 1951 elementary school. After nearly 80 years of service, the White School was razed in 1960.

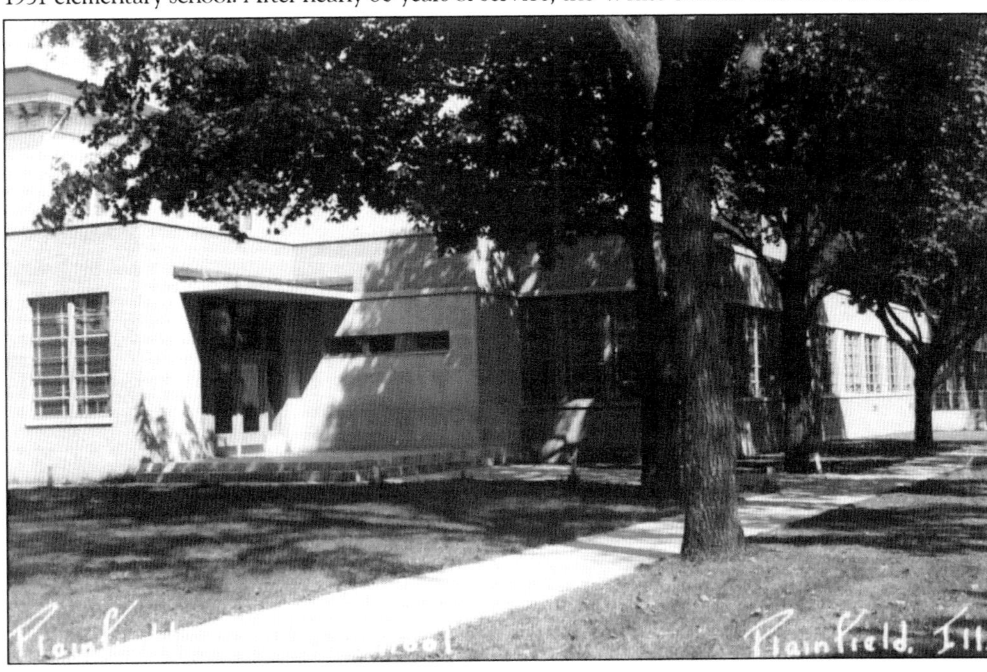

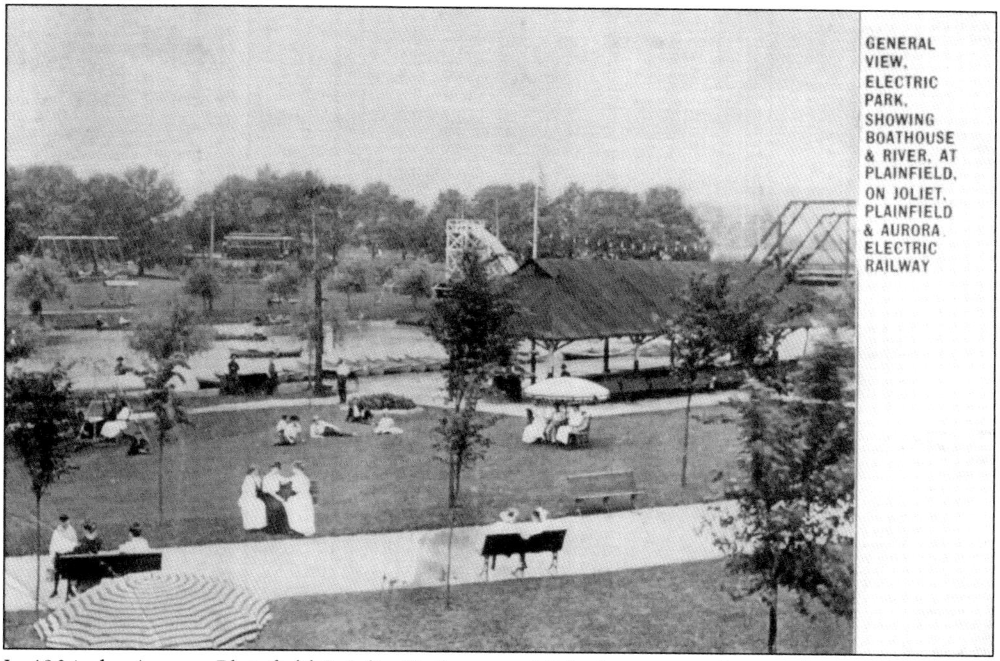

In 1904, the Aurora, Plainfield & Joliet Railway established a streetcar line with a popular 20-acre camping resort in Plainfield. Known as Electric Park, the attraction included camping cabins, a large auditorium, a dance pavilion, a restaurant, a bowling alley, a swimming pool, and boating along the banks of the DuPage River. A baseball diamond with an enclosed grandstand and horse-driving track were also included. Like many community parks across the nation, Electric Park was also used as an auto campground for travelers stopping along Lincoln Highway in Plainfield. The park officially closed in 1923, when the streetcars were replaced by buses. The top postcard photograph shows an overview of the park, including the boathouse, river, and toboggan slide. The bottom postcard shows the main entrance of the park at the corner of James and Lockport Streets.

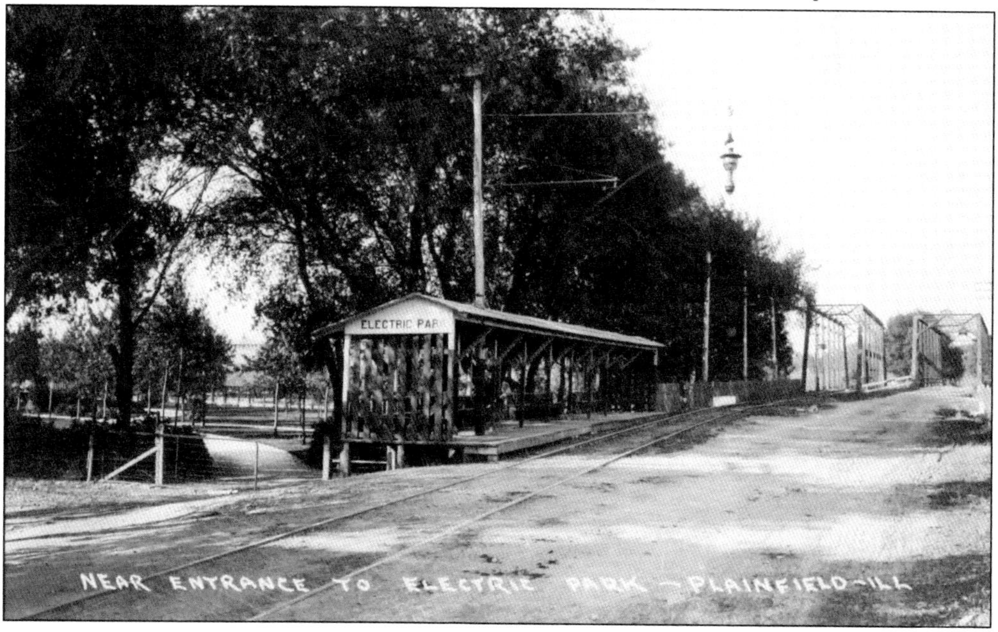

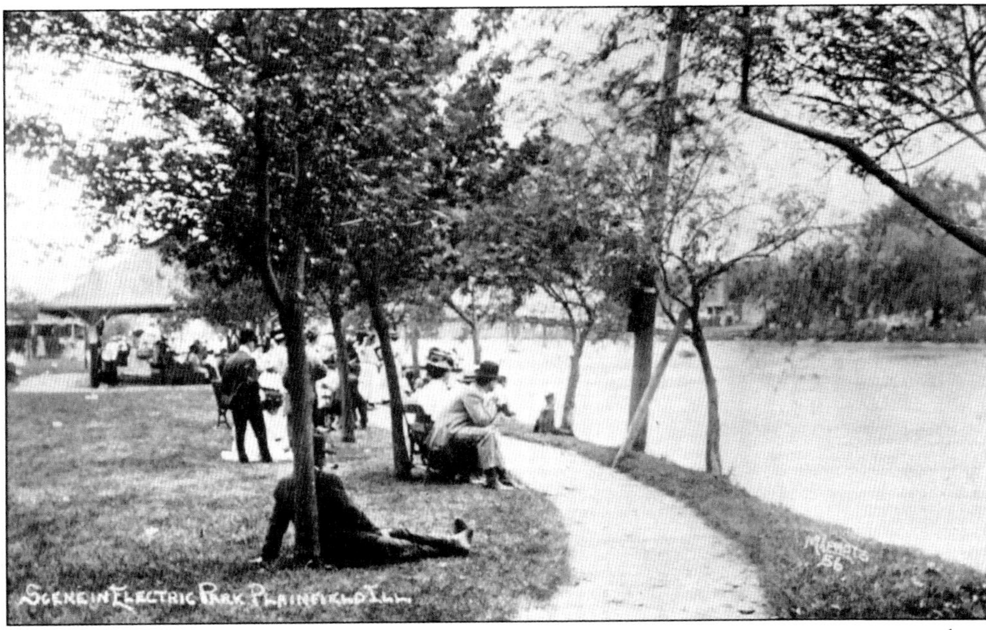

When constructed, Electric Park was intended to provide the trolley line excursionist with an ideal summer resort spot. Built along the banks of the DuPage River, the attractions at the park drew thousands every summer to enjoy camping, paddleboat rides, dancing, baseball, bowling, and balloon rides. This postcard photograph shows park visitors relaxing along the banks of the DuPage River.

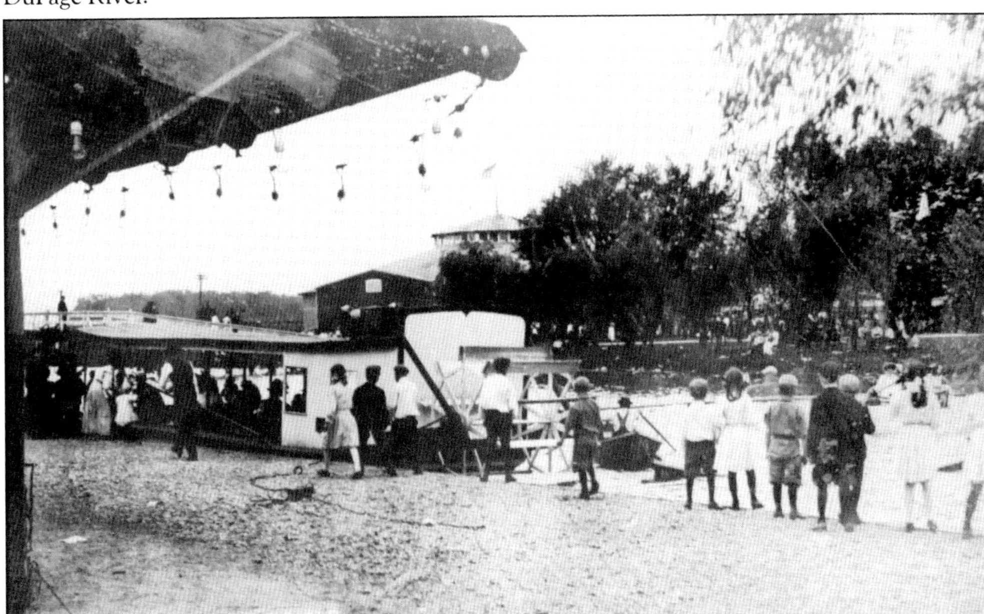

Another popular water activity at Electric Park was boating on the DuPage River. Not only could adventurous patrons rent rowboats for a nominal fee but also large groups could climb aboard the *Mary Lee* for a pleasure ride up and down the river. This picture postcard shows the east bank of the DuPage River with the boat pavilion to the left and patrons preparing to depart on the *Mary Lee*.

Three

Kendall, Kane, and DeKalb Counties

Those businesses that peddled petroleum in the 1920s soon began to view food, drink, and sleeping quarters as just another aspect of car commerce. With motorists already parked outside at the pumps, it was only natural to provide them with the stable necessities they were craving. With food that was quick to prepare and easy to consume, vendors prepared edibles for the road: snacks, sandwiches, carbonated drinks, coffee, and simple cooked foods like hamburgers and hot dogs.

Reflecting the newly found mobility in the 20th century, the uniquely American experience of the drive-in restaurant soon evolved and became linked with the growth of the automobile and the lifestyle changes that mobility created. Most drive-in restaurants built in the early years were simple structures. In cities and towns across Illinois and the nation, existing restaurants converted to curb service to attract the motoring public. In some instances, this meant simply adapting the structure as it was originally designed or augmenting the architectural details to invoke a drive-in image or theme. In time, some drive-ins became so popular that they were expanded to include dining rooms, counter service, cocktail lounges, and banquet rooms. Oftentimes, the inclusion of neon or enlarging a highway sign could quickly do the trick to get a motorist's attention.

For many travelers along the Lincoln Highway scanning the horizon for the right dining spot was not the only pleasurable experience. With clever, eye-catching billboards and signs by day and a flood of different neon colors at night, these advertising nuisances made these car-accommodating businesses along the route an instant hit. Traveling the Lincoln Highway through Kane, Kendall, and DeKalb Counties, there are numerous examples of these early automobile enterprises that can still be found, including gas stations, automobile showrooms, hotels, motels, theater buildings, motor courts, parks, historic sites, and drive-ins.

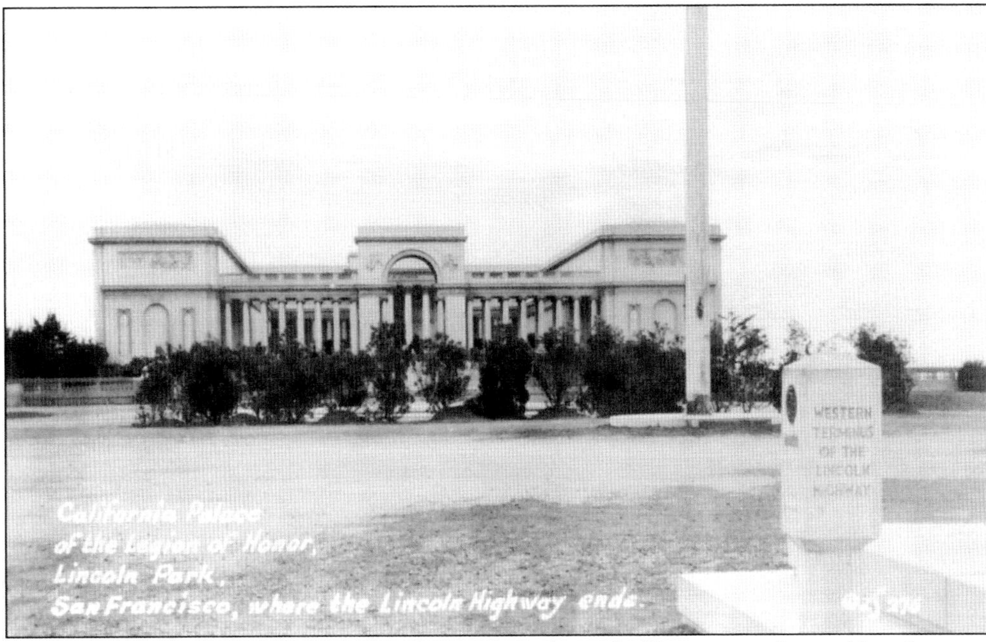

In the early years, sections along the roadway were only marked by posts, poles, and hand-written signs. In time, there was a need to develop a better marking system to aid the traveler along the highway. Some of the first markings were simple—merely a red, white, and blue band painted on a pole. Later, a more official-looking symbol consisting of a red, white, and blue rectangle with the letter *L* and the words "Lincoln Highway" were used. It was not until the late 1920s that the Lincoln Highway was officially marked and dedicated to the memory of Abraham Lincoln. On September 1, 1928, groups of Boy Scouts helped to place concrete markers at sites along the route. They were placed along the outer edge of the right-of-way at important crossroads, minor crossings, and other intervals along the road. While these original concrete markers can still be found along the route, there are very few remaining in Illinois. These images show early route markings along the highway. (Both, courtesy of Russell Rein.)

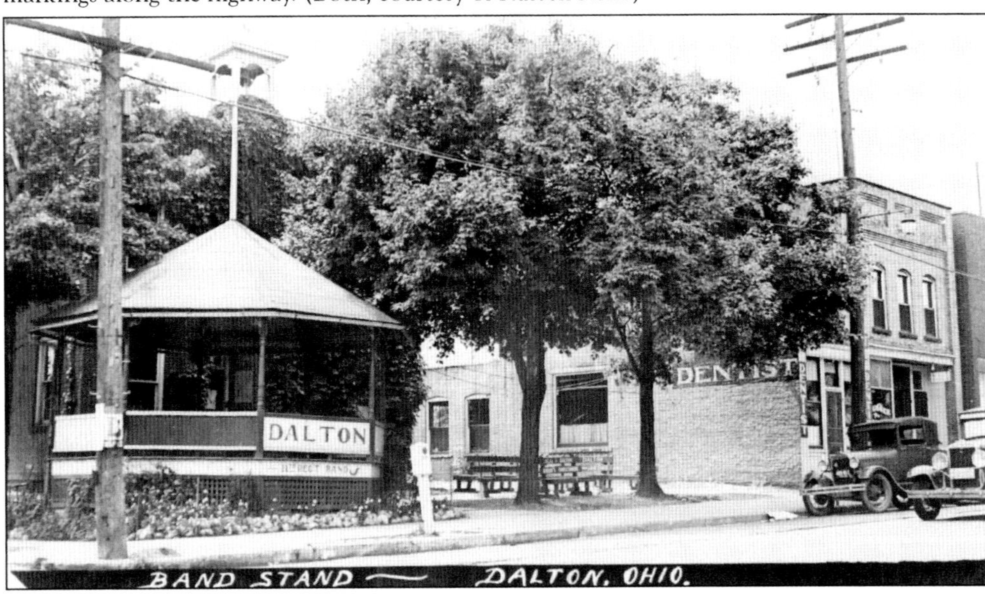

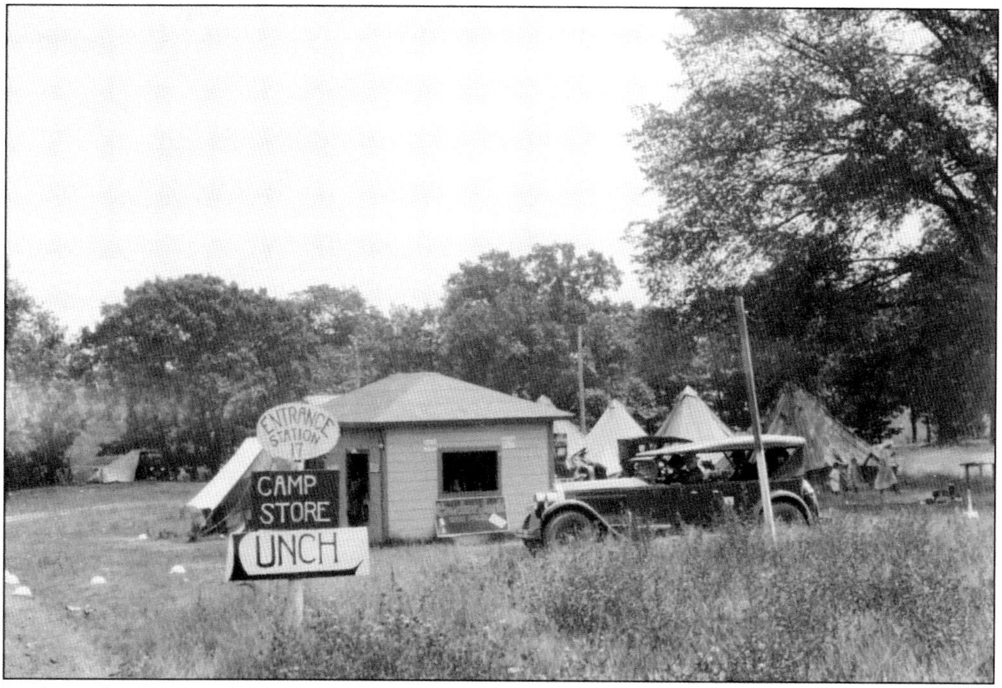

By the early 1920s, road improvements and highly publicized expeditions along the Lincoln Highway generated enough interest that Americans felt more confident about taking up the adventure of cross-country motor travel. Travelers who could afford to pay for comfort would welcome the excellent accommodations found in many local hotels. Those motorists on a budget or eager for adventure found "motor hoboing" or camping along the route a more appealing alternative. By the mid-1920s, municipal organizations across the country established auto camps in order to prevent motor tourists from "squatting" in areas where they were not welcome. The Aurora Automobile Club established an auto camp along the Lincoln Highway in 1923 near the outskirts of town near Phillips Park.

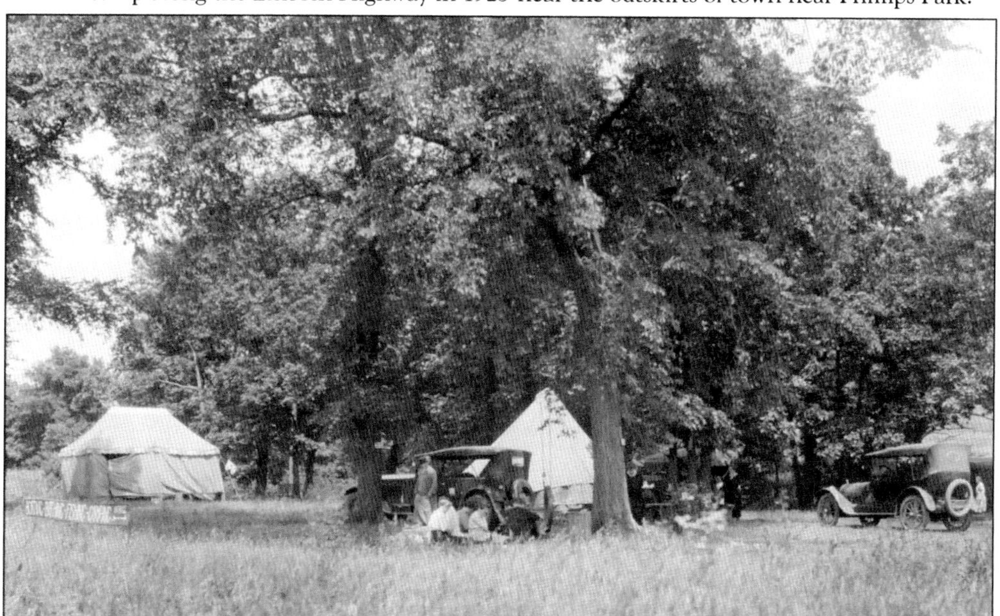

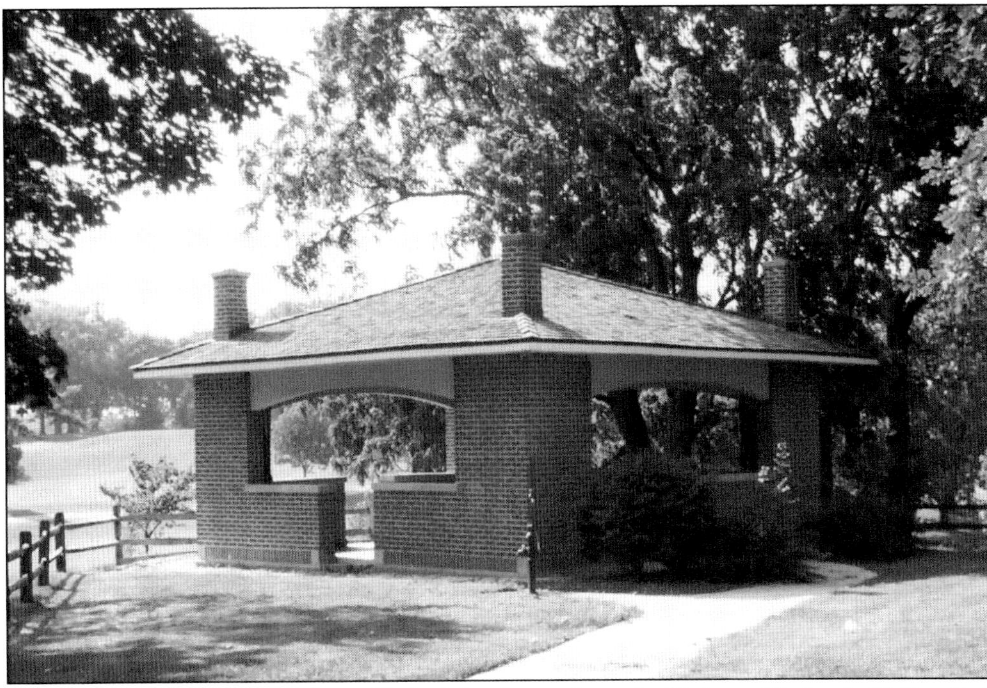

In 1923, the Aurora Auto Club established the Aurora Lincoln Highway Shelter in Philips Park to provide the highway motorist with certain amenities a tired traveler might need on the road. According to the 1924 edition of the *Complete Official Road Guide of the Lincoln Highway*, the auto camp provided "free camping [along with] fireplaces . . . ovens and a sink." The guide also mentioned the availability of "pure drinking water just outside the [shelter] building." The Aurora Shelter fell into disrepair by the late 1940s and faced demolition by the late 1990s. To help save the historic structure, the Aurora Preservation Commission raised money to restore the structure to its original 1924 appearance.

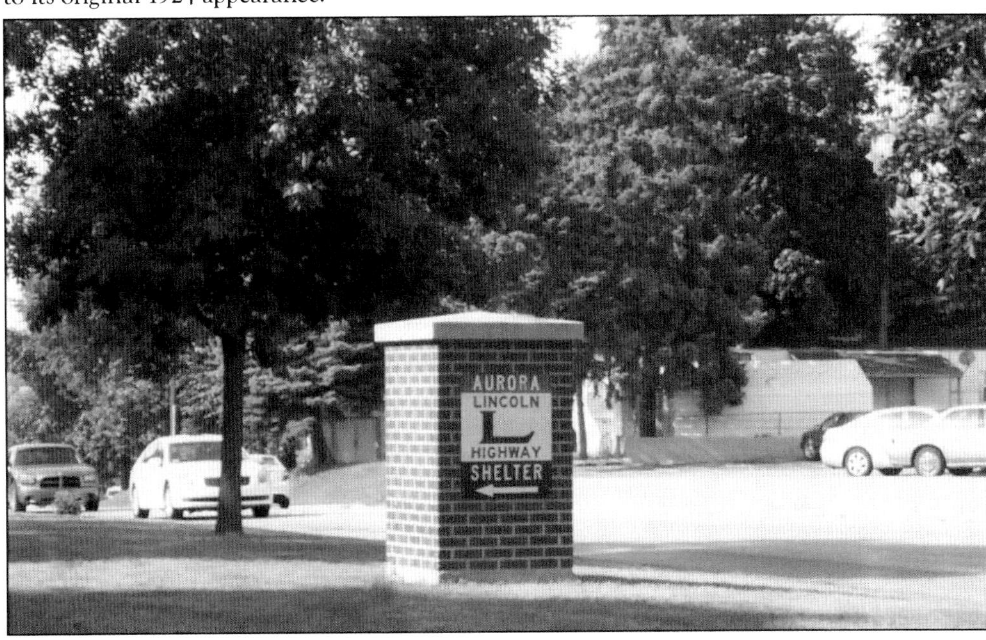

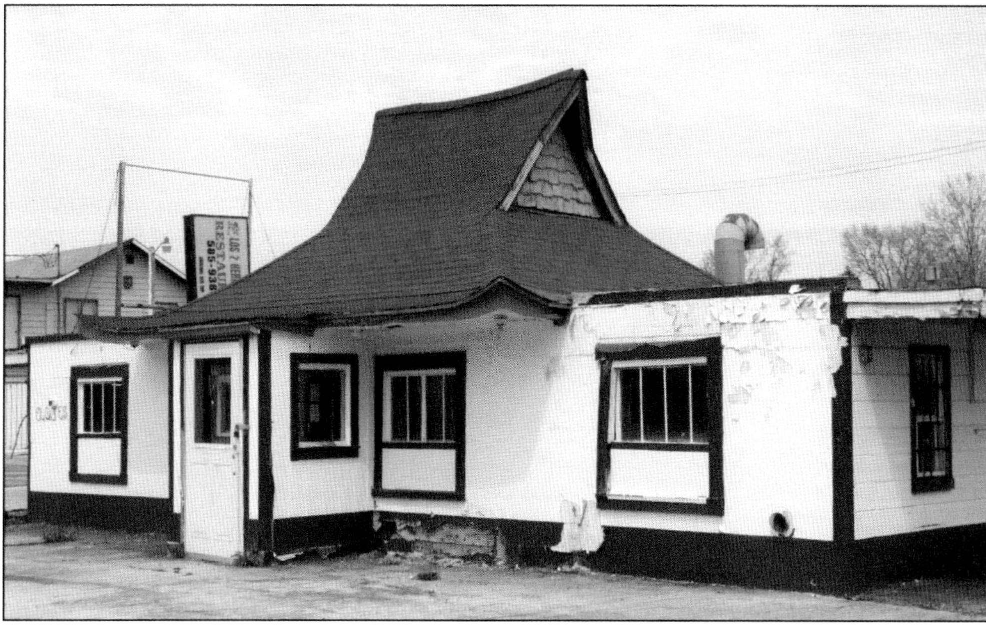

The remnants of this building, located on the northeast corner of Hill Avenue and Binder Street, harken back to an era when gas stations pumped gas and the local station owners tried to make their stations unique looking in order to attract the traveling customer. Constructed in the early 1920s and facing the century-old Phillips Park across the street, this thematic building's pagoda-style roof reveals this to have been a Wadhams gas station along the Lincoln Highway in Aurora. The Wadhams Oil Company hired Milwaukee architect Alexander C. Eschweiler to design a small building that was both functional and efficient, as well as eye-catching to the motoring public. Eschweiler developed an easily recognizable, red-roofed, Japanese-looking, pagoda-styled station that would be repeated in over 100 Wadhams stations across the Midwest. For many years, this building was also home to Hinterlong's Red Top Restaurant before it was converted to a Mexican restaurant.

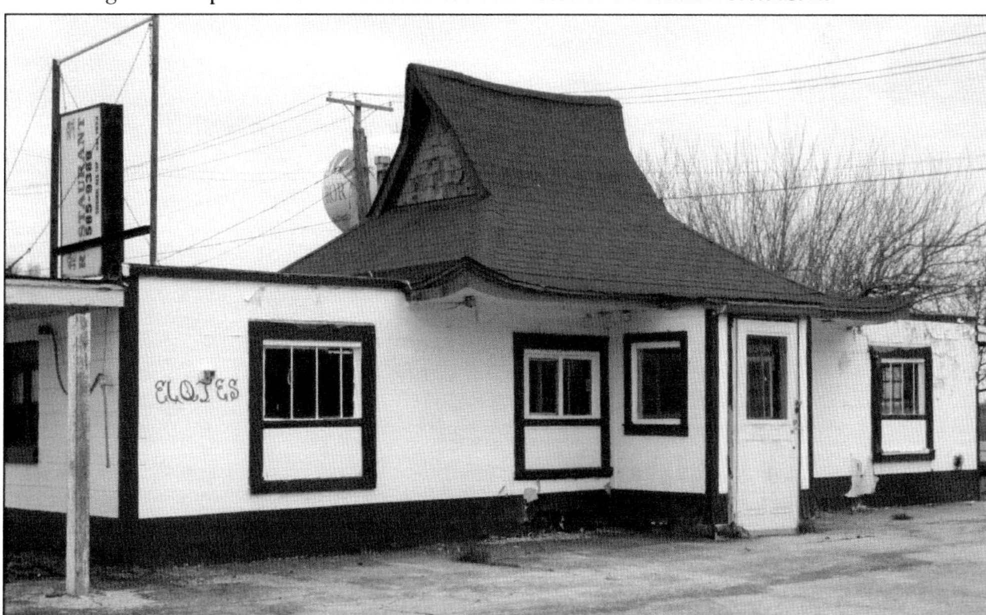

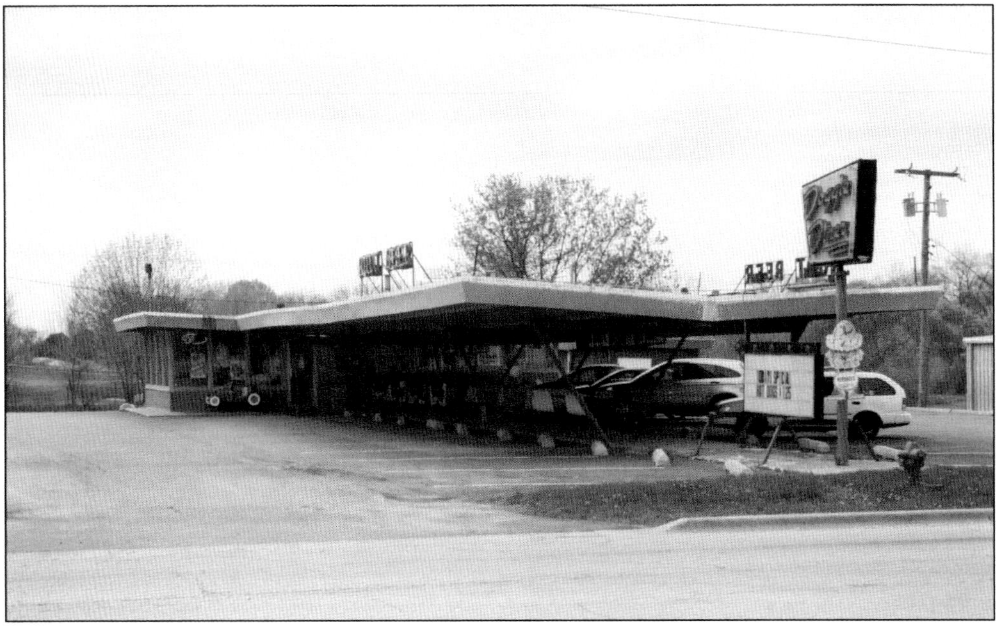

From their beginnings in the 1920s until their fall from grace by the 1970s, the drive-in restaurants on the American road provided weary road travelers with an enjoyable diversion and the chance to dine in the comfort of their automobile. Businesses would have women (or in some cases men) hand-deliver food on special trays that would hang from the window. Employees who were known collectively as "carhops" or "curb girls" usually performed this unique style of serving customers in their cars. Their uniforms consisted of many different things from roller skates to sneakers or dresses to jeans. Everything depended on the image or theme of the restaurant. Doggie Diner, located in Aurora, with its yellow and red neon sign, is an example of an old themed drive-in restaurant that was a common site along the Lincoln Highway.

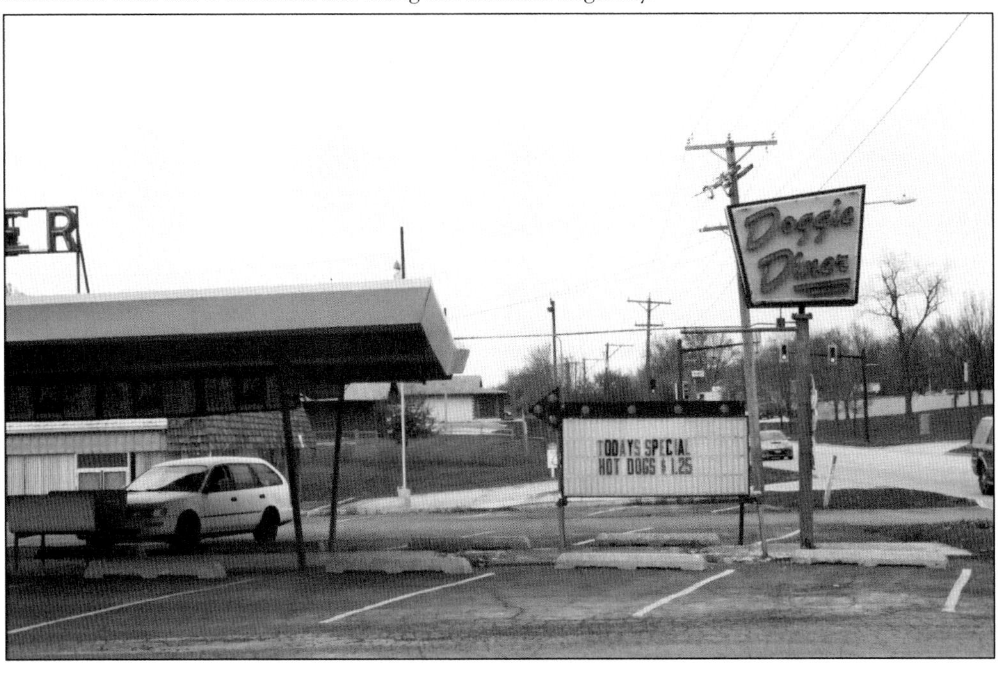

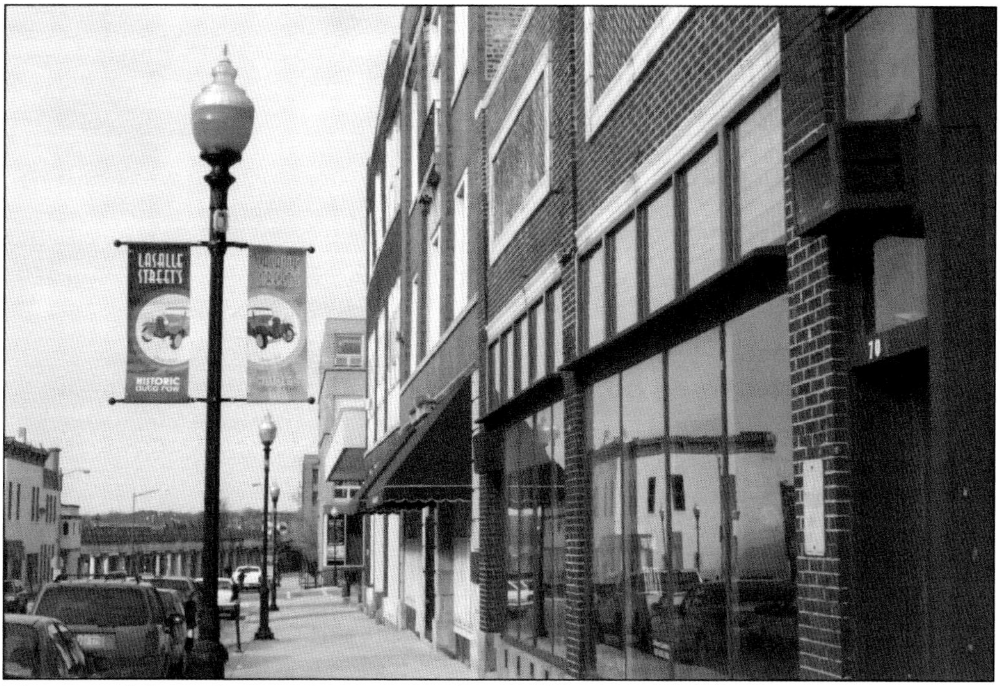

The automobile revolutionized American culture and society during the early 20th century. With the new availability of reliable and affordable automobiles, dealers began to see their sales numbers rise. As automobiles increasingly became a common necessity for rural and urban life, many large cities developed a location where many automobile sales service center companies clustered. In time, service companies and other business concerns that sold batteries, tires, and other auto supplies also sprang up within the vicinity of the commercial dealers. In most cities, the areas where auto companies and suppliers gathered were typically near downtown and along major arterial streets. In Aurora, LaSalle Street between Downer Place and Benton is where the early automobile commercial center flourished. The buildings located on this block are fine examples of early-20th-century commercial style structures. This stretch of LaSalle Street, listed in the National Register of Historic Places, was also on the original Lincoln Highway route through Aurora.

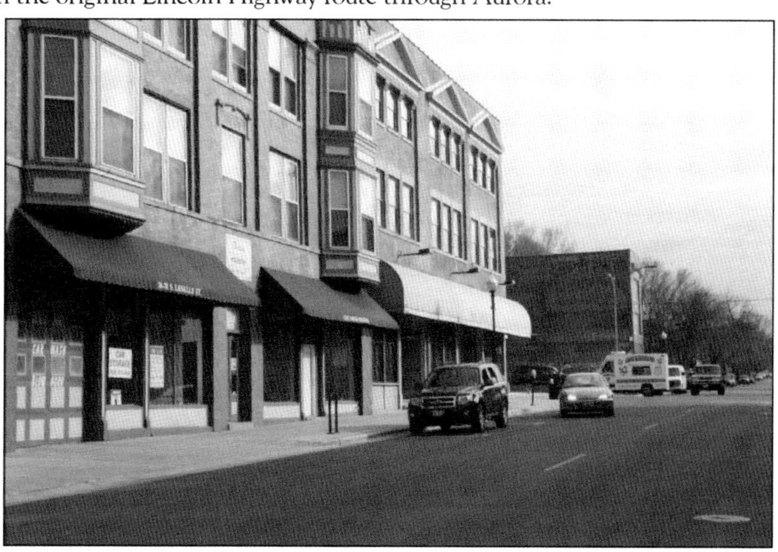

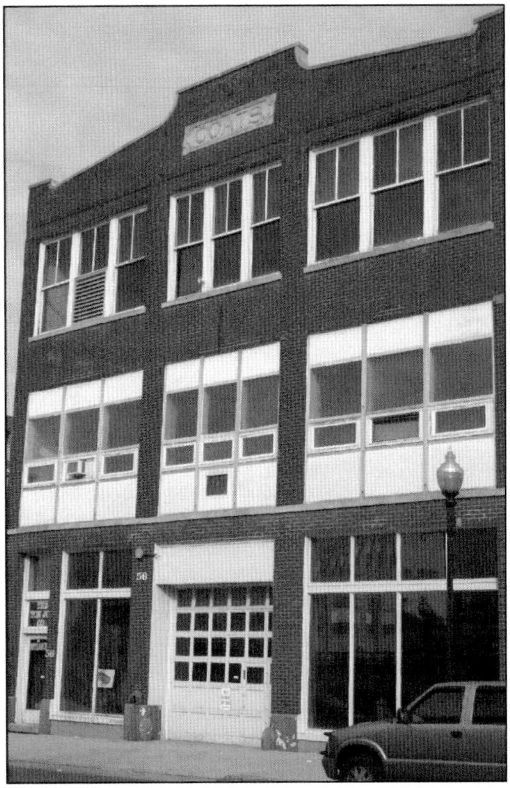

Early-20th-century automobile showroom buildings were typically one to three stories in height and usually built of reinforced concrete, clad with brick, and ornamented with stone. These buildings also featured large, first-floor storefront windows that allowed the passerby to see the floor models and often included large open spaces on all floors for the display of automobiles. Constructed in 1907, Coats Garage—shown in the photograph on the left and located at 56 South LaSalle Street—was the first automobile sales and service building constructed on LaSalle Street. To hold the weight of the showroom floors, this building was constructed with large I beams that span the width of the building. Theiss' Central Garage Building, shown in the bottom photograph, was constructed around 1912 and reflects the commercial style of architecture that was common in urban centers. This building utilized the new technique of fireproof reinforced concrete slabs for the floors and large rectangular windows at street level.

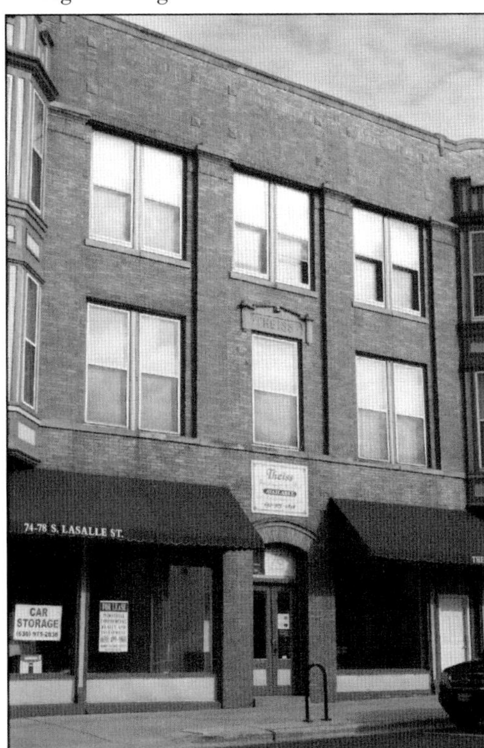

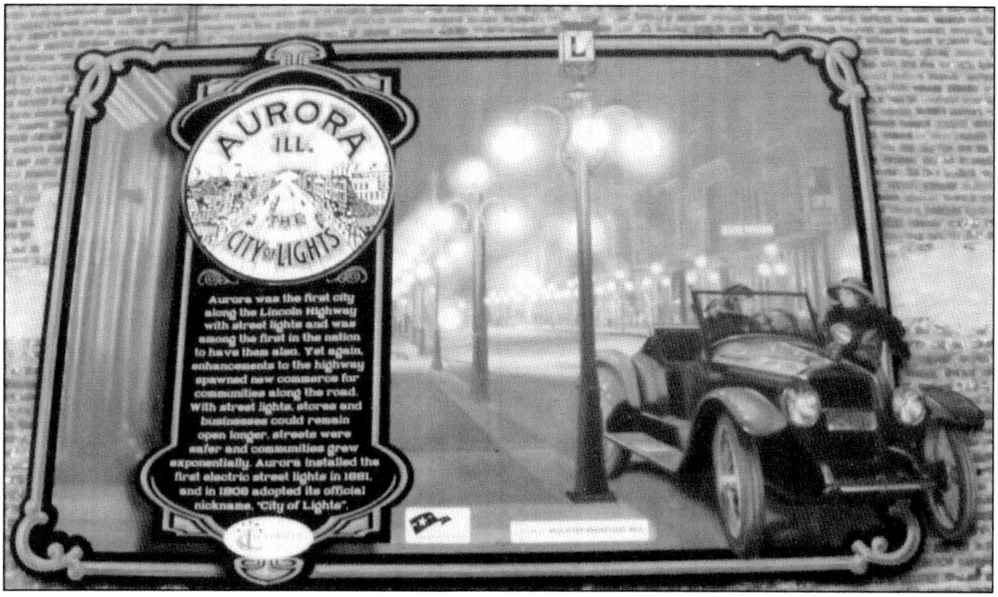

Illinois is fortunate to be the only state to have the Lincoln Highway designated as a national scenic byway. From the Indiana border to the Mississippi River, numerous murals and gazebos that offer historical information and trivia about the road have been installed in communities along its route. The Illinois Lincoln Highway Coalition, through a collaborative process with local historians, civic leaders, and talented artists, has raised the funds to help make these projects a reality, along with promoting tourism along the 179-mile stretch of the road in the state. The top photograph shows the Lincoln Highway Interpretive Mural located on North Broadway Street just north of New York Street in Aurora. This mural brings to life early-20th-century Aurora with a nearly three-dimensional view of a car traveling in a newly illuminated downtown "City of Lights." The bottom image is a postcard showing downtown Aurora illuminated with lights. (Below, courtesy of Russell Rein.)

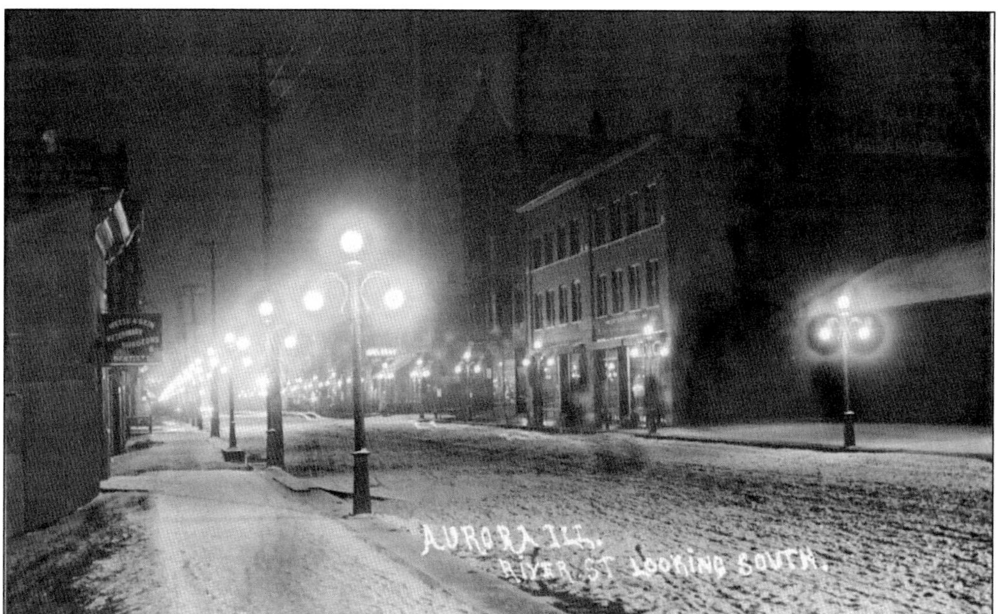

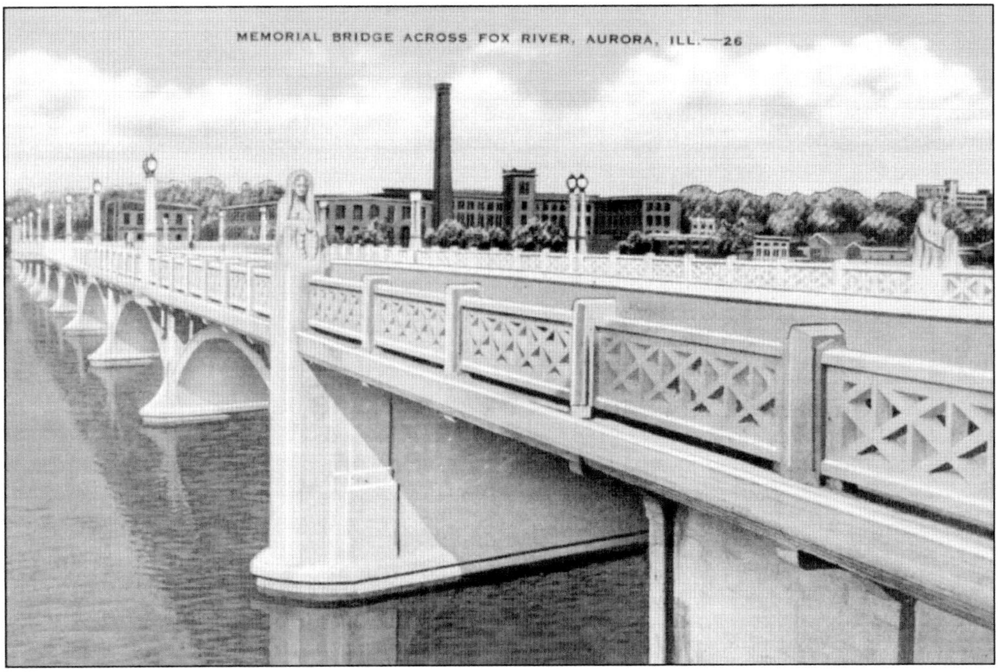

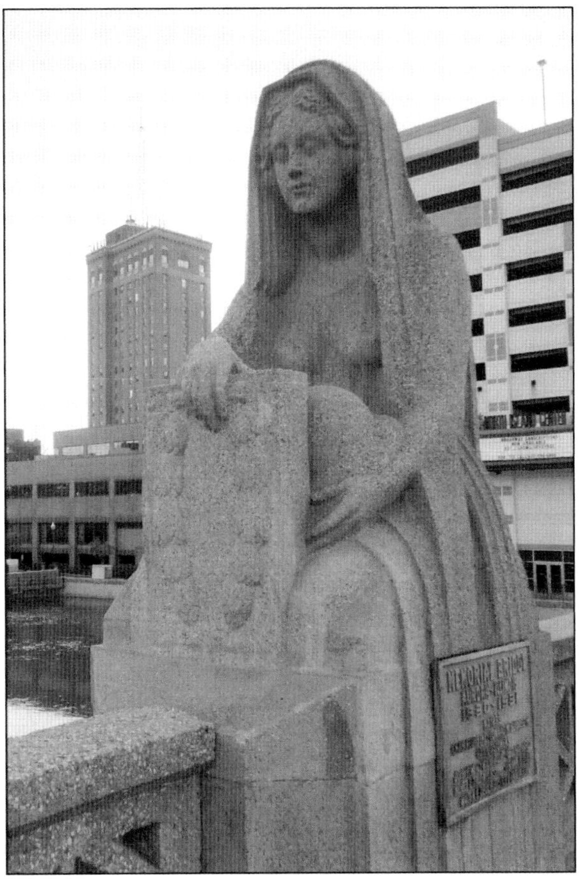

Many of the bridges along the Lincoln Highway reflect the cultural awakening that spread across America as society began to shed its Victorian-era architectural style for one that reflected progress and independence. The New York Street Memorial Bridge spanning the Fox River in Aurora, Illinois, is one such example. Dedicated on Armistice Day, November 11, 1931, as a memorial to World War I veterans, the bridge was designed by sculptor Emory Seidel. Built in the art moderne style, Seidel integrated several sculpted figures into the concrete structure. These decorative figures are located in the bridge pylons and in niches at the center of the bridge deck. The New York Street Memorial Bridge is located just north of the original 1913 Lincoln Highway route and bridge over the Fox River. The top postcard photograph shows the Memorial Bridge looking west over the Fox River. The photograph to the left shows one of the sculpted figures on the south side of the bridge. (Above, courtesy of Russell Rein.)

Local architect Eugene Malmer designed the historic Hotel Arthur, located on the northwest corner of North Broadway Street and East Galena Boulevard. Constructed in 1905, the six-story brick and Bedford stone building is consistent with the Second Renaissance Revival architectural style and was once the tallest building in Aurora. In 1915, the building was leased to the Aurora, Elgin & Chicago Railroad Company to serve as the company's traction terminal station and corporate headquarters. The Hotel Arthur was added to the National Register of Historic Places in 2005.

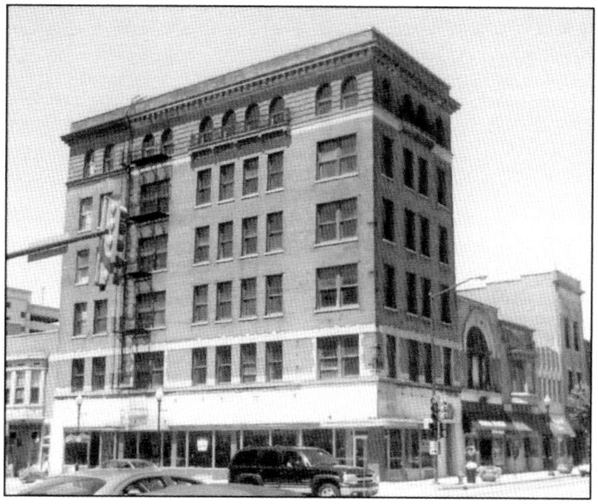

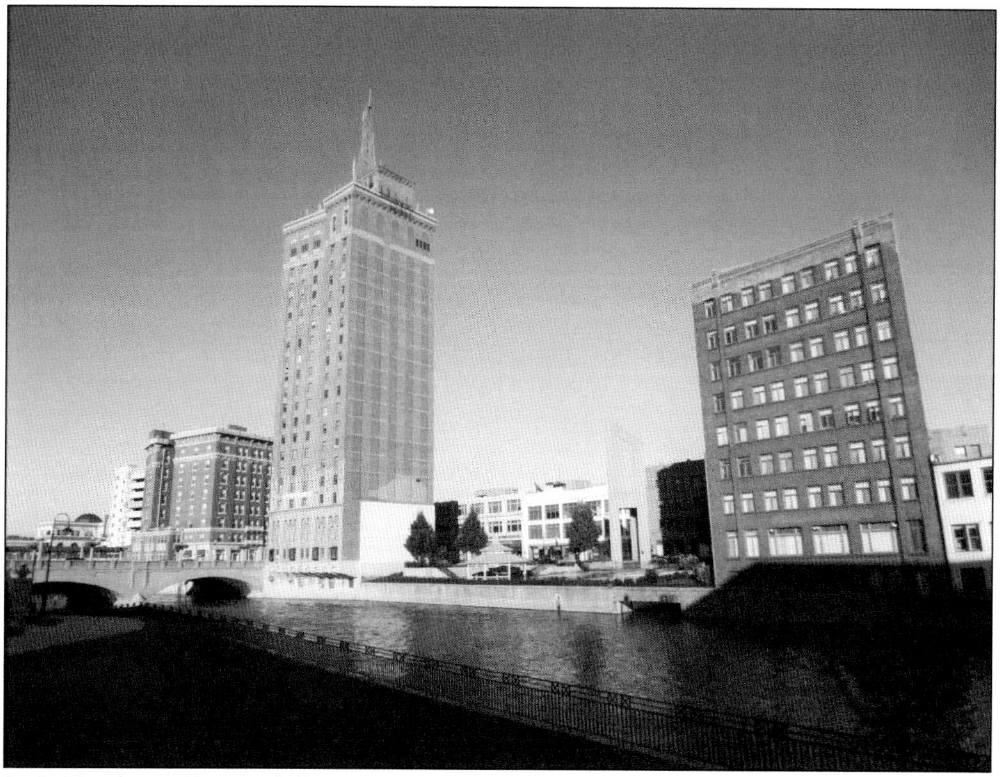

Stolp Island initially provided an ideal location for early industrial development that relied on the river as a source for power. As the community of Aurora grew, the island became a demarcation between the bustling settlements on the east and west banks of the river. Due to its central location in the growing community, Stolp Island became not only a functional transportation link between communities but also the location for many of Aurora's public buildings and private organizations.

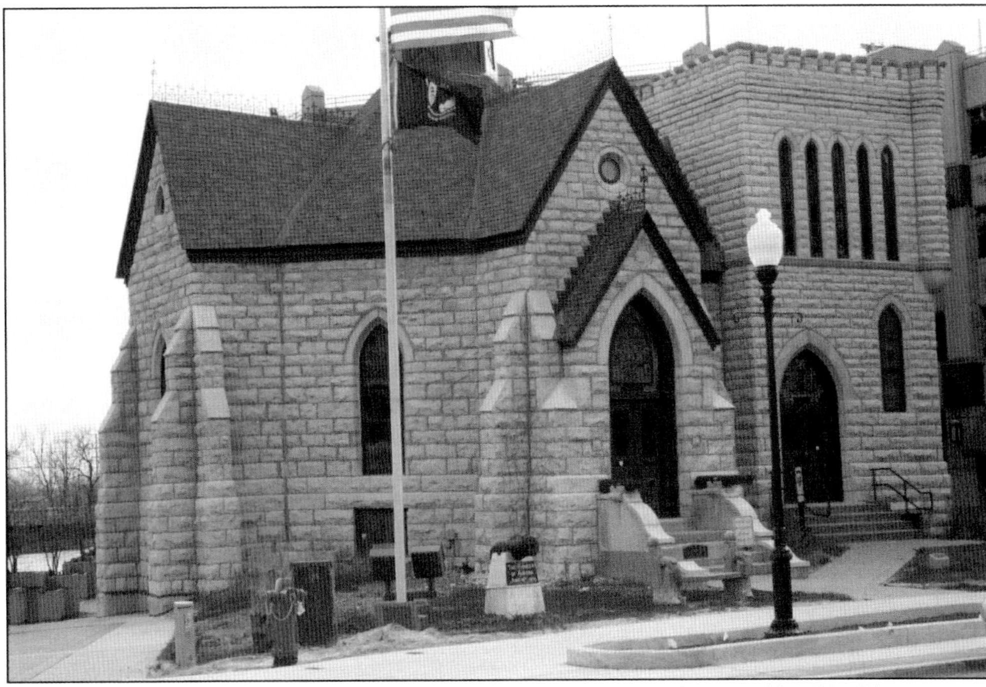

Located on Stolp Island in the Fox River, the Grand Army of the Republic (GAR) Memorial Hall is one of Aurora's most recognized historic landmarks. Completed in 1878, the structure was built as a memorial for Civil War veterans. Constructed with locally quarried limestone, the Gothic Revival–style structure was designed by Aurora architect Joseph P. Mulvey and built by money raised from the Soldiers Monument Association and the Ladies Monument Association. The GAR Memorial Hall was added to the National Register of Historic Places in 1984.

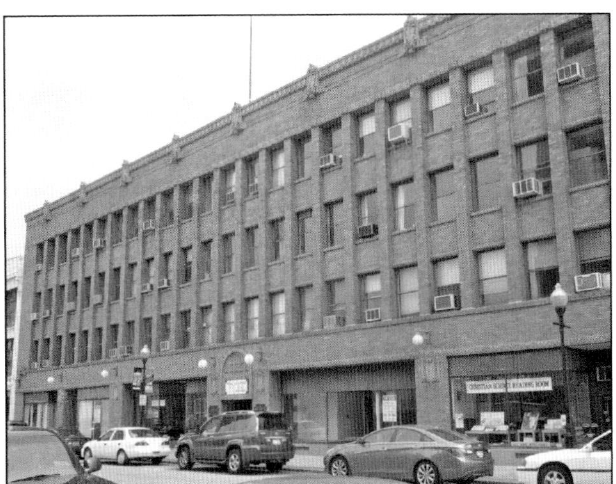

Constructed in 1923, the Keystone Building was designed by George Grant Elmslie and is one of five buildings designed by Elmslie in the Aurora area. Located at 30 South Stolp Avenue, the four-story Keystone Building features long horizontal planes; decorative, arched screen over the entryway; bronze light fixtures; and terra-cotta detailing along the roofline—all examples from the Chicago School of architecture. The Keystone Building was listed in the National Register of Historic Places in 1980.

Constructed in 1917 by the Inland Development Company, the eight-story Aurora Hotel was designed by the architect firm of H. Ziegler Dietz and was once the tallest building on Stolp Island. Located at the northwest corner of Glena Boulevard and Stolp Avenue, the Second Renaissance Revival–style hotel was the first large hotel in the city and was known for its finer touches. After decades of neglect, the battered landmark closed in 1984, and the city condemned the building and purchased the structure for $129,000. In 1996, the city sold the building to Harold D. Rider & Associates of Chicago for $1. With the help of a series of local and federal loans and tax breaks, Rider reconstructed the building and transformed it into a 56-unit apartment complex for low-income senior citizens. The photograph on the right shows a postcard image of the Aurora Hotel looking north from the Fox River. The bottom image shows a view of the hotel today. (Right, courtesy of Russell Rein.)

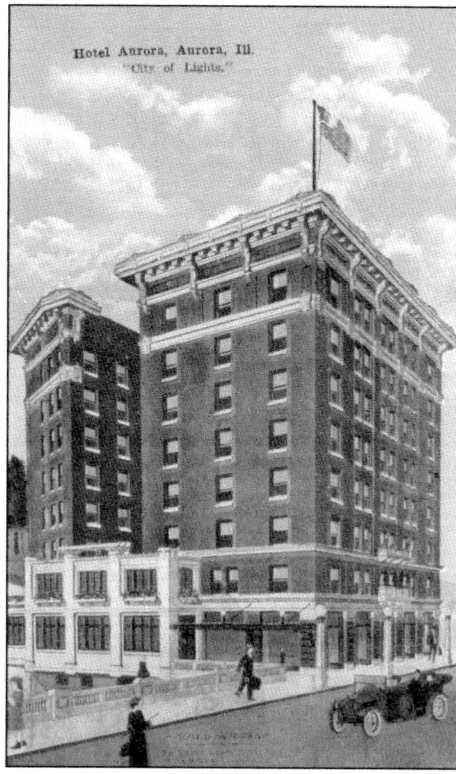

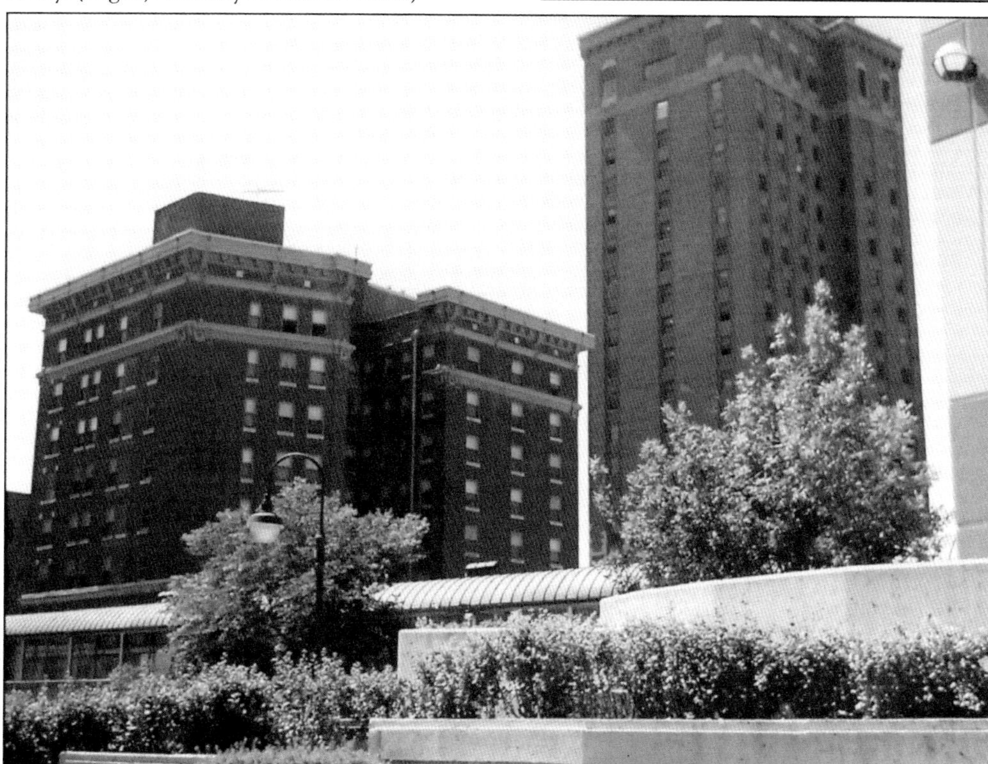

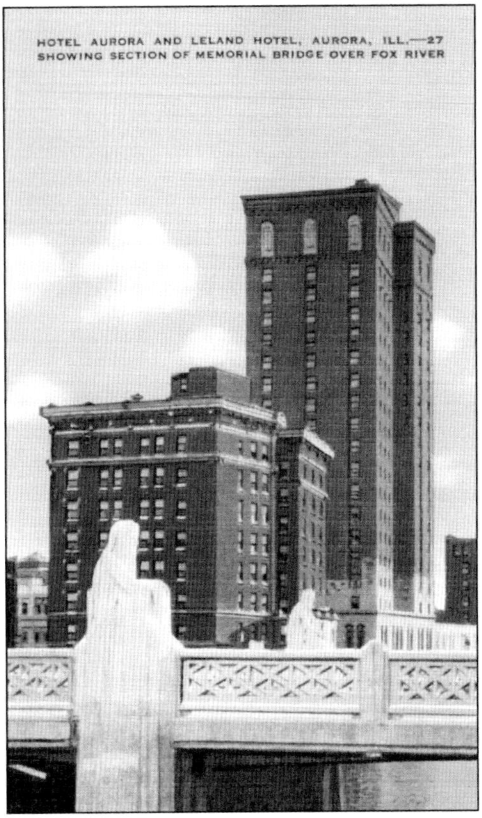

Located on the southwest corner of Stolp Avenue and East Galena Boulevard, the Leland Tower was constructed in 1928 as a first-class hotel and entertainment center on Stolp Island. The building's exterior has an Italian Romanesque appearance and was designed by the architect firm of Anker Sveere Graven and Arthur Guy Mayger of Chicago. Besides being a first-class hotel, the Leland also became an important entertainment venue for the region. The top of the Leland Tower once housed the Sky Club, and for many years, the club, with its spectacular view, was a center for local social life. The hotel ceased operations in the 1960s and was later converted to an apartment complex that is known today as Fox Island Place. The postcard to the left shows an image of the Leland Hotel looking north from the Fox River. The bottom image shows a view of the hotel today. (Left, courtesy of Russell Rein.)

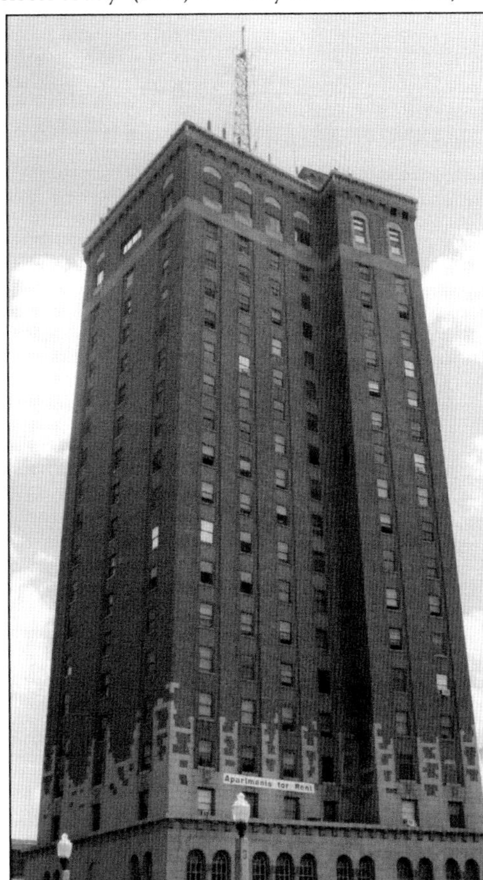

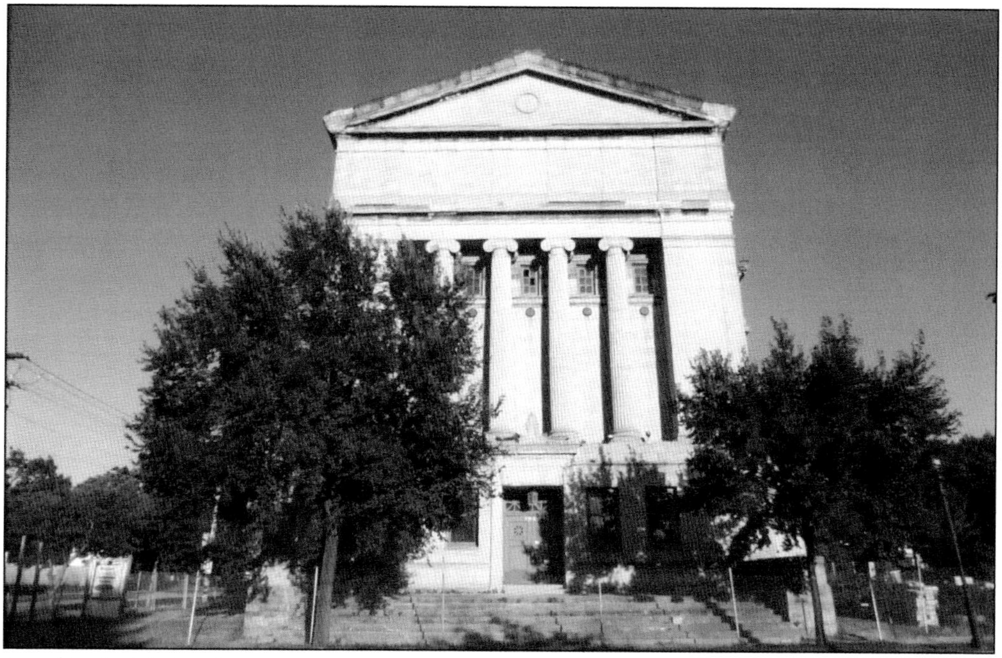

Listed in the National Register of Historic Places in 1982, the Aurora Masonic Temple was designed by architect William Q. Bendus in 1922. Constructed in the neoclassical style, the building is located on the southeast corner of East Benton Street and South Lincoln Avenue and occupies a prominent place in downtown Aurora. The five-story steel and custom-formed cast-concrete building was constructed by the Aurora Masonic Alliance, a group of 10 Masonic organizations. The temple served Masonic members until the mid-1980s, when the alliance sold the temple and it was converted to a banquet facility and offices. The building was closed in 2006 and has suffered from a lack of maintenance, which has resulted in damage to the various architectural features both inside and outside of the structure.

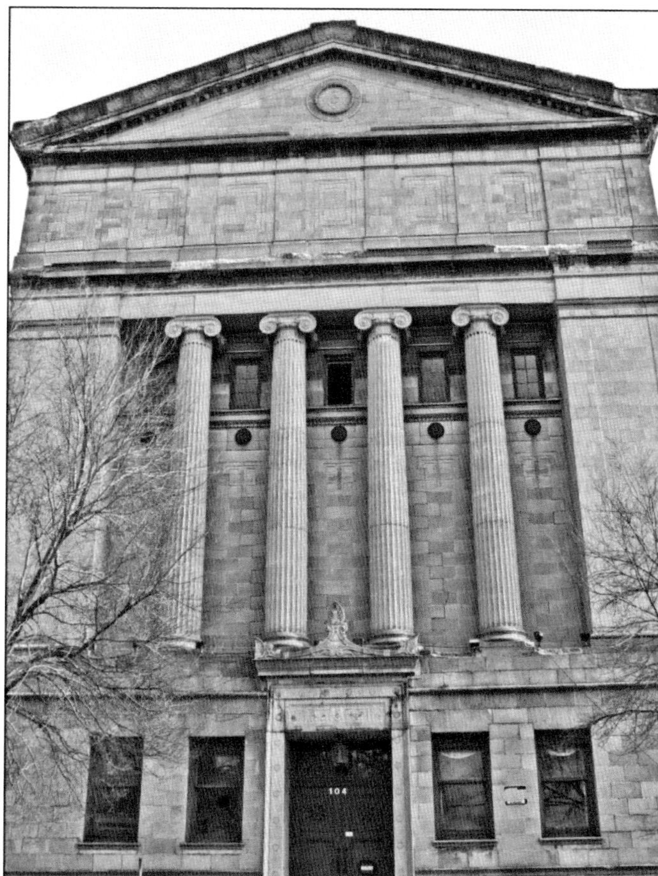

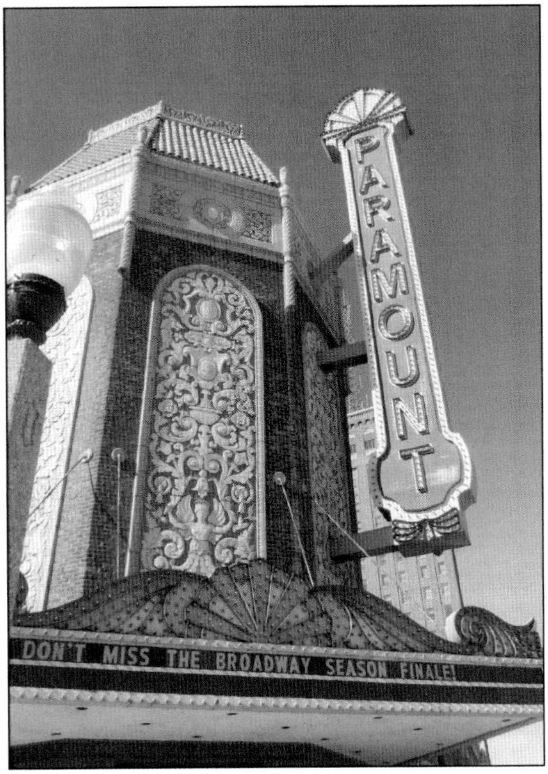

The Paramount Theatre was designed by noted Chicago theater architects Cornelius Ward Rapp and George Leslie Rapp, nationally famous for their opulent movie houses in cities across the country. During the 1920s, Rapp and Rapp designed hundreds of theaters that included interior designs featuring opulence and exterior decorations common with the increasingly popular art deco style of the decade. Over the years, the Paramount Theatre offered its patrons a mix of movies, vaudeville performances, concerts, and other artistic performances. By the 1970s, age began to take its toll on the old building, and in 1976, the Aurora Civic Center Authority purchased the Paramount, and a nearly two-year restoration effort began in earnest on the structure. In 2006, a 12,000-square-foot Grand Gallery lobby was added with a new, state-of-the-art box office, café, and art gallery. Today, the Paramount Theatre offers a variety of theatrical, musical, comedy, dance, and family programming.

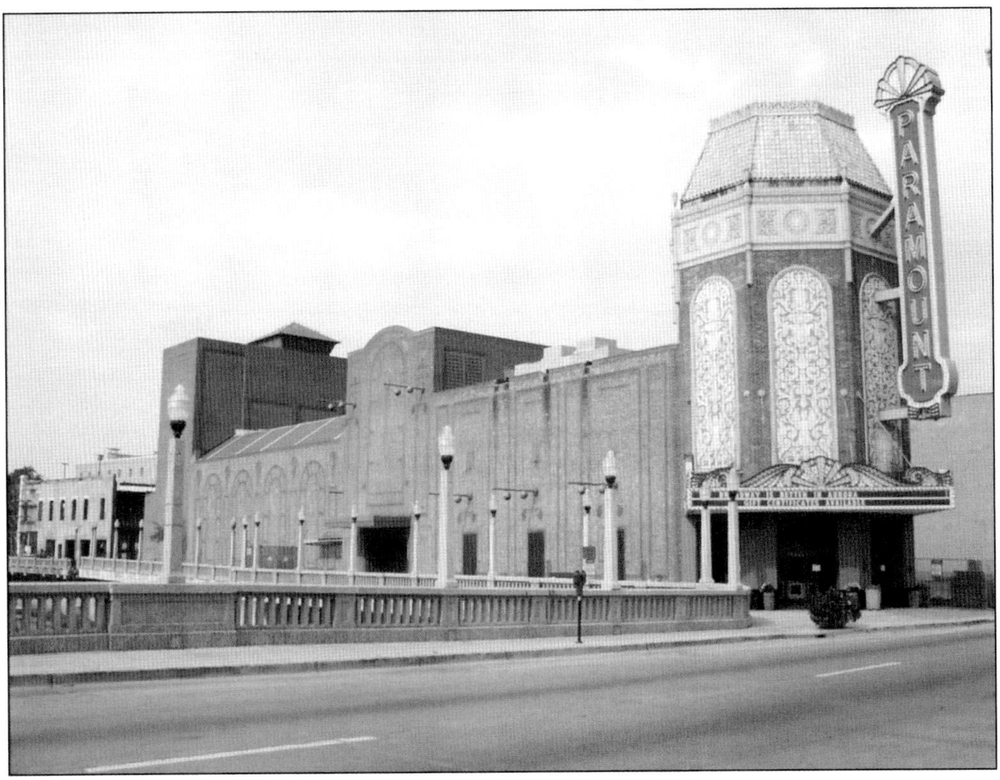

Motor courts were usually structured like the cottage courts except that room units were integrated into a single building. In the early years, the courts were arranged in a geometric *U*-shaped configuration, and often this was dependent on the depth of the lot or the distance from the roadway. The typical motor court contained a separate office building and another building that might contain a coffee shop. Like the early-era cottage courts, motor courts relied on the outdoors for public space. Not all motor courts, however, had courtyard configurations. Many later-era courts were constructed as a simpler row or *L*-shaped room arrangement. At the same time, these courts began to erect large signs that dominated the motel grounds and could be visible from the highway. The postcard on the right shows Daniel's Auto Court, located along the Lincoln Highway in Aurora. The bottom photograph shows the simple single-line configuration of the Geneva Motel. (Both, courtesy of Russell Rein.)

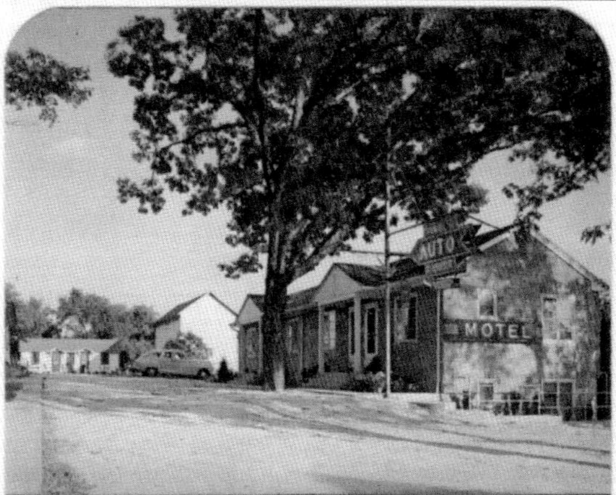

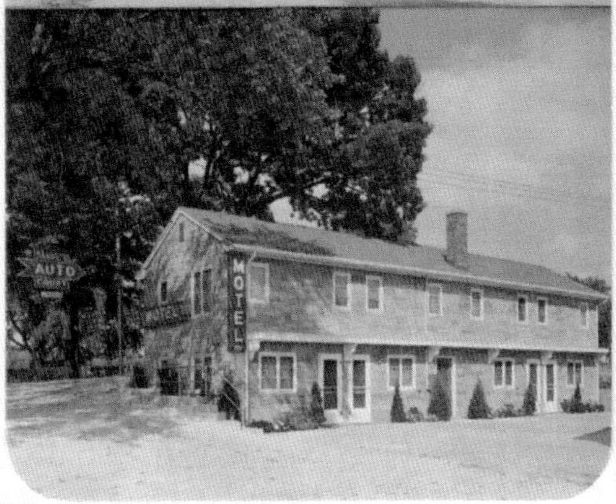

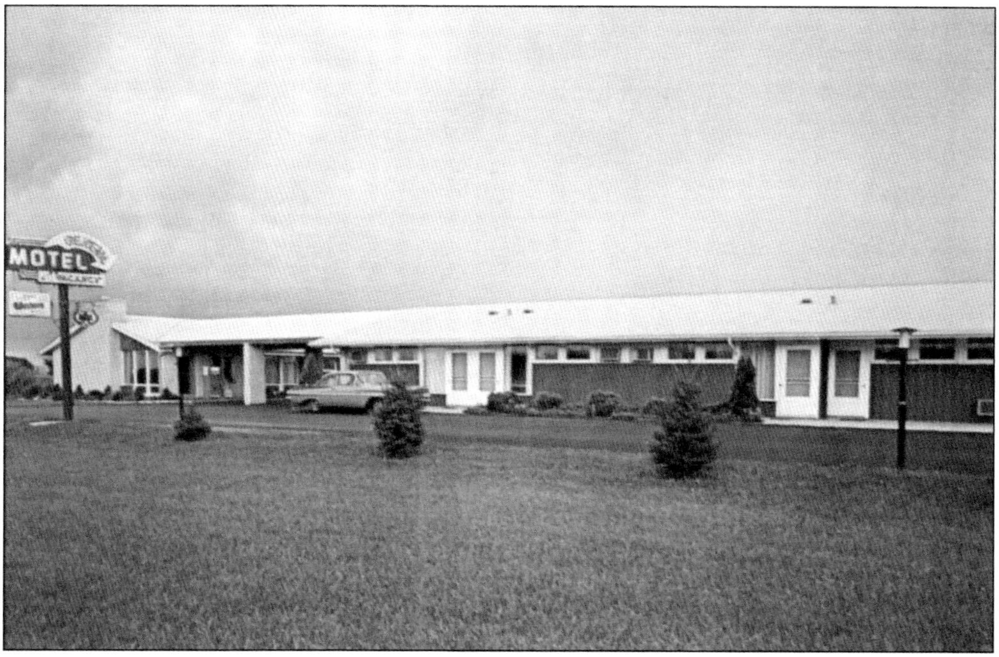

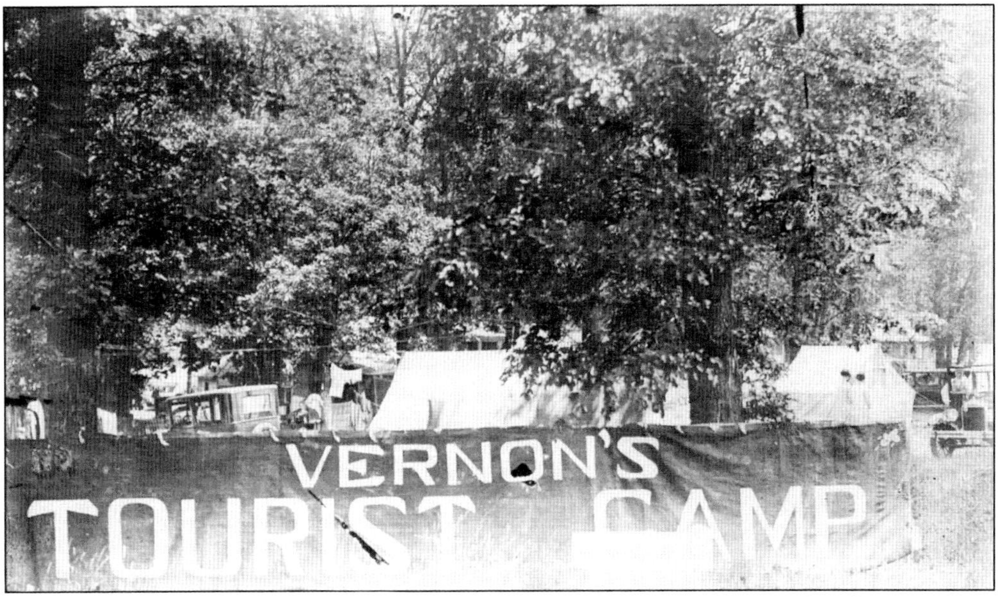

As free municipal auto camps grew in popularity, they soon became overcrowded, and communities had trouble keeping them maintained. It was not long before the urge to compete with other towns and their auto camps led to expensive improvements, and there was a growing pressure to levy a charge for the use of the facilities. By the mid-1920s, auto camps offered private cabins that provided travelers with all the comforts of home, including a bed, electricity, heating, and, if lucky, a kitchenette. These auto camps were soon known as motor courts, and their cabins were arranged in a row parallel or perpendicular to the highway, often in a *U* or *L* shape, with a central courtyard in the front. The top image shows Vernon's Tourist Camp, located north of Aurora. The bottom image shows Metzger's A-1 Cabins, which were located just north of the original route of the Lincoln Highway along New York Street. (Both, courtesy of Russell Rein.)

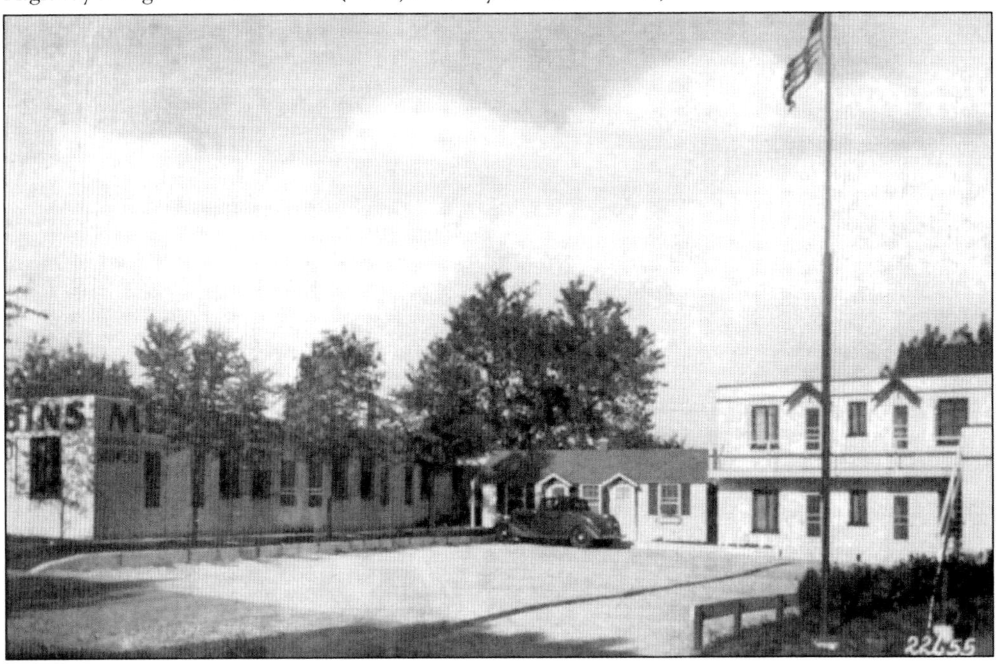

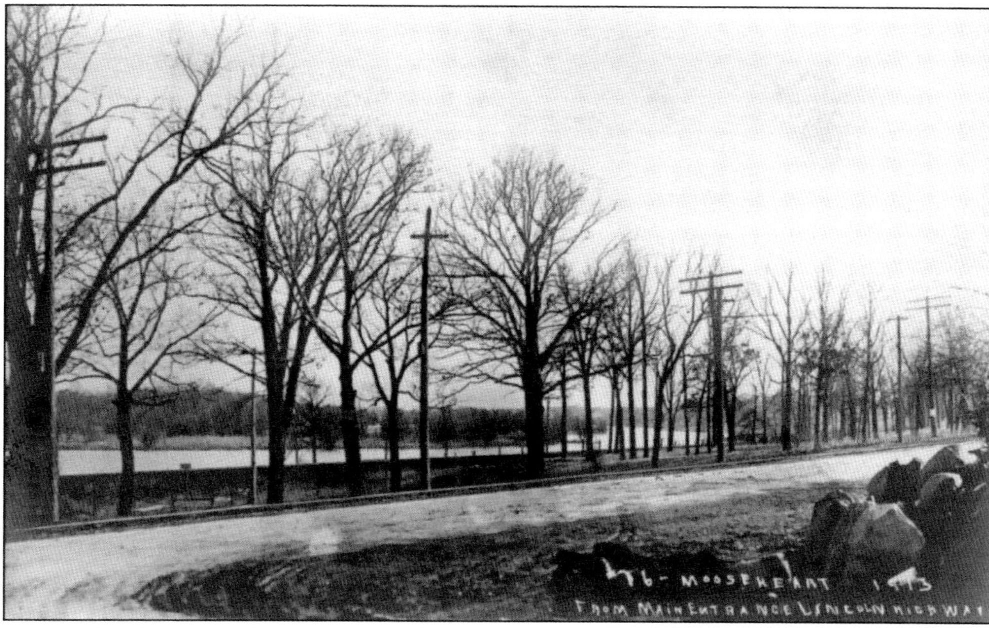

In late 1912, the Moose Supreme Council approved the purchase of what was known as Brookline Farm, nearly 1,000 acres west of the Fox River along the dusty, dirt-surfaced Lincoln Highway. Located between the towns of Batavia and North Aurora, the cornerstone was placed for Mooseheart on Sunday, July 27, 1913, and construction began in earnest. Mooseheart cares for youth whose families are unable to care for them and provides these children with a wholesome environment and the best possible education and training. These photographs show views of the Lincoln Highway from the main entrance of Mooseheart. In the top photograph, a section of the Lincoln Highway looking south can be seen. A view of the Fox River is also visible. In the bottom photograph, automobiles leaving Mooseheart can be seen nearing the highway. (Both, courtesy of Russell Rein.)

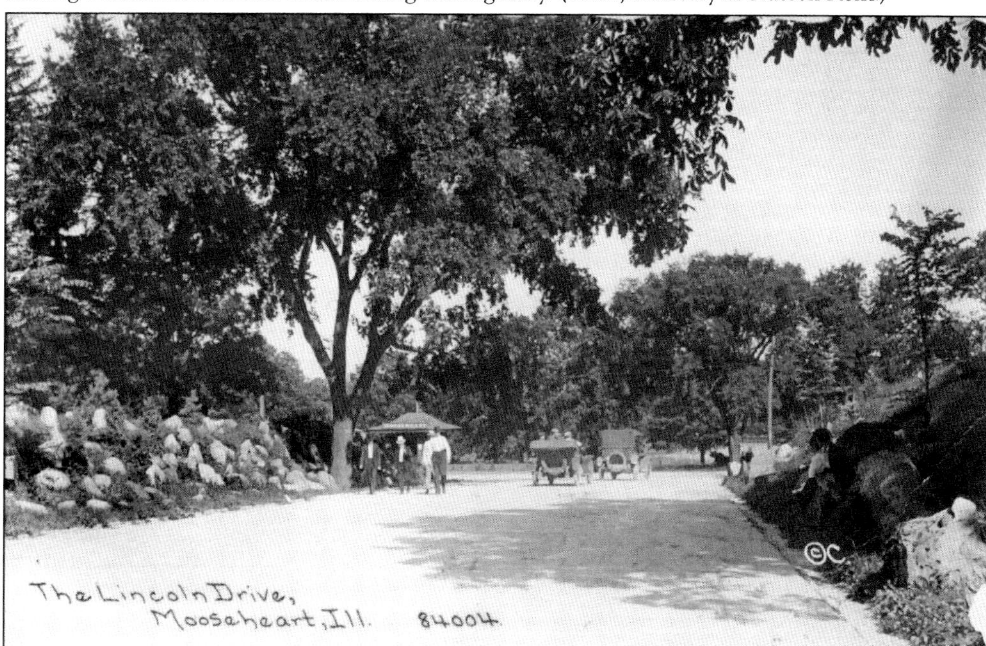

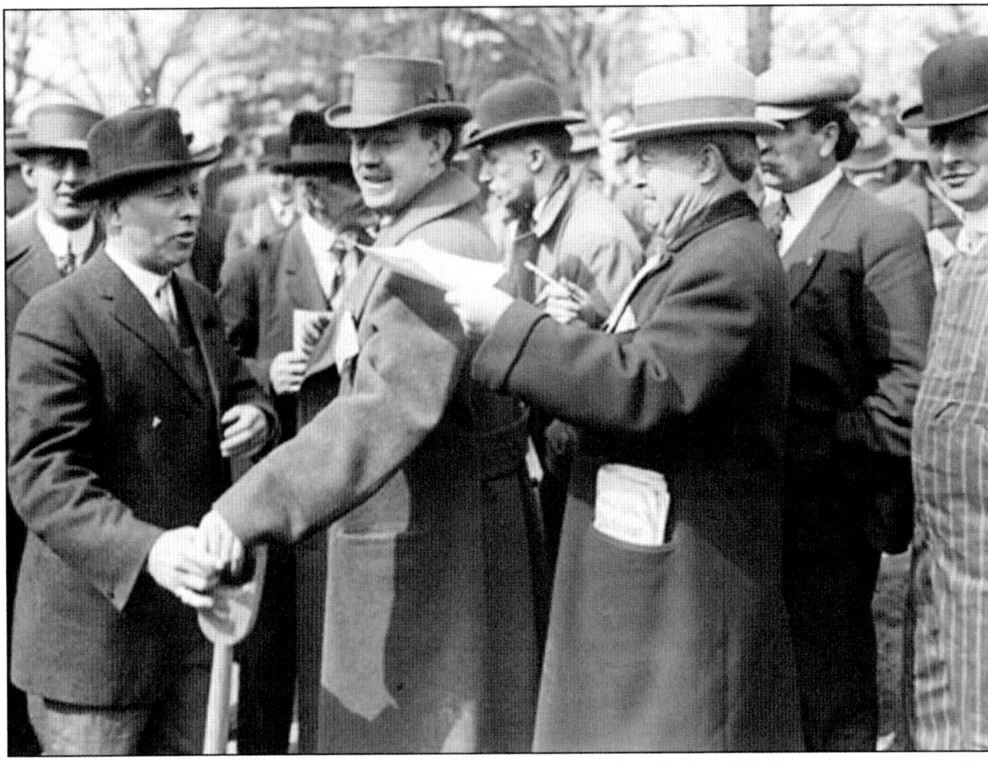

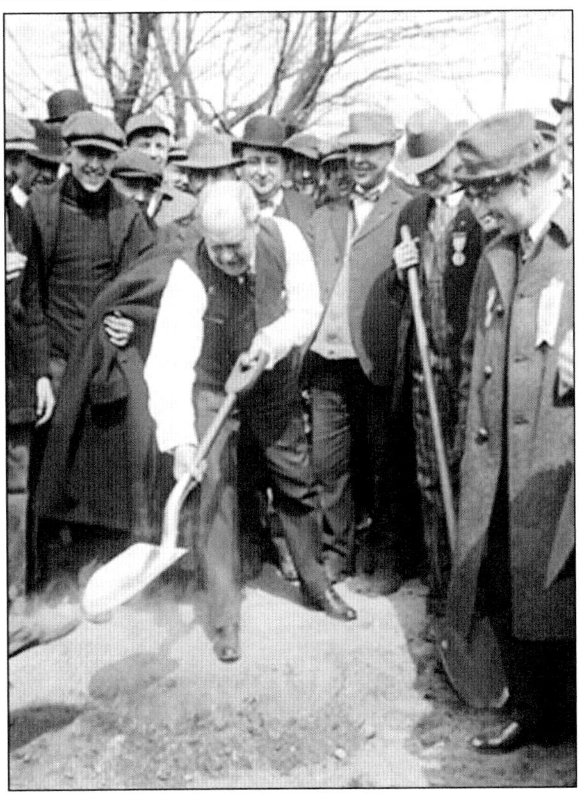

Gov. Edward F. Dunne, members of the Illinois state legislature, members of the state highway department, and others involved in highway improvement efforts formed a line of 15 touring cars and began a motor trip across six of the northern counties of the state. Traveling nearly 25 miles an hour, the day-long endeavor included stops at 20 towns to make "Good Roads" speeches and usher in a new era of highway improvement in the state. Besides shaking hands and addressing crowds along the route, Governor Dunne also assisted workers in certain locations by raking sections of the road or steering a steamroller near Mooseheart. The top photograph shows Governor Dunne standing in front of a group of men holding papers and promoting "Good Roads" as part of his tour. The image on the left shows the governor shoveling dirt along the Lincoln Highway near Mooseheart. (Both, courtesy of the Chicago Daily News Collection, Chicago History Museum.)

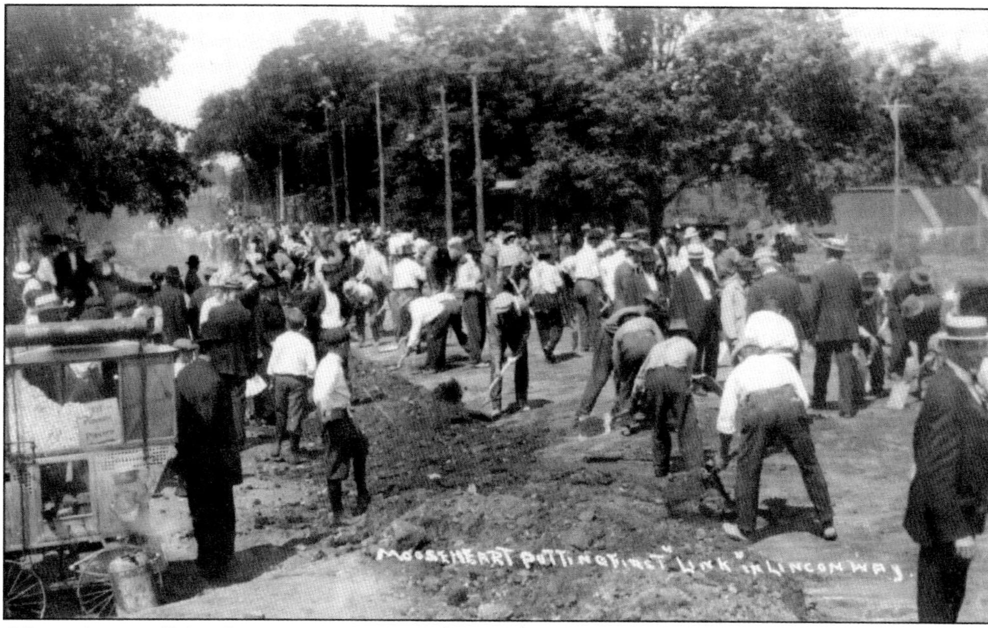

After taking a 134-mile motor trip across the north counties of Illinois on the Lincoln Highway, Gov. Edward Dunne began the crusade of transforming the mud and dirt roadways of Illinois into more user-friendly roadways. On April 15, 1914, thousands of residents in communities along the Lincoln Highway turned out to labor with picks and shovels to begin to make the roadway better. The top photograph shows volunteers working a two-mile stretch near the Moose Lodge headquarters near Batavia. When the route of the Lincoln Highway was established to run past Mooseheart, the members made a deal with the state to help pave a two-mile section in front of the lodge if the state would provide the equipment. The bottom image shows a view of the first concrete section constructed between Mooseheart and Batavia. (Above, courtesy of Russell Rein.)

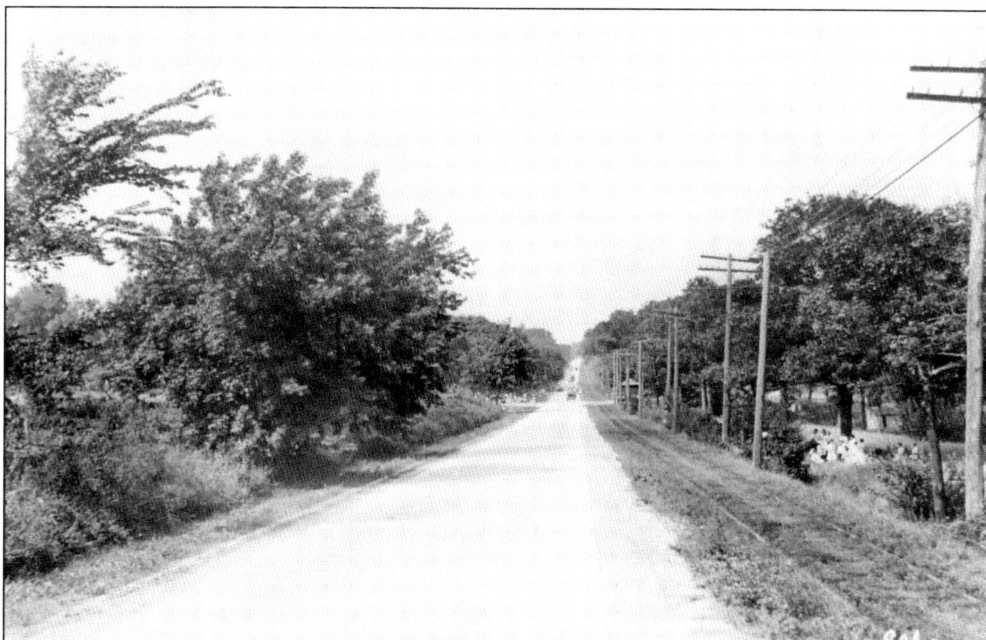

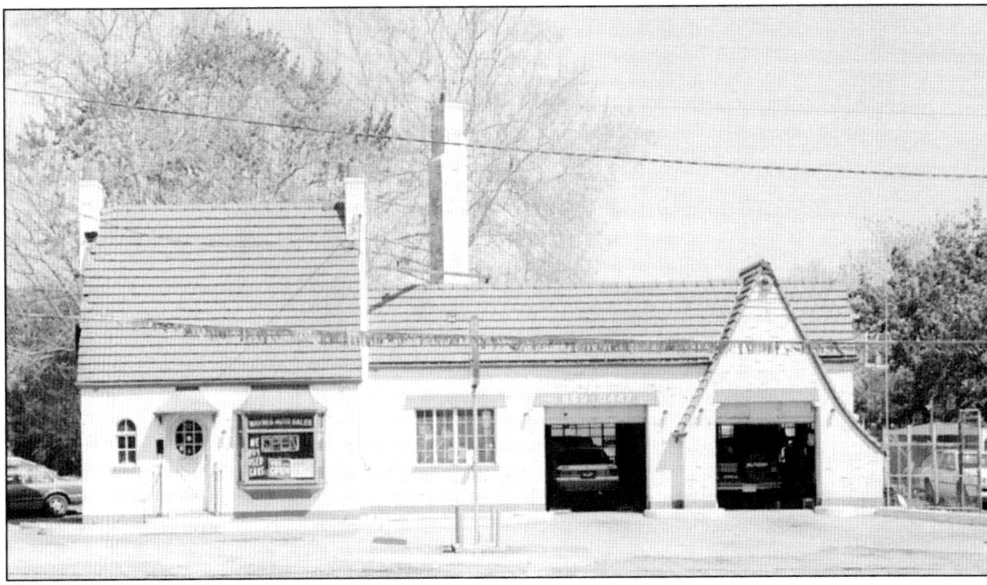

In the first two decades of the 20th century, petroleum corporations embraced a corporate packaging idea and began to adopt trademarks, brand names, and look-alike gas stations. Soon, prospective customers were able to easily identify and recognize the standardization that appeared regardless of the location. The Pure Oil Company was a pioneer in the movement to use architecture as a corporate symbol. Beginning in 1927, the company created a new corporate identity by adopting a standard English cottage design that was repeated hundreds of times across the Midwest. The standardization adopted by the company, as shown in these images, included the station design, the signage, the logo, and a blue color scheme. Illinois is home to several old Pure Oil structures, including one in Geneva. Located on the southwest corner of State (Lincoln Highway) and Fifth Streets, Geneva's historic gas station was originally built in 1937 by August Wilson and was an integral and vital part of the Lincoln Highway in this area.

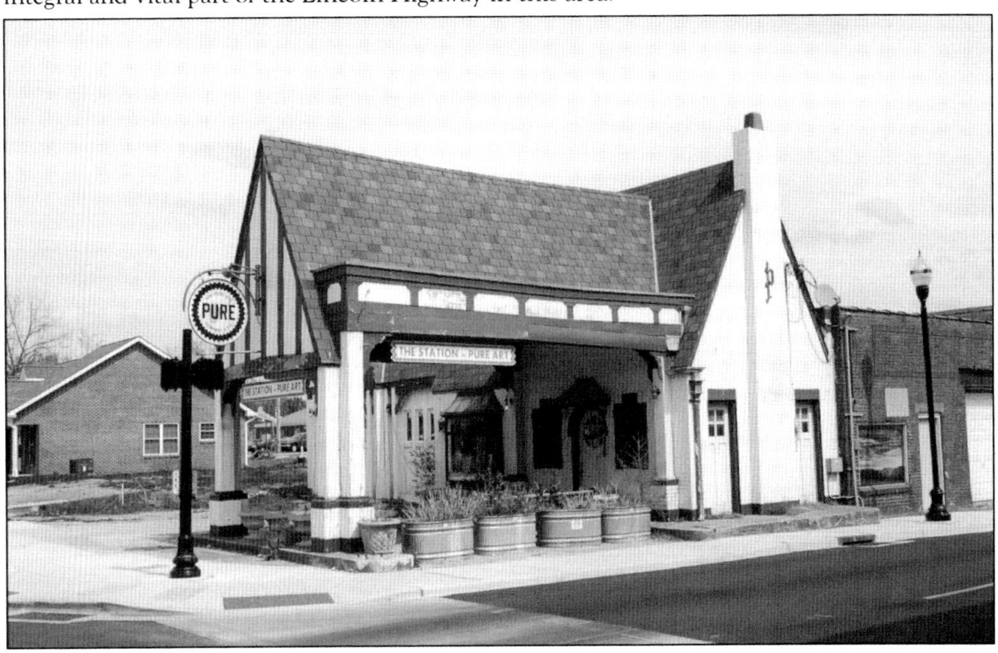

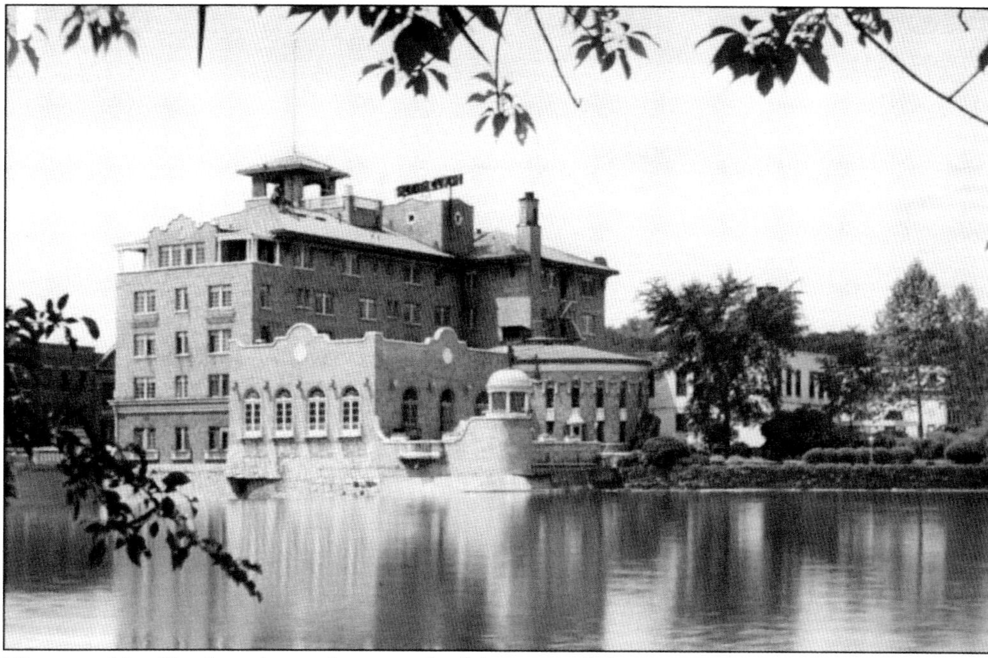

The city of St. Charles is located just north of the original alignment of the Lincoln Highway and is a quick detour for many travelers along the route. The Hotel Baker was constructed in 1928 by Edward J. Baker, a native of St. Charles, Illinois, who dreamed of building a luxurious hotel in town. The Hotel Baker was at first the site of the Old Haines Mill, which was built in 1837 and burned down in 1919. Baker bought the property and used his inheritance to fund construction costs, which neared $1 million. Located along the west branch of the Fox River on Main Street, the hotel was one of only a few hotels in the world to generate its own power by channeling the Fox River to generator turbines located below the building. The Hotel Baker was added to the National Register of Historic Places in 1978.

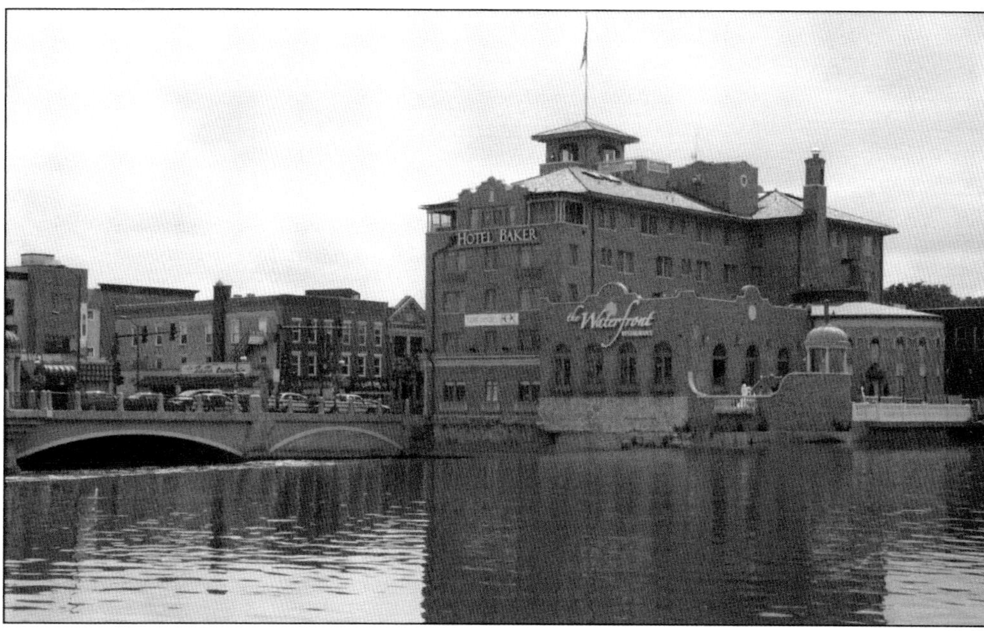

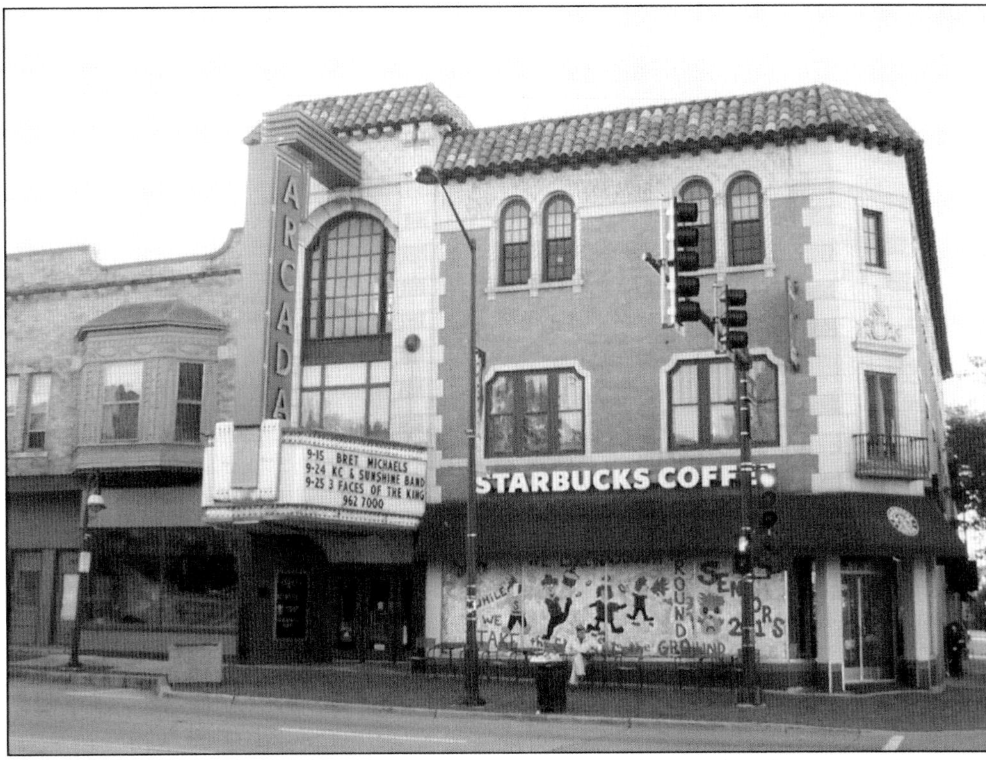

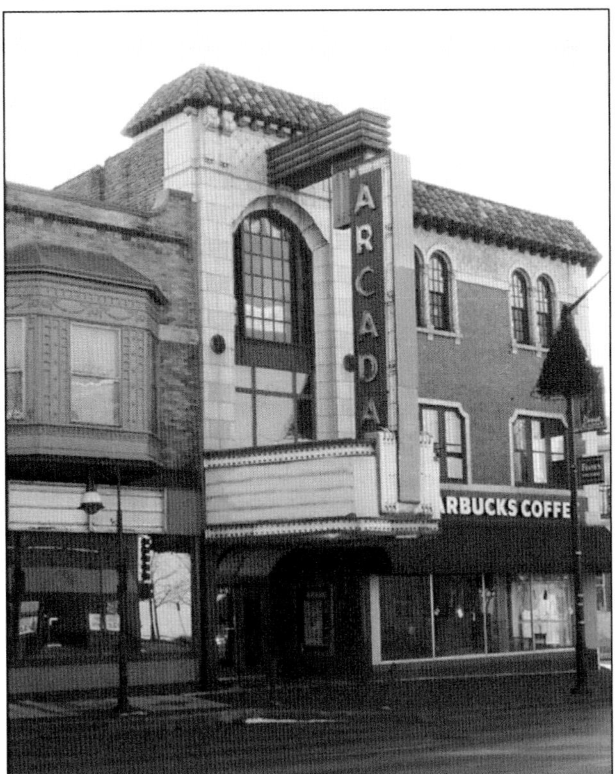

Located at the corner of East Main Street and First Avenue, the Arcada Theater was constructed in 1926 by Lester Norris, a St. Charles millionaire, with plans drawn by Chicago architect Elmer F. Behrns. It was Norris's idea to bring the city of St. Charles a playhouse theater that would offer the customer every element of comfort surrounded by an elegant grandeur that is simple yet ornate and allows the patron to feel an atmosphere of intimacy. Opened in 1926, the Arcada soon become known as one of the greatest playhouses in the Fox River Valley and attracted many of the stars of the Vaudeville era. Today, the theater still attracts today's greatest acts and still boasts the original pipe organ that rises from the stage floor. The Arcada Theater was placed in the National Register of Historic Places in 1994.

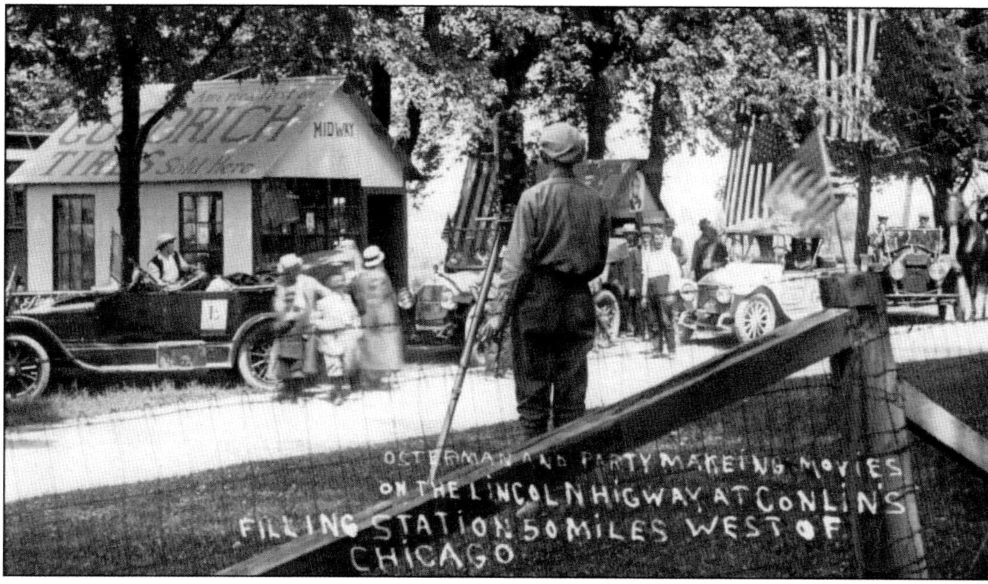

The poor condition of the nation's roads led states to begin to pass laws that gave direct financial aid for local road building or created road commissions to help control the development of new roads. In 1916, the Federal Aid Road Act was enacted by Congress and was designed to ease the problem of poor roads across the nation by providing matching funds to states for certain highway construction. In order to determine the condition of the Lincoln Highway, the Lincoln Highway Association sponsored the Motion Picture Caravan to travel the entire length of the road and film the journey. Directed by Henry Ostermann, *The Three Mile Picture Show* is believed to be the first motion picture made of an automobile trip. The final version of the film was shown at the 1915 Panama-Pacific Exposition in San Francisco. These two photographs show Henry Ostermann and his crew filming sections of the Lincoln Highway at Conlin's Filling Station, located about 50 miles west of Chicago. (Both, courtesy of Russell Rein.)

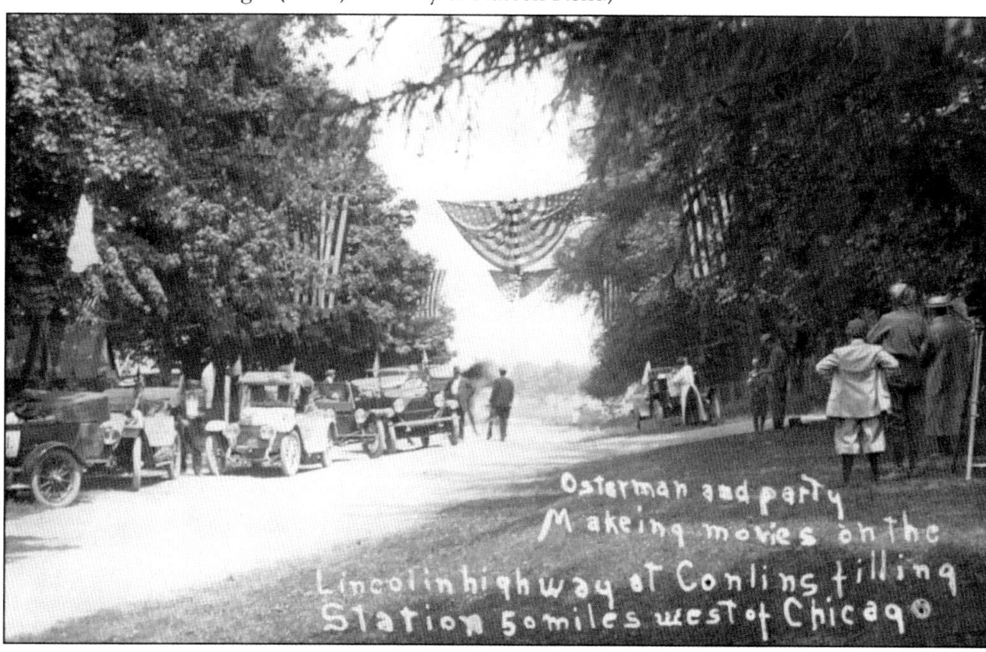

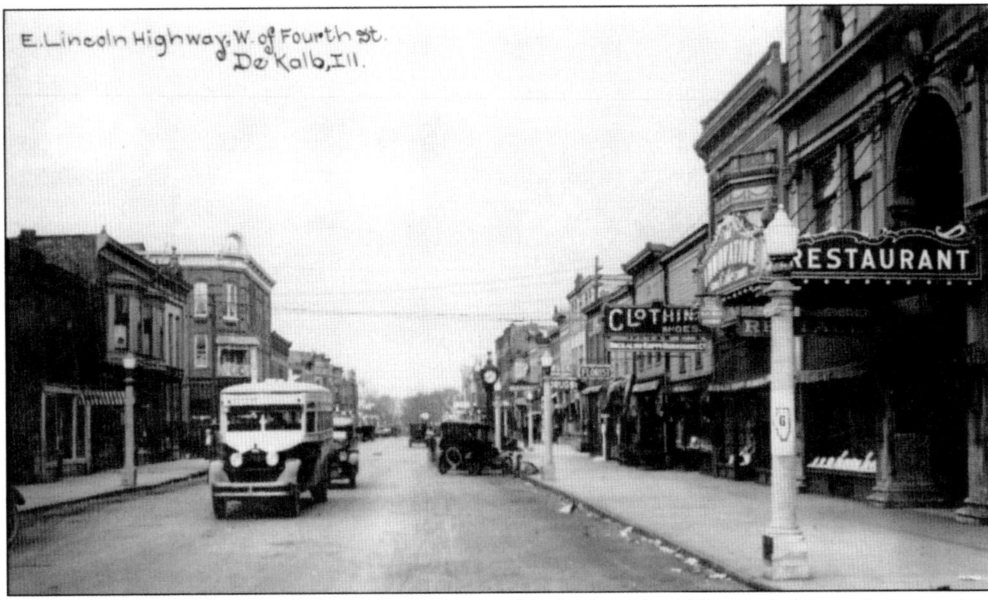

A number of buildings in DeKalb's business district date back to the 1880s and often included various retail businesses at the ground floors and served as office space on the upper floors. East of Fourth Street, the commercial and retail area transitions into an industrial character, as many businesses, including the railroad depot, are located there. These photographs show East Lincoln Highway through DeKalb, Illinois. The top image shows the Lincoln Highway looking west from Fourth Street. The bottom photograph shows the Lincoln Highway looking east near Third Street. Notice the Soldiers and Sailors Memorial Clock in both photographs. The memorial clock was dedicated on February 13, 1921, and was located in the road for several years until it was moved to an adjacent sidewalk. Today, the clock has been fully restored and is located in Memorial Park, which is located on the northeast corner of First Street and the Lincoln Highway. (Both, courtesy of Russell Rein.)

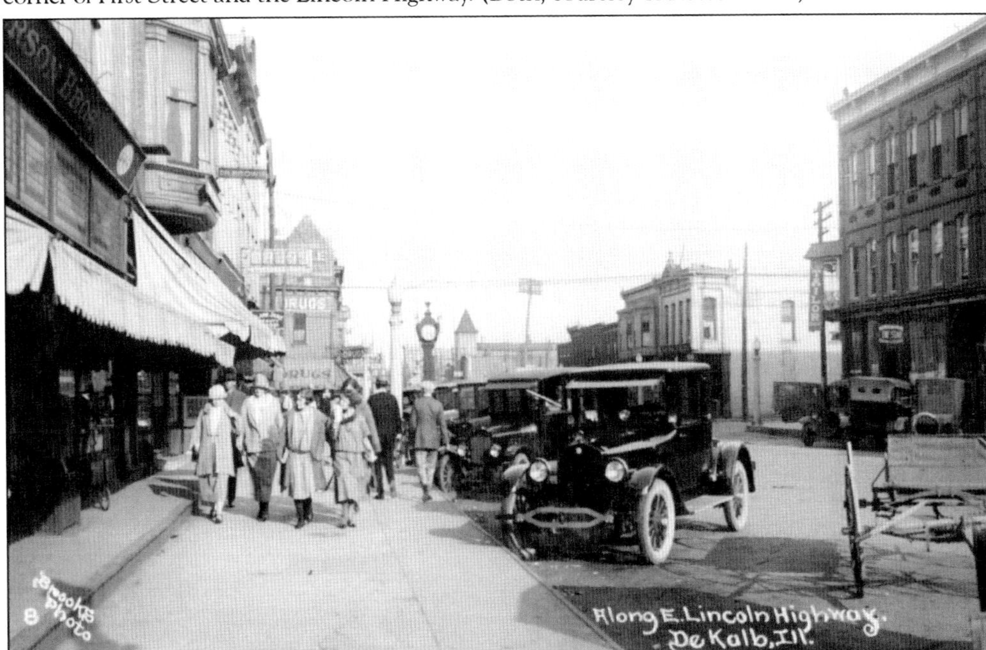

The Egyptian Theatre in DeKalb has its roots in the nationwide interest in Egyptian archeology during the early 1920s. When the DeKalb Theatre Company was searching for a construction theme for a new motion picture house, it hired architect Elmer F. Behrns to design an exterior structure to reflect Egyptian cultural symbols. Construction on the theater building began in 1928, and on December 19, 1929, the theater opened to the public. Over the decades, the theater was used to show movies and sometimes hosted concerts. By the late 1970s, the theater was in disrepair and nearly fell victim to condemnation. In 1978, a local group of citizens banded together to save the theater and formed an organization to help restore the building. The same year, the building was placed in the National Register of Historic Places. The Egyptian Theatre is located at 135 North Second Street, just north of the Lincoln Highway in downtown DeKalb.

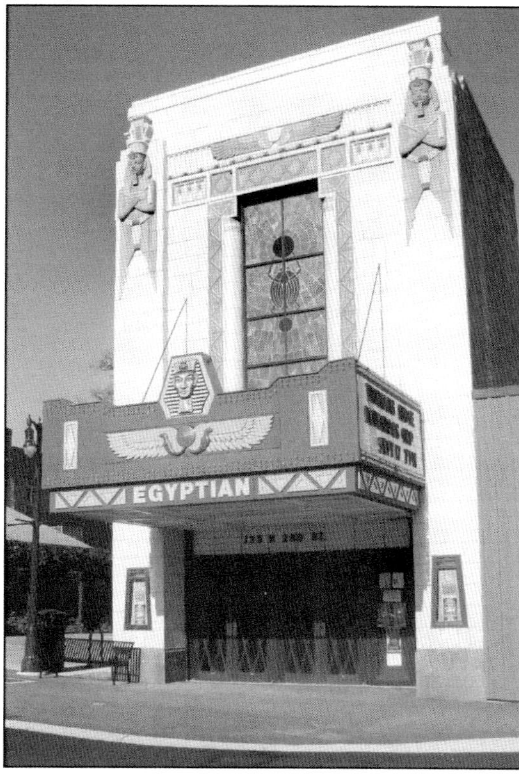

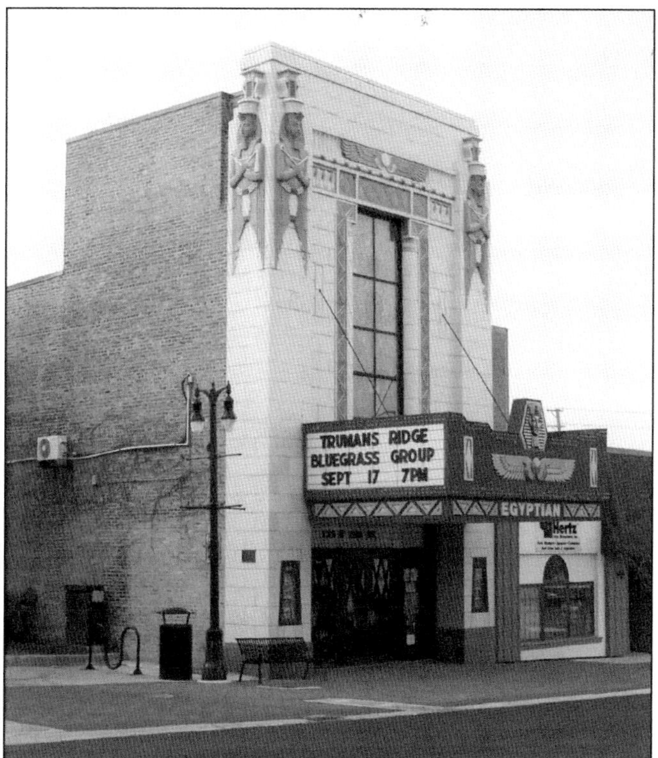

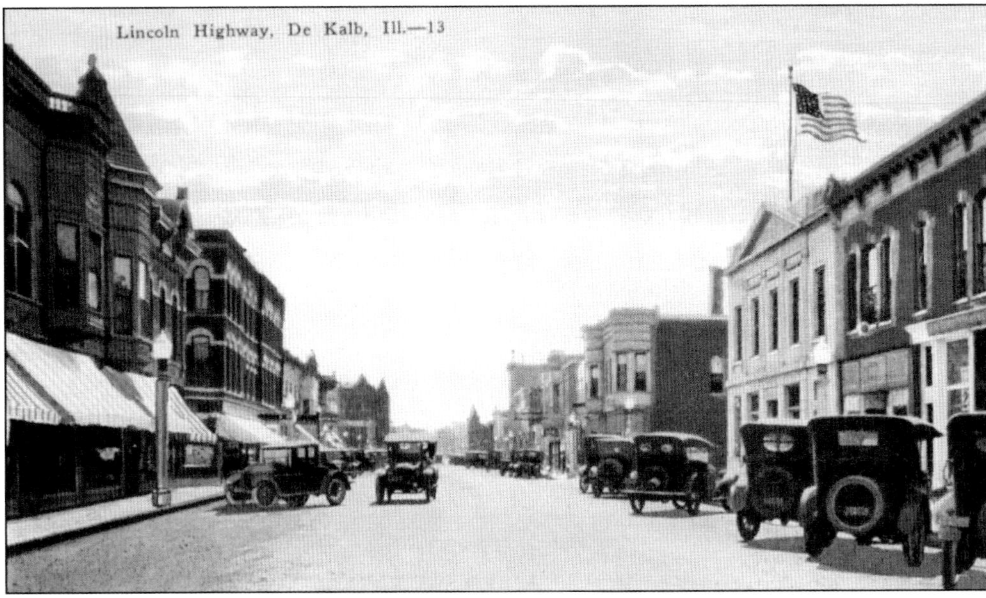

The early residential development occurred in areas south of the Lincoln Highway. As the town prospered, the downtown area north of Locust Street between First and Fourth Streets developed as the residential area for the city's prominent citizens. The business area between First and Fourth Streets, running along the Lincoln Highway, was the core retail area of the growing city. Some of the town's early retail businesses, including meat markets, dry goods stores, bakeries, furniture stores, tailors, banks, restaurants, and hotels began to appear. The top postcard shows a view of the Lincoln Highway looking east near Second Street. The First National Bank Building can be seen on the right in the image. The bottom image shows automobiles leaving DeKalb and traveling west along the Lincoln Highway. Notice the arched sign for the city in the distance. (Above, courtesy of Russell Rein.)

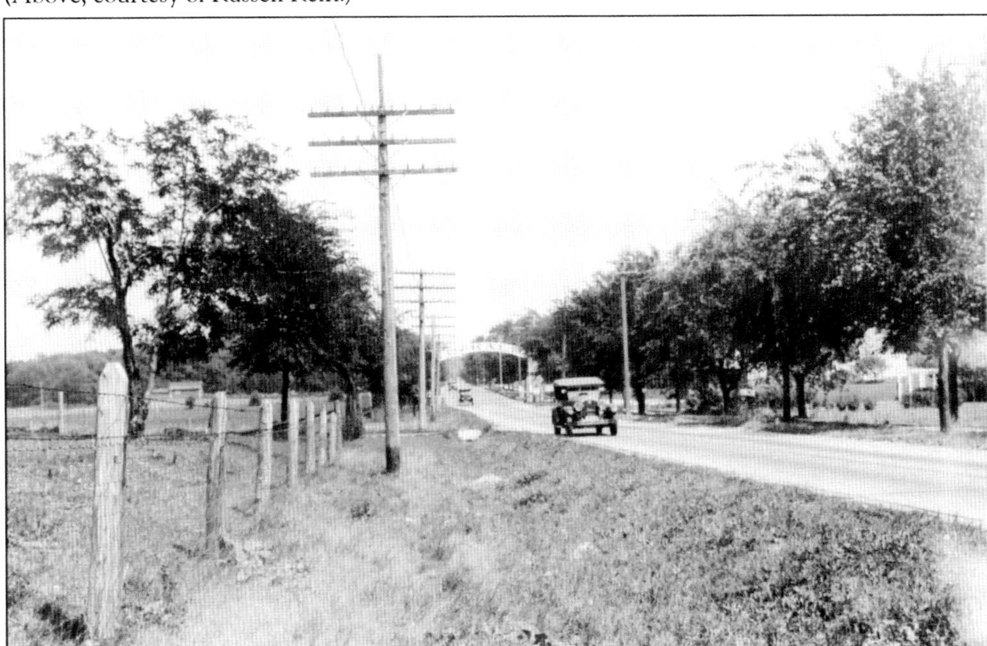

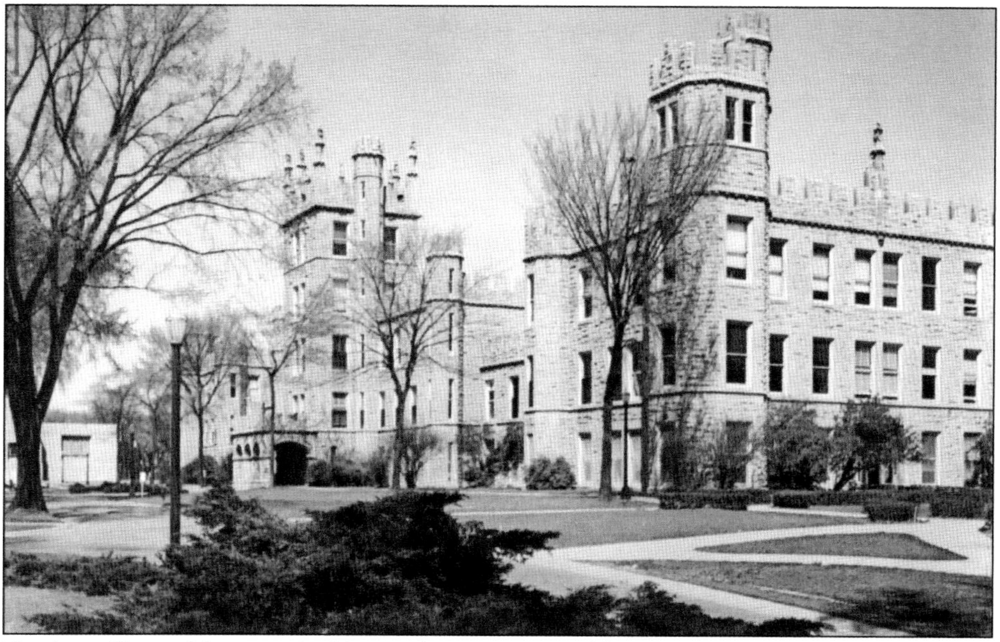

Northern Illinois University's oldest and most recognizable campus building is Altgeld Hall, or what was originally called "Castle on the Hill." Shortly after the board of trustees chose DeKalb as the site for the new school in 1895, Chicago architect Charles E. Brush was hired to design the new building. Constructed in Tudor Gothic style, the castle facade of the new building was the idea of Gov. John P. Altgeld, who wanted to change the character of public buildings around the state, particularly at the five Illinois university campuses. On October 1, 1895, the cornerstone was laid as more than 30,000 people attended the event, including Governor Altgeld himself. As a champion of higher education in Illinois, the progressive-minded governor's idea of building a new palace on the prairie came at a time when America was on the edge of new prosperity and new technological achievement. These photographs show views of Altgeld Hall.

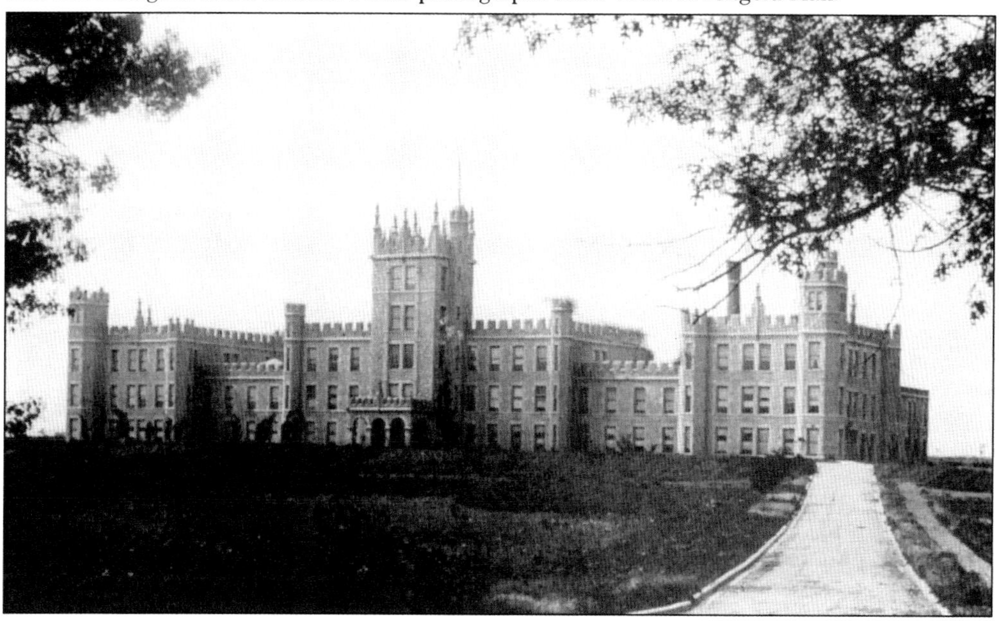

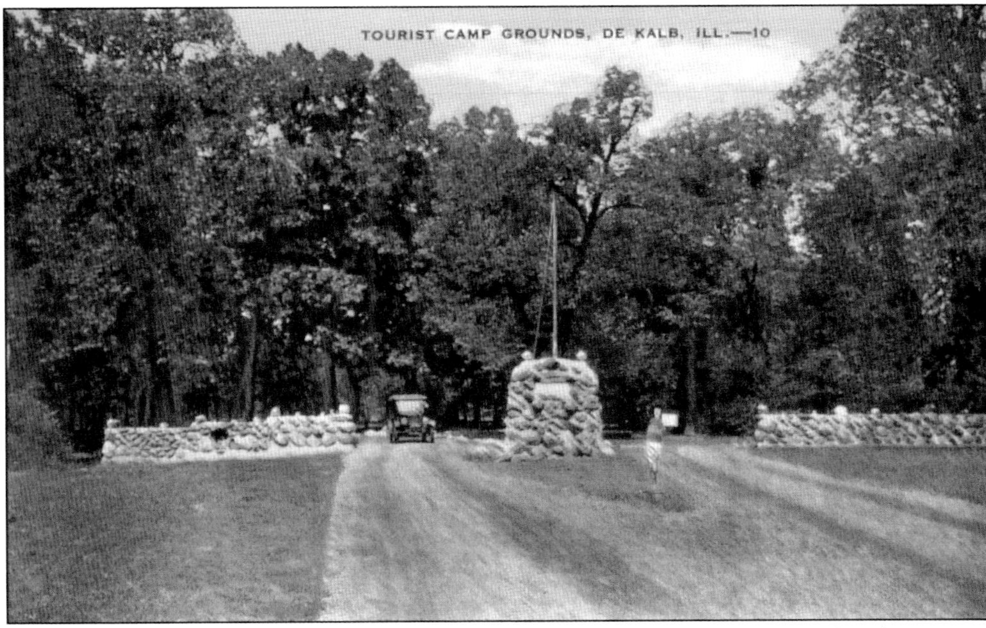

For early Lincoln Highway motorists, there was nothing to match the elegant hotel amenities enjoyed by the railroad traveler. Few downtown hotels had space for automobiles, and motorists pitching tents alongside the roadway risked upsetting local farmers and landowners by squatting without permission on their property. By the 1920s, cheap, basic accommodations for road travelers appeared in the form of motor camps. Soon, sites providing individual cabins containing beds would replace these outdoor facilities. Within a decade, these types of businesses morphed into the typical motor court arrangement, with individual cabins or huts arranged in a semi-circular or linear arrangement. These images show typical tourist camps found along the roadside in Illinois. The top image shows an auto camp in DeKalb County, and the bottom image shows the pavilion shelter erected at the campground. The sign in the tree reads: "The Shelter erected in 1922 by the DeKalb Kiwanis Club." (Above, courtesy of Russell Rein.)

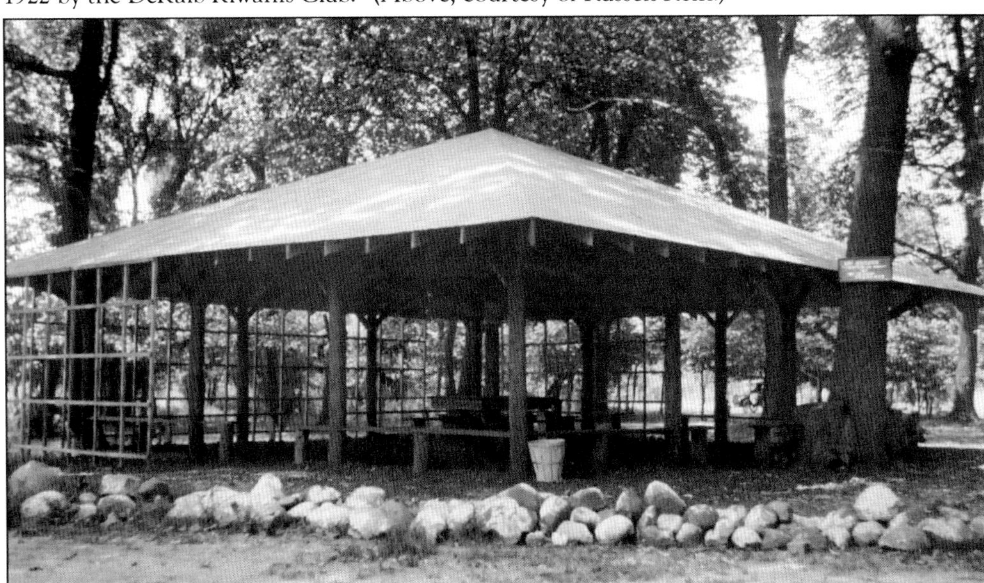

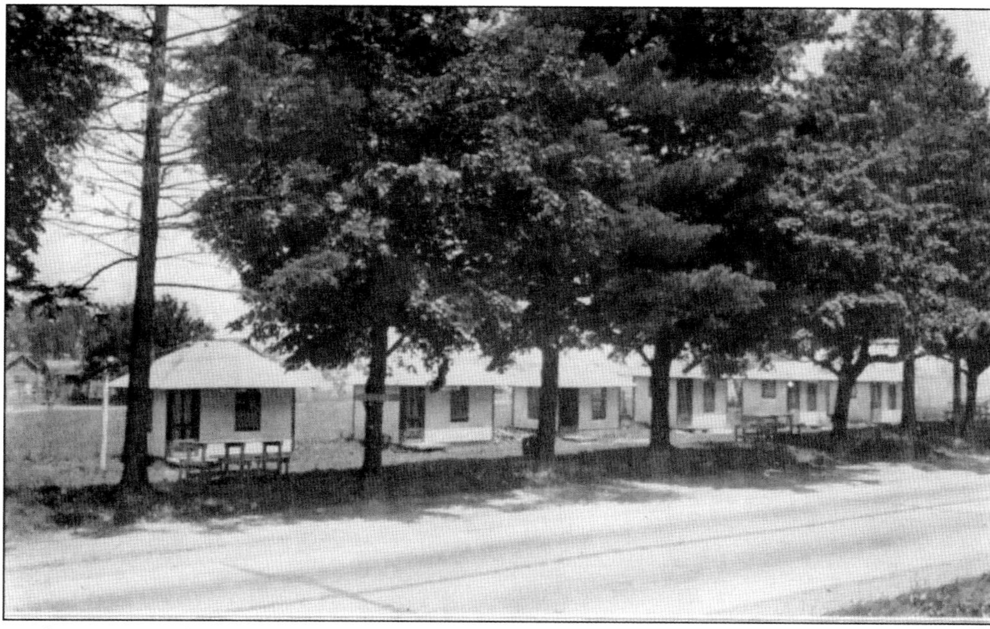

In the 1920s, early motels were referred to as "camps," reflecting the fact that the traveling customer slept in tents rather than actual rooms. As more permanent structures were erected a decade later, the vernacular shifted to include "cabin" or the more charming word "cottage." By the late 1940s, the nomenclature shifted to include the word "court" or the more generic term "motel." This photograph shows a view of Treadwell's Cozy Cottages, located along the Lincoln Highway in Maple Park. (Courtesy of Russell Rein.)

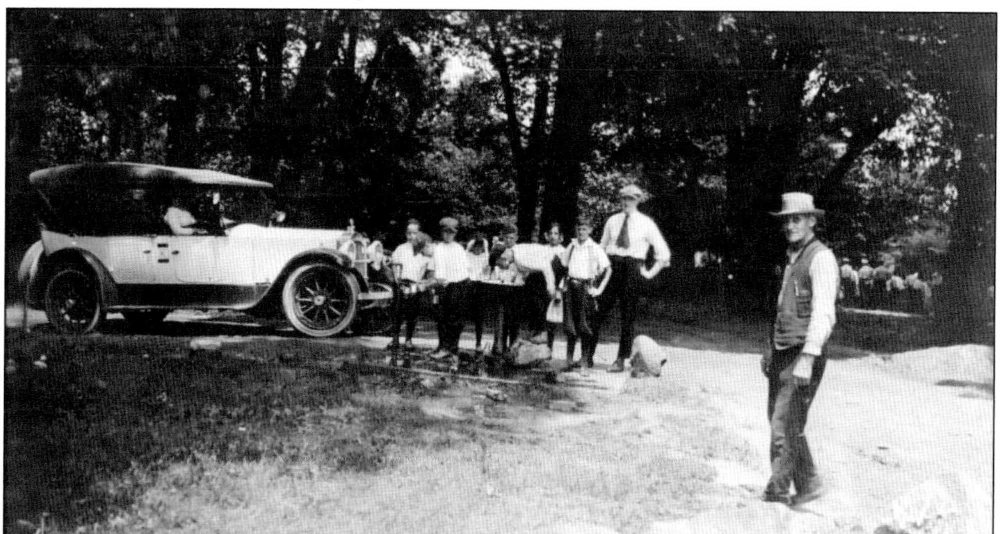

The auto camping fad peaked in the years following World War I. The popularity was spurred, in part, by the fear of breaking down on poor roads, miles from any town or city with a hotel. Unrestricted camping was inexpensive and offered the tourist family easy access to their vehicle, informality, and above all, fresh air. Soon, communities across America sought to cash in on the number of affluent auto travelers and tried to situate a camp in a centrally located city park, such as this auto camp in DeKalb.

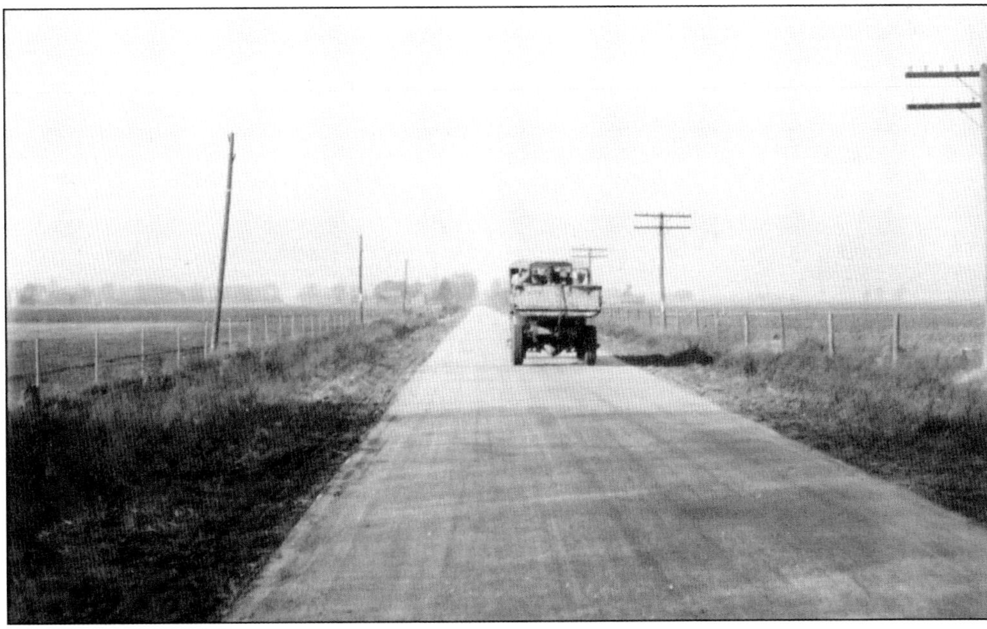

Location and agriculture are two important elements in the growth of DeKalb. Besides agricultural products, DeKalb also helped give rise to a unique invention that would transform American agriculture in the 19th century. DeKalb was known as the "Barb City" because of the invention and production of barbed wire and the economic wealth it brought to the region. Barbed wire pioneers Isaac Ellwood and his partner Joseph Glidden patented a type of wire in 1874 that would lead to the development of a production company that would revolutionize livestock fencing throughout the United States. Visitors to DeKalb can learn more about these entrepreneurs by visiting the Joseph F. Glidden Homestead at 921 West Lincoln Highway and the Victorian home of Isaac Ellwood, located just north of the highway at 509 North First Street. These images along the Lincoln Highway through DeKalb show how rural the area was in the early 1920s.

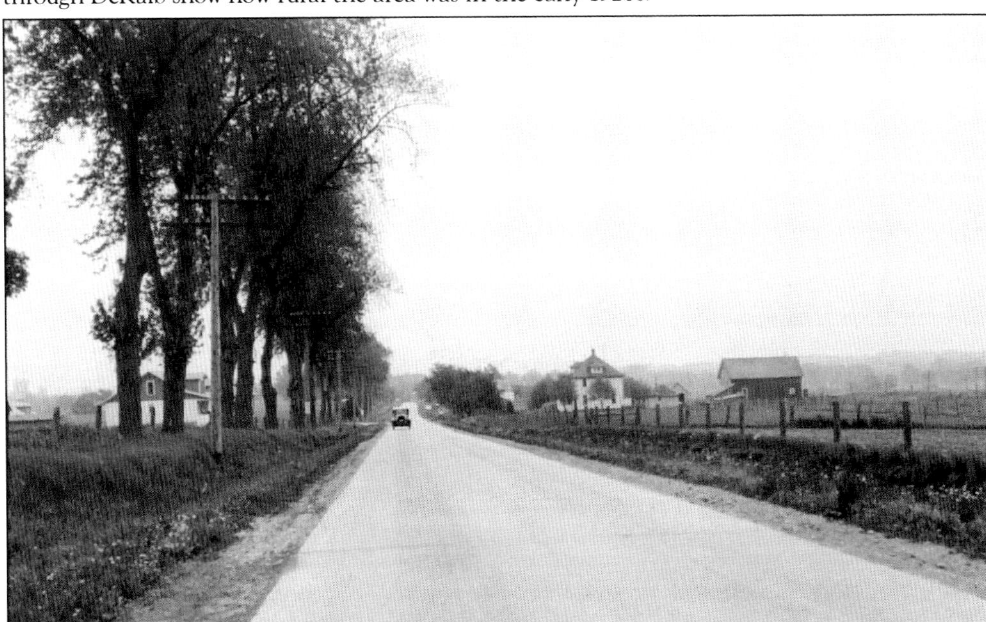

Four

Lee and Whiteside Counties

Undoubtedly the automobile had the single most important impact on the economy of the United States in the 1920s. Not only were there millions of automobiles being produced every year, but by the end of the decade, an estimated 23 million private automobiles filled the arteries of roads and highways across America, an average of nearly one per family.

The automobile industry also helped to kick-start industries that revolved around the production of the auto, including those that manufactured tires, spark plugs, rubber, paint, glass, nickel, and petroleum products, among others. Together, these industries helped to trigger an explosion in road building across the nation. These new roads helped not only to facilitate a population shift from the cities to the suburbs but also to change recreational patterns and family life.

In time, the automobile changed the patterns of American life and the way Americans think. It provided a freedom and mobility never imagined a generation before. Not only did individuals become more mobile, it also created generations of salesmen, mechanics, tinkerers, and adventurers. And the benefits of automobile ownership were only just being realized. The vacationing nuclear family, the traveling businessman, and the commercial traveler all helped to create a passion for mobility that changed American culture. As symbolic as it might be, an automobile gave the owner a feeling of power and status that might only be equaled by becoming a homeowner.

However, the growth of the automobile industry was not without a downside. There were undesirable, even dangerous results of this mobile revolution, namely traffic jams, rising accident rates, air pollution, roadside advertisements, and an aging public transportation system that was soon neglected. While all these disadvantages were noticeable during this decade of growth, they collectively took a backseat to the unbridled blessing this new technological tool had to offer America. After all, the automobile was a symbol of American freedom, prosperity, and rugged individualism.

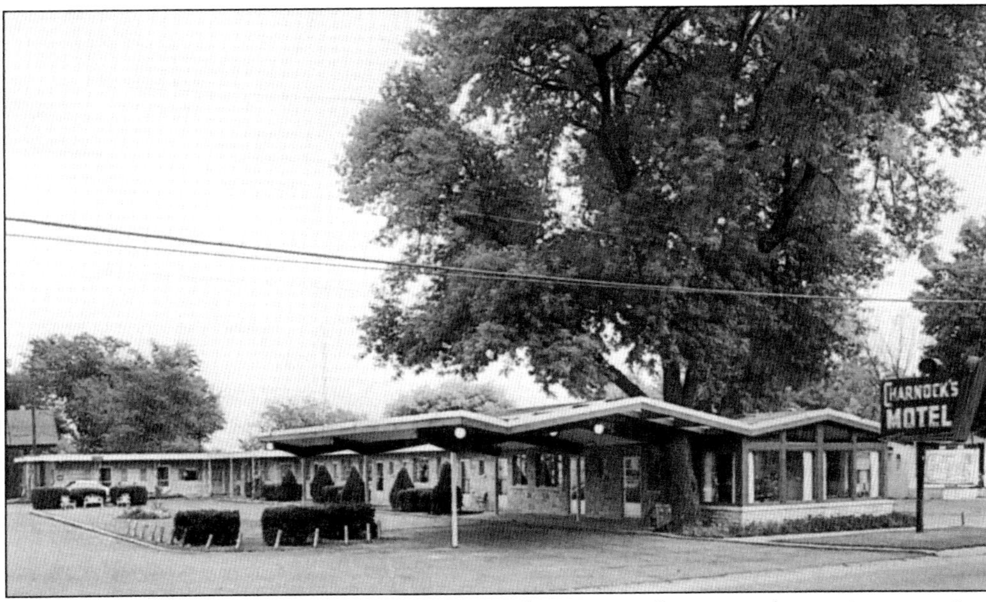

The postcard was one of the motel's primary means of promotion. Consequently, artistic conventions were utilized that created aesthetic satisfaction for the creators and the consumers alike. Looking at the postcard requires looking into the scene while the borders and frames help to create an emotional distance to the image. This c. 1954 postcard shows a view of the Charnock Motel, located along North Seventh Street in Rochelle. This motel building is still in operation today. (Courtesy of Russell Rein.)

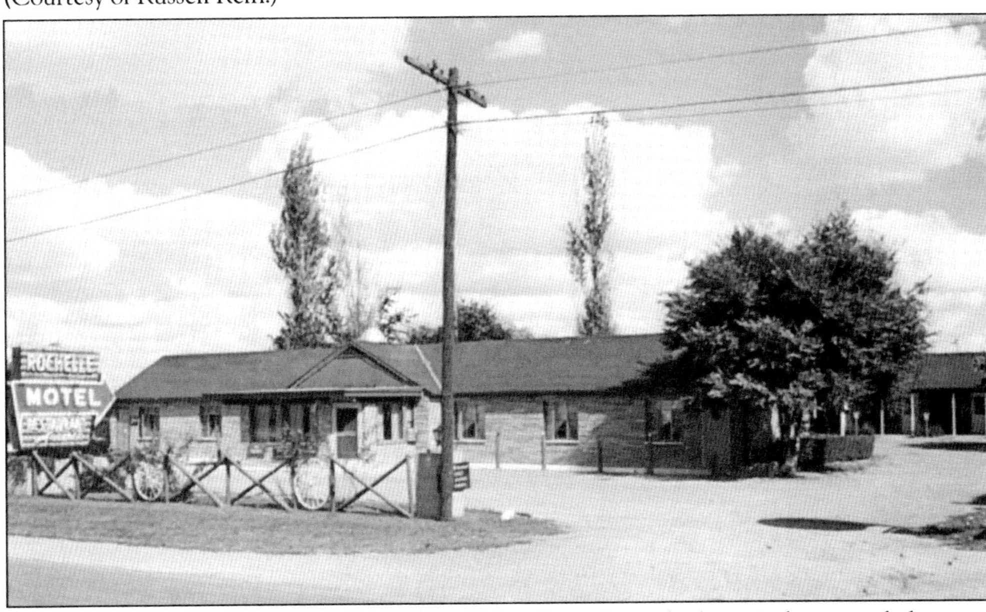

Motels were significantly cheaper to build than hotels, and very little capital was needed to start a business. Along recently laid sections of new highway, the prices of land were cheap, and in some circumstances, converting old land or buildings was easier than new construction. Many of the early motel novices were mom-and-pop entrepreneurs who responded to the growth in the travel market and entered the business. This image shows the Rochelle Motel, located north of town on Route 51. (Courtesy of Russell Rein.)

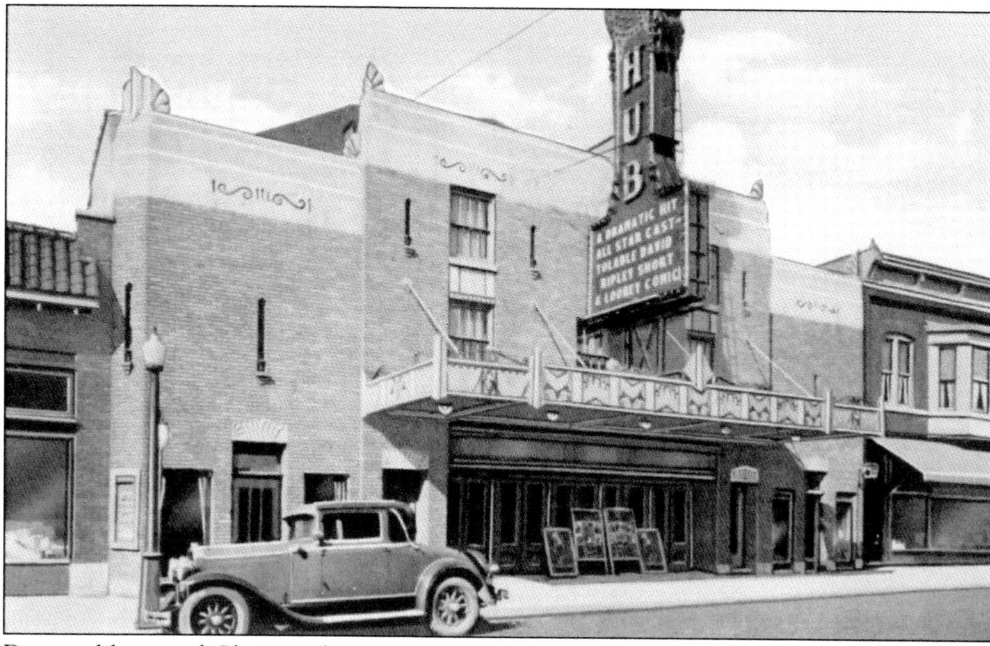

Designed by noted Chicago theater architect Elmer F. Behrns, the historic Hub Theatre in downtown Rochelle opened its doors for patrons in 1931. Behrns—who also designed the Arcada in St. Charles, the Egyptian in DeKalb, and the York in Elmhurst, among others—created the Hub in an art deco style with nearly 950 seats. Originally part of the Alger Theaters chain, the Hub Theatre would serve the entertainment needs of Rochelle and the vicinity for many decades. By the 1980s, the theater was split into a multiscreen facility, and it would continue to show first-run movies until in it closed in early 2011. The top postcard photograph shows the front of the theater from the Lincoln Highway. In the bottom image, the Hub Theatre is visible on the left along the west side of the block. (Both, courtesy of Russell Rein.)

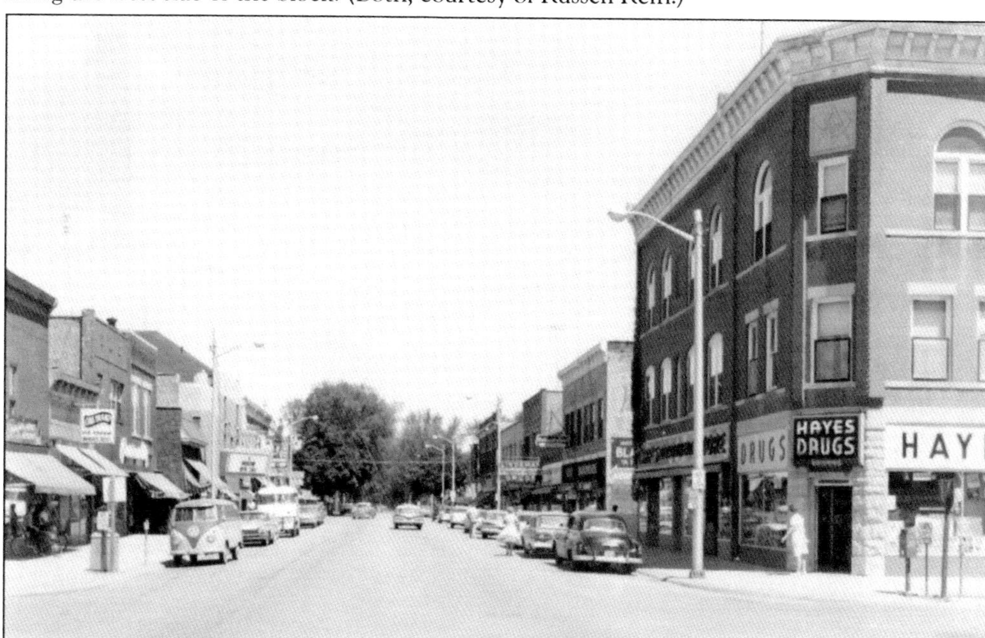

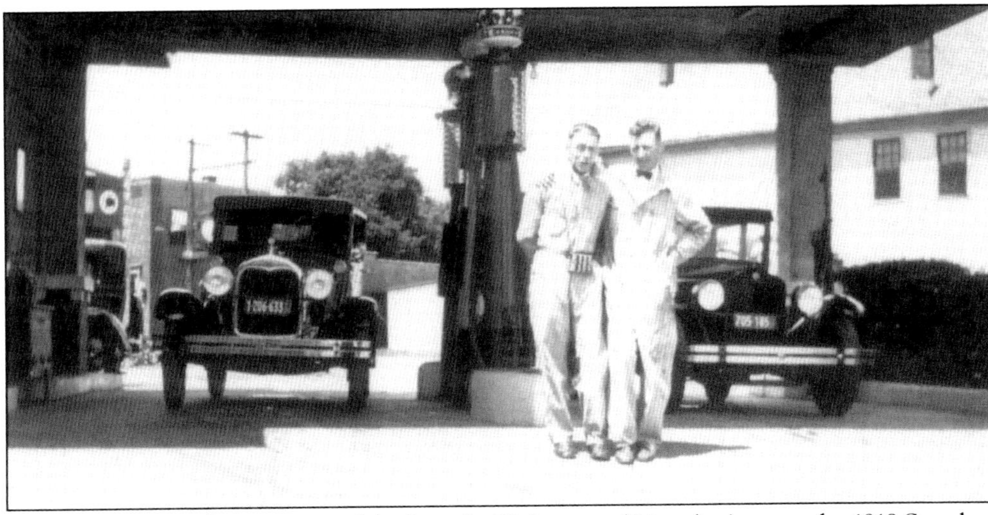

Located on the southwest corner of the Lincoln Highway and Lincoln Avenue, the 1918 Standard Oil filling station is the first filling station on the highway in Rochelle. In 1918, Standard Oil of Indiana acquired the property from Carrie E. Stocking for $6,200 and considered this a decent spot due to its corner location. Originally, the property contained a two-story building dating from the mid-19th century that once served as a restaurant and boardinghouse. This building was moved to the south side of First Avenue to make room for the construction of the new station. The filling station operated until 1942, when it closed and the canopy and the pumps were removed. In 2001, the filling station was restored to its 1918 design, accomplished through two State of Illinois Tourism grants and a City of Rochelle hotel tax. The top photograph shows a view of the old station from the Lincoln Highway. The bottom photograph is a contemporary view of the old filling station.

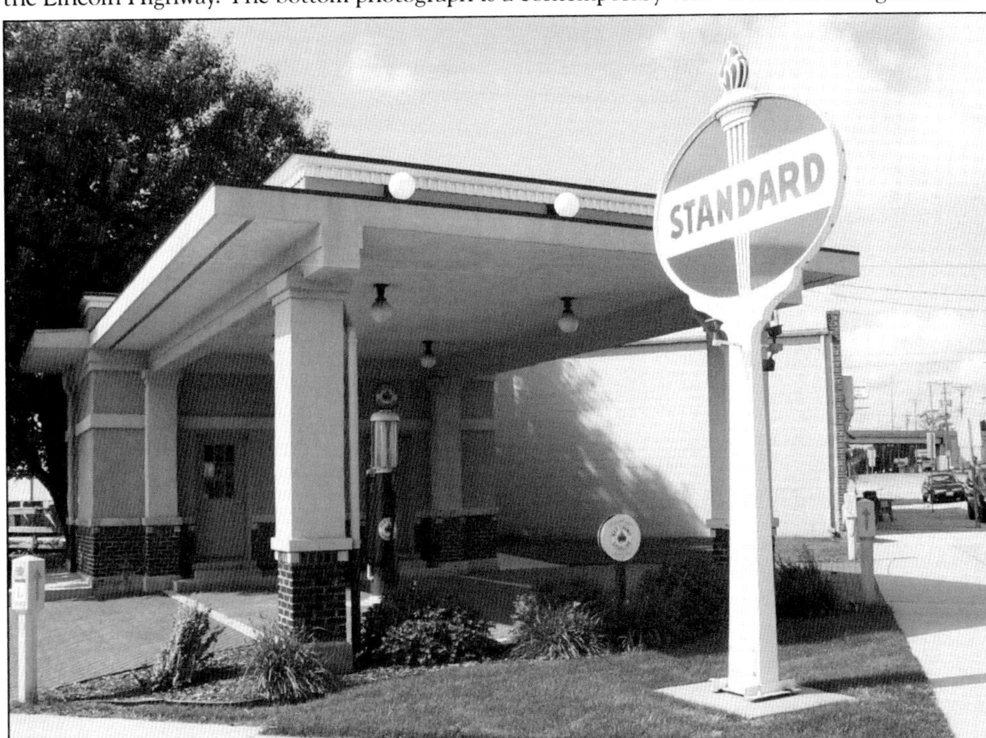

Like many vintage hotels in small cities, the Collier Inn was not designed for the automobile traveler. Instead, the hotel's advertising emphasized the building's modern conveniences, such as rooms with baths, running hot and cold water, electric lights, and steam heat. Some hotels offered full-range amenities such as dining rooms and coffee shops, as these were important considerations for a road traveler. No town or city could prosper without a modern hotel to accommodate visitors, especially automobile travelers. Emily Post, who made a cross-county trip along the new Lincoln Highway in 1915, got stuck in some mud outside of town and stayed for a few nights at the Collier Inn. The postcard on the right shows the Collier Inn from the highway. The bottom image shows a view of the west side of the Lincoln Highway looking north through the town of Rochelle. (Right, courtesy of Russell Rein.)

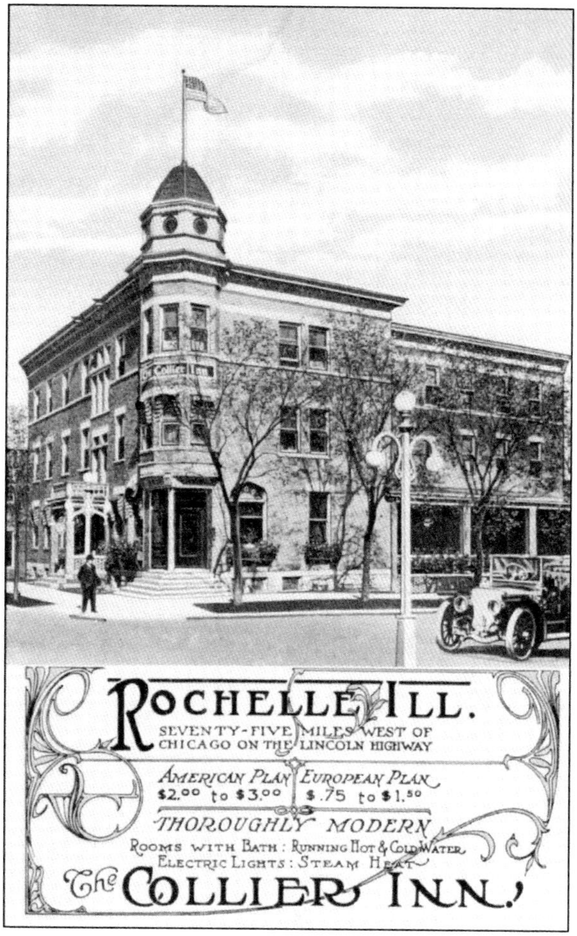

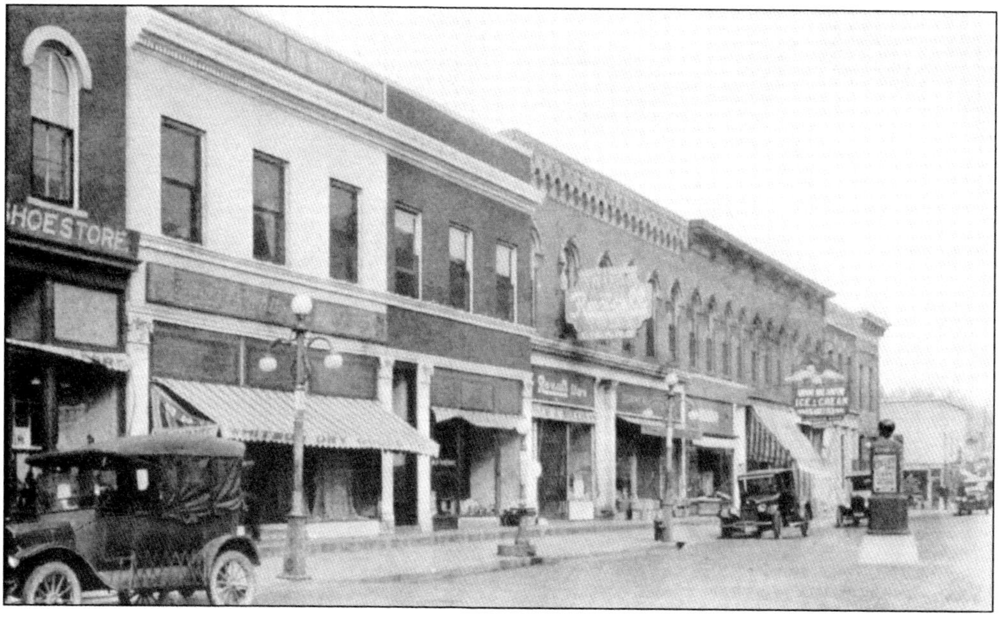

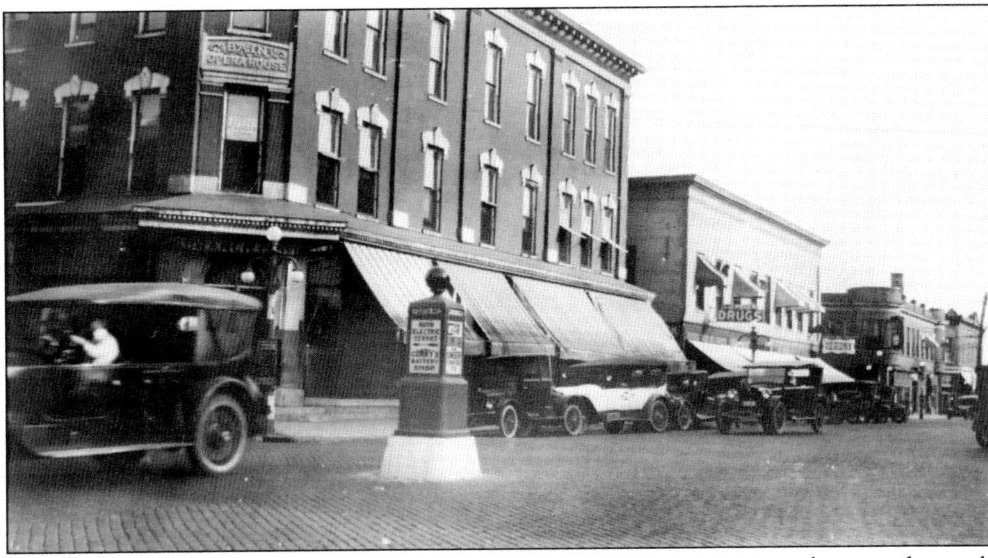

In April 1915, Emily Price Post decided to venture out and travel America's roads across the newly created Lincoln Highway and chronicle her travels and adventures for *Collier's Magazine*. Her trip began in New York City and ended 45 days later in San Francisco, California, where she attended the Panama-Pacific Exposition. On May 6, 1915, Emily Post arrived in the town of Rochelle and was stranded in the area due to heavy rains that made the roads difficult to navigate. Post found the town of Rochelle to be a "sweet" and "clean" town with its streets "all wide and smoothly paved with brick." A mural depicting the story of Emily Post's adventures along the road is mounted at the corner of the Lincoln Highway and Fifth Avenue in downtown Rochelle. The images shown here are of the Lincoln Highway through Rochelle in the early 1920s, not long after Emily Post came through the area.

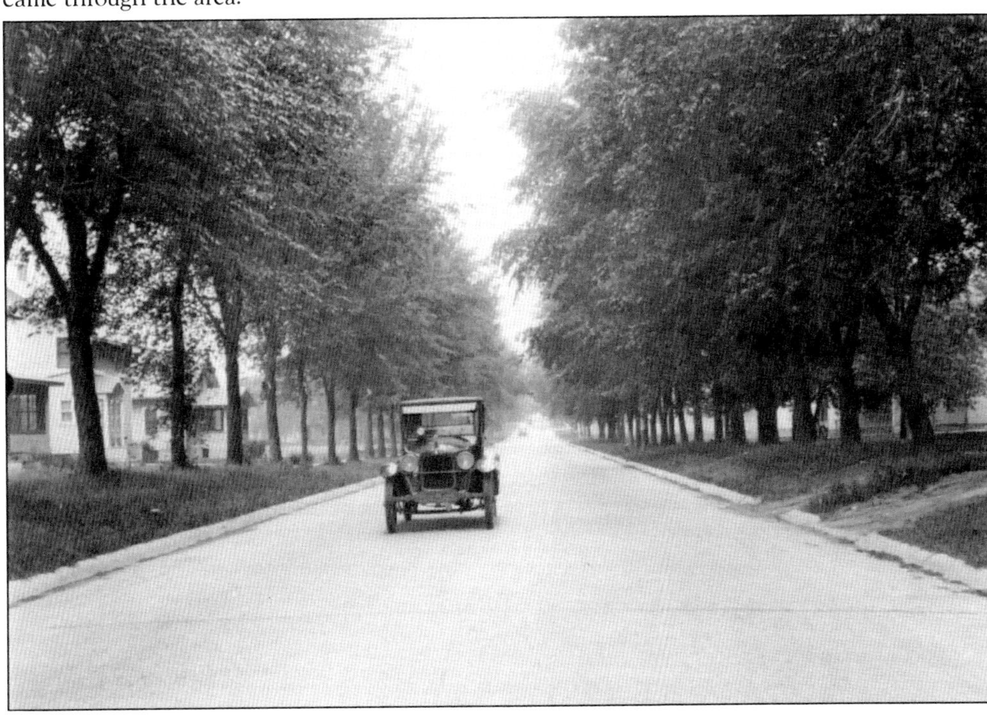

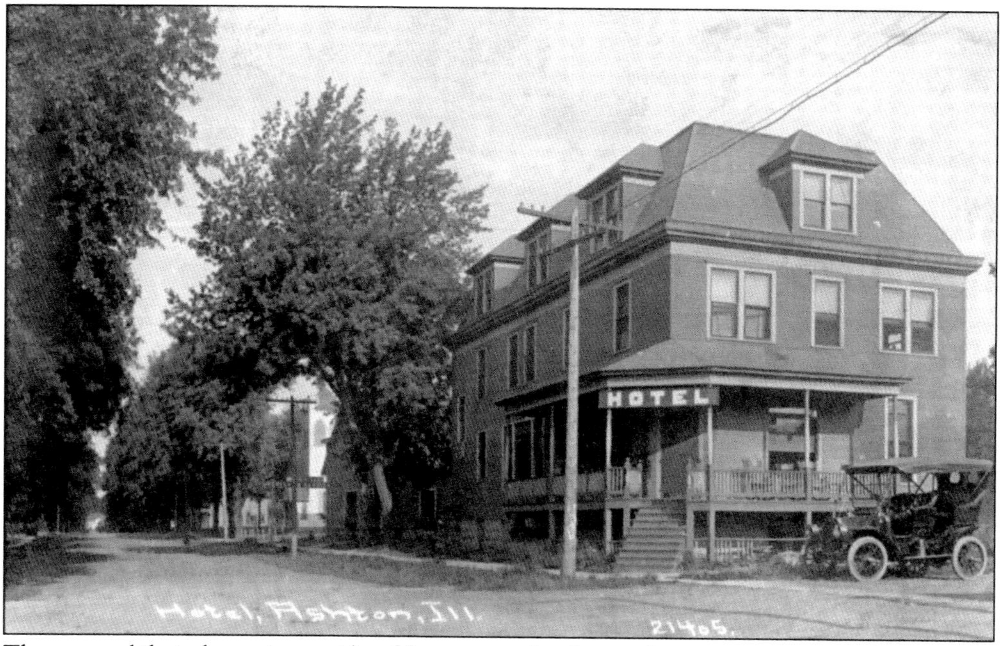

The automobile industry is considered by many to be the single most important industry in the United States since the 1920s. The value of its related products exceeds that of any other industry. Other industries—such as plastics, aluminum, oil, steel, glass, rubber, and machine tools, just to name a few—are dependent on automobile production and are important to the nation's economic health as well. Many other industries that came into existence at the same time as the automobile also owe their existence entirely to the car industry, including road construction, car insurance companies, gas stations, car repair shops, motels, and hotels. These photographs show two such businesses located along the Lincoln Highway in Ashton, Illinois. The top photograph shows the Ashton Hotel, and the bottom image shows Wright's Tourist Camp. Motorists along the Lincoln Highway could get gas and a quick lunch and stop for a rest at the auto camp. (Both, courtesy of Russell Rein.)

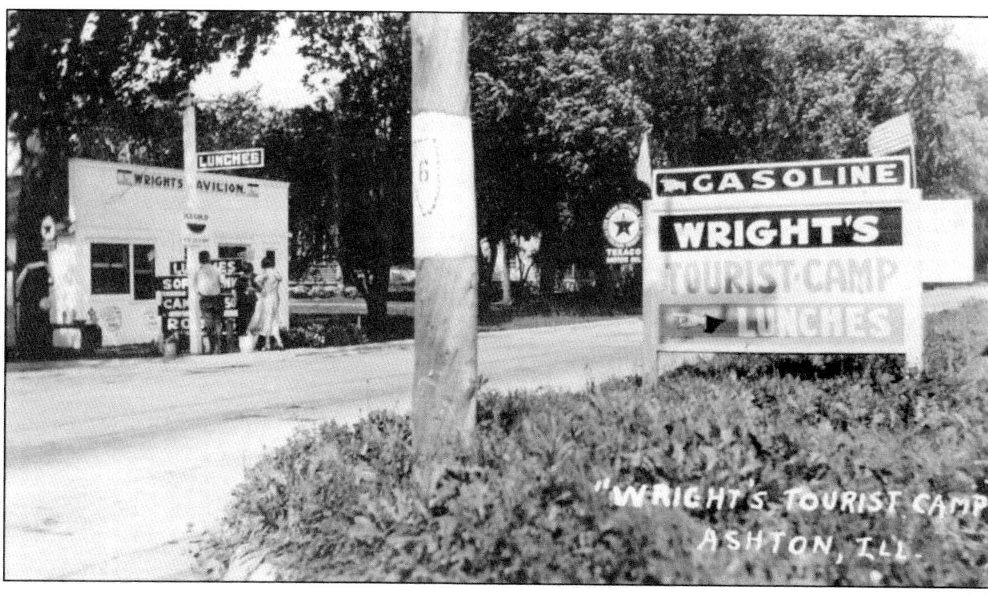

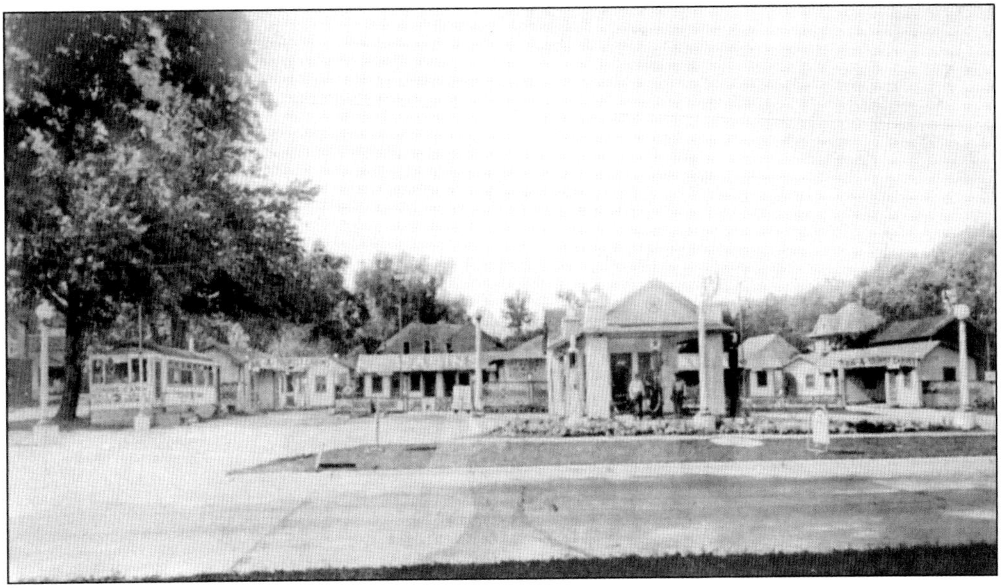

During the early decades of road travel, common names used along the roadside to lure automobile travelers included "camp," "cottages," "village," or "cabins." Often, these terms were combined with a proprietor's name or other unique modifiers that helped to differentiate the location or surroundings. While some terms provide a rustic or woodsy ideal, all of them express a feeling of security that many people valued in the early years of road travel. As with many tourist courts, a typical *U*-shaped or crescent layout included an office building, a coffee shop, and rows of cabins. These images show the Big A Tourist Cabins, located along the Lincoln Highway in Ashton. Notice in the top image, the service station is located in the front, the diner building to the left, and the tourist cabins arranged in rows in the rear. (Both, courtesy of Russell Rein.)

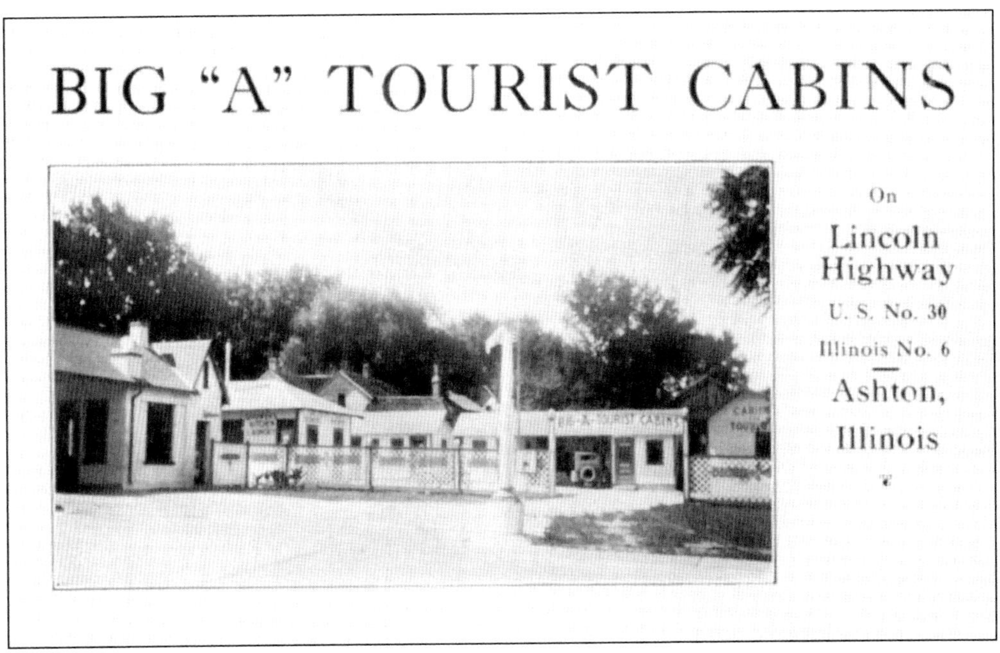

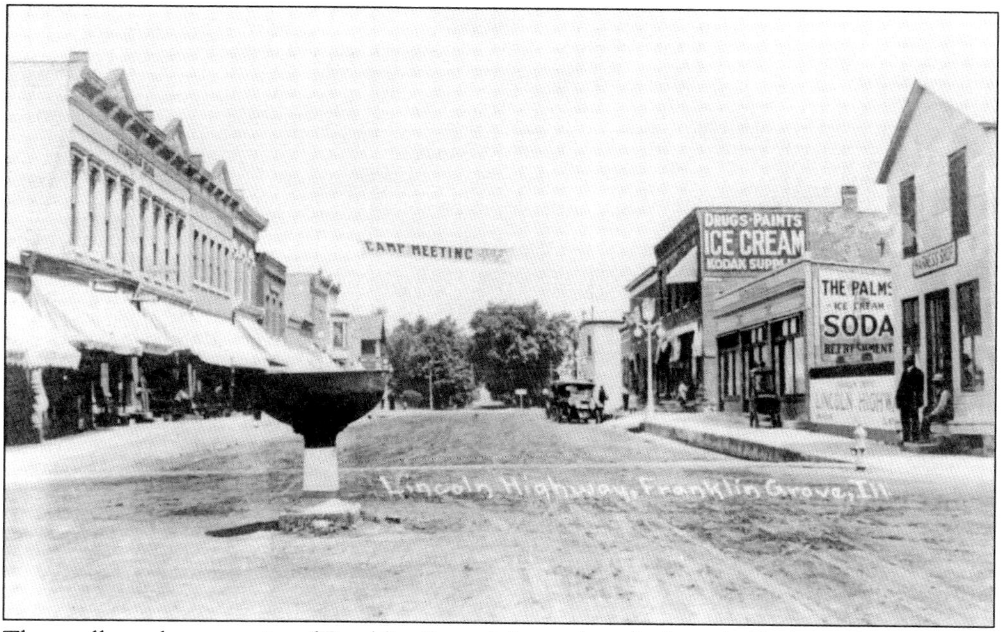

The small, rural community of Franklin Grove is located on the Lincoln Highway about 90 miles west of Chicago. The town began as Chaplin in the 1830s, and after an initial burst of growth and development, the area has remained mostly unchanged today, as travelers through the area can still see a pastoral countryside dotted with farmstead, cattle, fields, and a passing landscape that a traveler in 1913 would find idyllic. In 1914, Henry C. Ostermann, the first Lincoln Highway field secretary, stopped in Franklin Grove to gather support from locals by selling the very first Lincoln Highway cloisonné pins at the historic H.I. Lincoln Building. A mural describing this story was installed in town in 2013. The top image shows the Lincoln Highway through downtown Franklin Grove. Notice the painted Lincoln Highway sign to the right. The bottom image shows a stretch of the highway just west of town. (Above, courtesy of Russell Rein.)

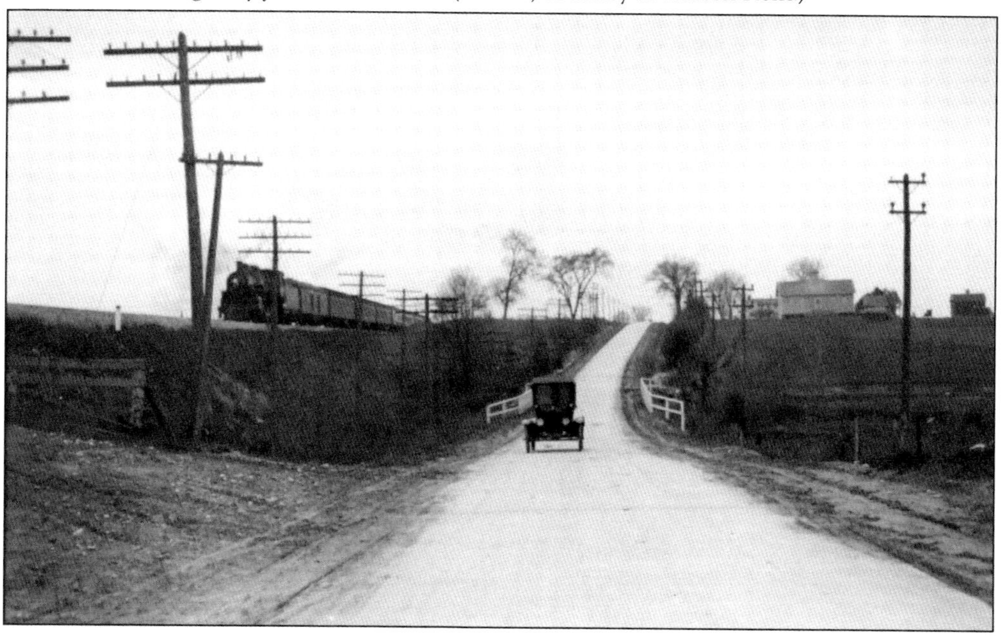

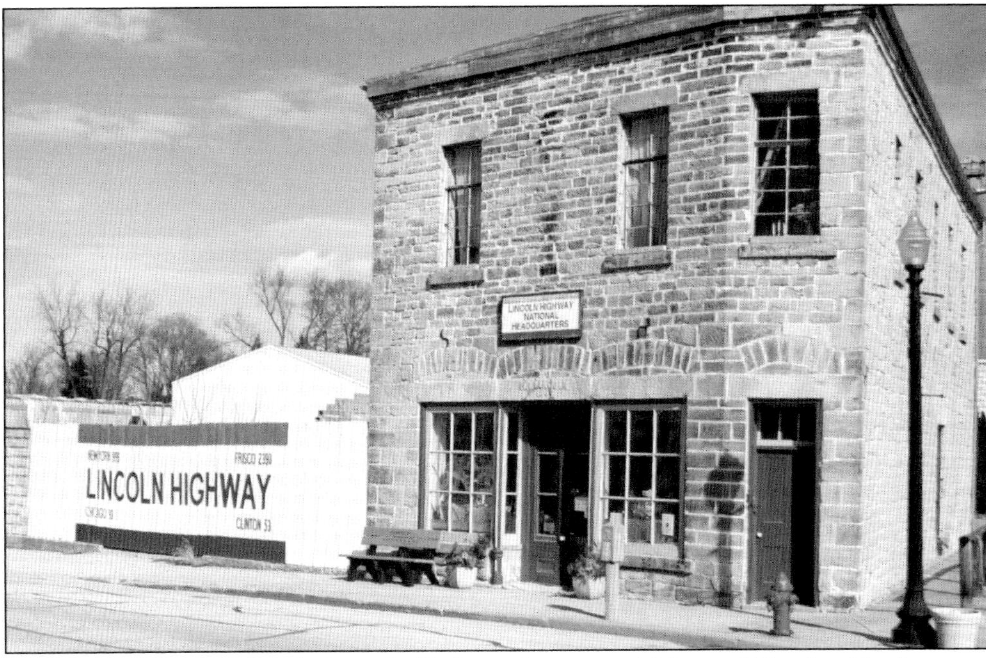

Franklin Grove is home to the Lincoln Highway Association's National Tourism Headquarters. The building dates to 1860, when a distant relative of Abraham Lincoln, Henry Isaac Lincoln, built it as a dry goods store. Lincoln came to the area shortly after the railroad came through in the 1850s and eventually found success in the retail trade. After serving as the location for Lincoln's dry goods store, the building continued to serve a number of needs, such as a post office, a newspaper office, and a dance studio. By the 1990s, the building was in disrepair after years of neglect, and members of the Franklin Grove community decided to work together to preserve the history and heritage of the area in one location. They bought the building and started restoring it, and by 1999, the building became the Lincoln Highway Association's national headquarters. These images show views of the H.I. Lincoln Building from the highway.

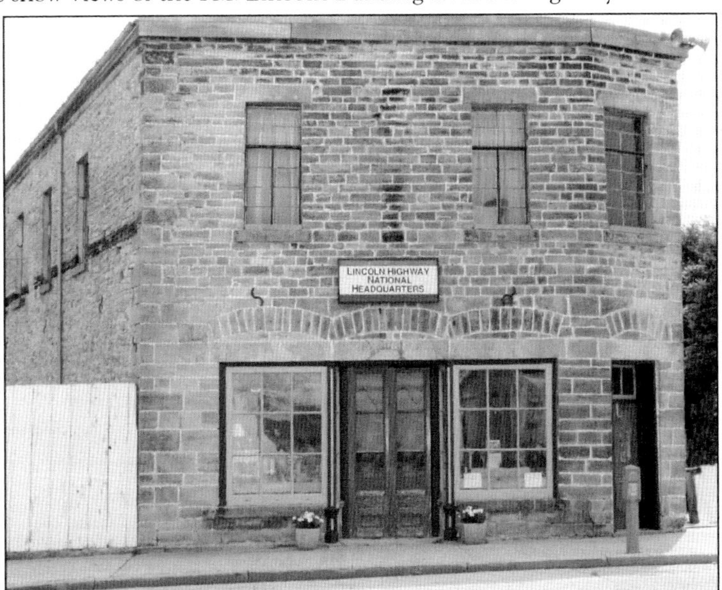

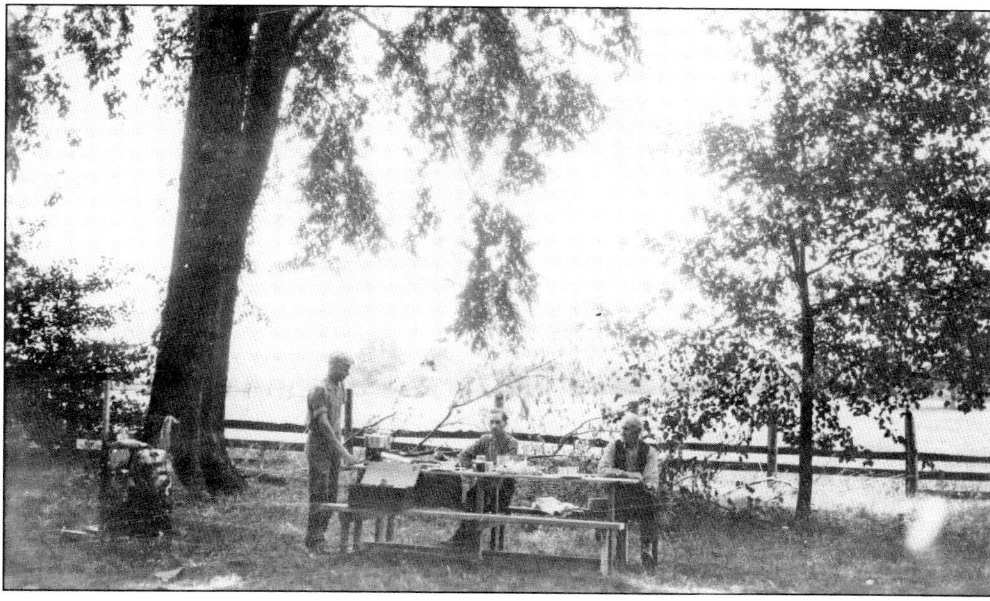

In the early years of the Lincoln Highway, the open space that bordered the road on the outskirts of towns or in certain city parks became attractive venues for adventurers to set up temporary sleeping accommodations. For the motorist, veering off the road and coasting to the nearest clearing provided certain outdoor natural amenities that could not be found in a traditional hotel. The surge in popularity of municipal camps was soon followed by manufacturers that saw the great potential for sales in travel gadgets geared to the automobile enthusiast. For instance, the Tentobed Company manufactured special rigging that allowed the owner to sleep inside the automobile. Another common product available was an auto tent and bed kit that was usually carried on the running board. The L.F. Schilling Company sold a tent kit that attached to the automobile for support. These images show different views of an auto campground in Dixon.

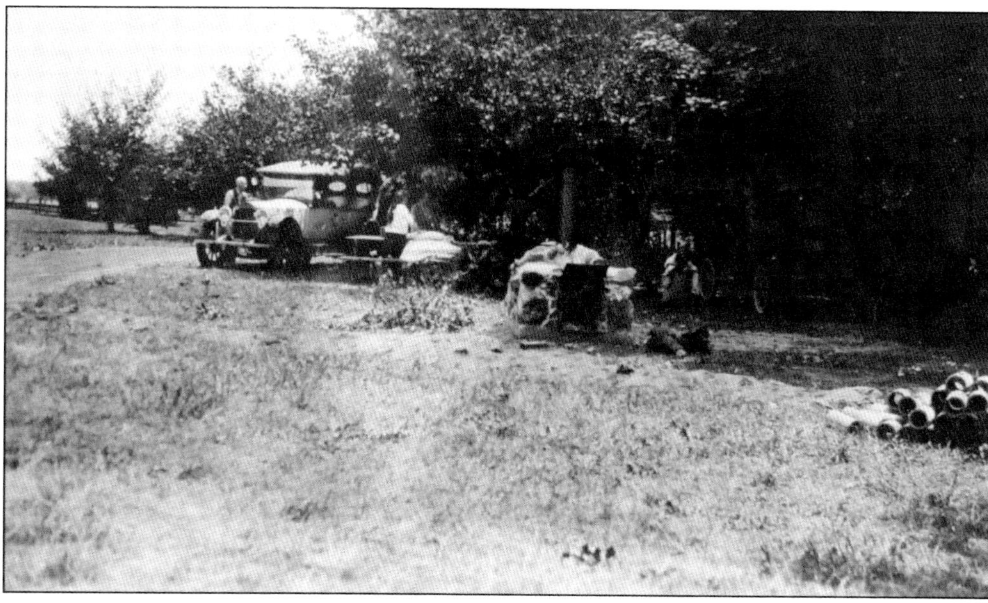

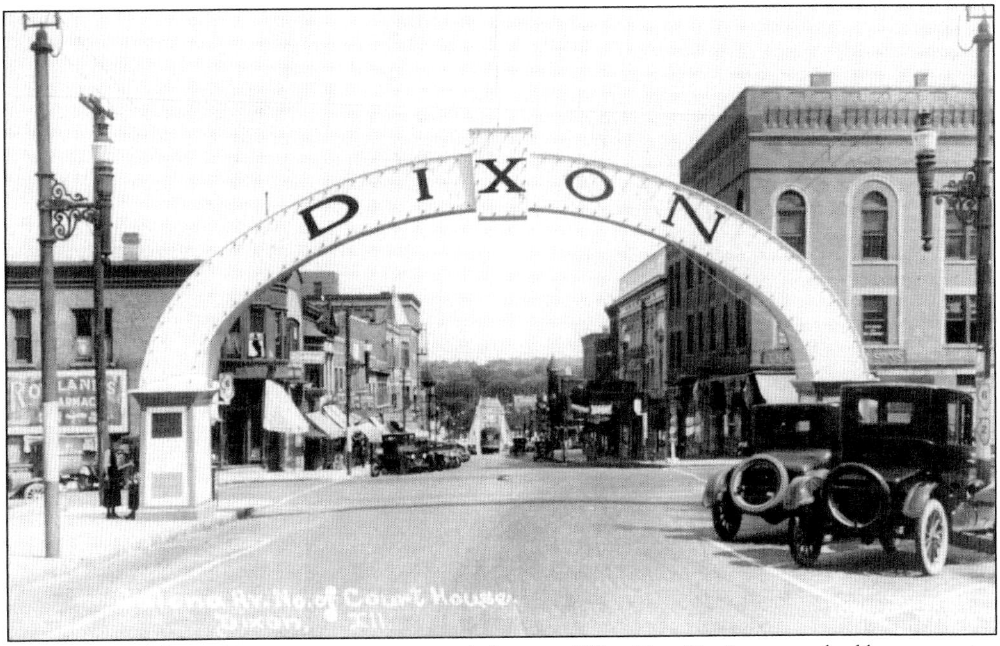

The decade of the 1920s, or as it was commonly known, "The New Era," was marked by prosperity and new opportunity in the aftermath of World War I. The war ended officially on November 11, 1918, and America came out of it relatively unscathed. American soldiers (called "doughboys" because the large buttons on their uniforms resembled a deep-fried bread of the same name) returned home beginning in May 1919 to ticker tape parades in many towns, amid hopes for a prosperous decade. The War Memorial Arch in Dixon was first constructed for Lee County's celebration of the homecoming of soldiers from World War I with a parade and speeches on June 12, 1919. The first arch was temporary, and in time, a more permanent arch memorial was erected. (Above, courtesy of Russell Rein.)

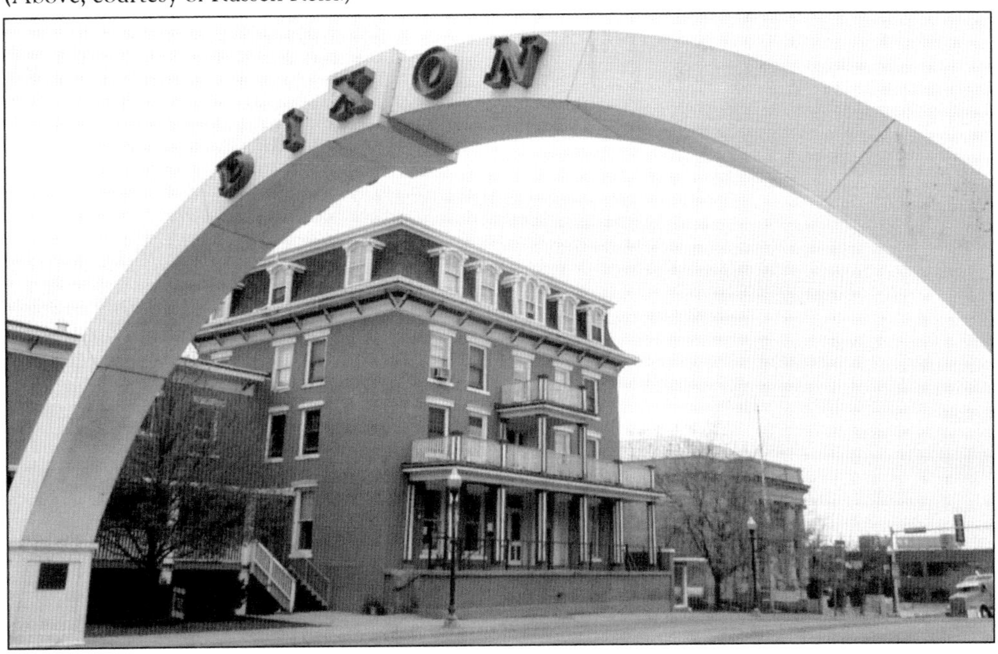

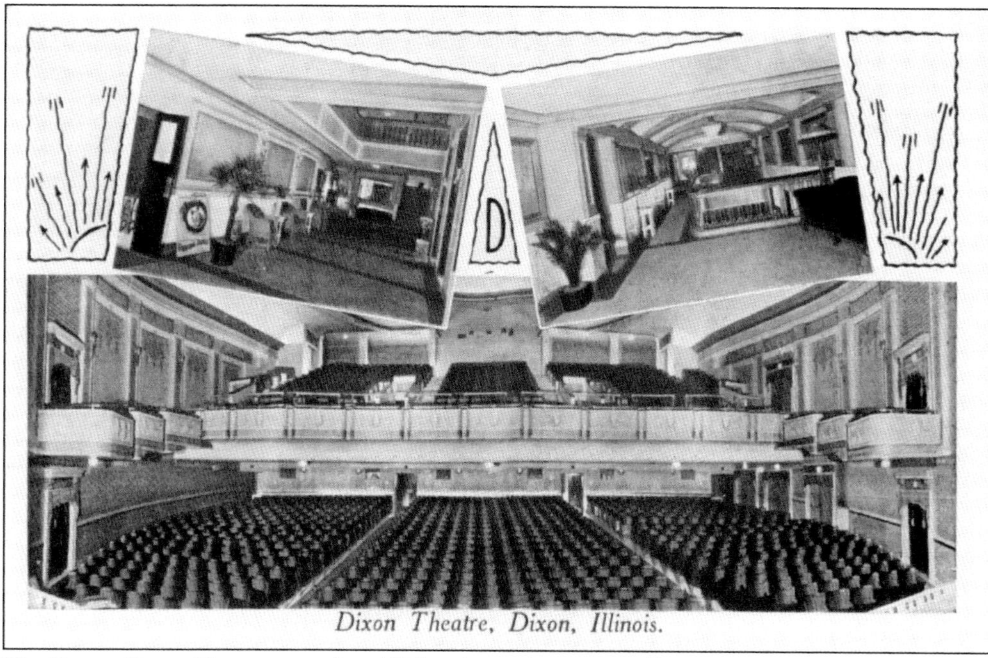

The Dixon Opera House opened in 1876 and was the center of local entertainment activities for many years until it was destroyed by fire in 1920. The same year, Leonard G. Rorer, the manager of Dixon's Family Theatre, announced publicly that he was going to erect a new theater building on the site of the old opera house. Constructed by local architect William J. McAlpine, the 1,200-seat Dixon Theatre opened to the public in 1922. The historic theater served the needs of the community of Dixon for many years until it was closed in 1984. Currently the theater is in various stages of renovation and is available as a rental facility. The top postcard shows an interior view of the Dixon Theatre, located along the historic Lincoln Highway. The bottom image shows the exterior of the theater from the highway. (Above, courtesy of Russell Rein.)

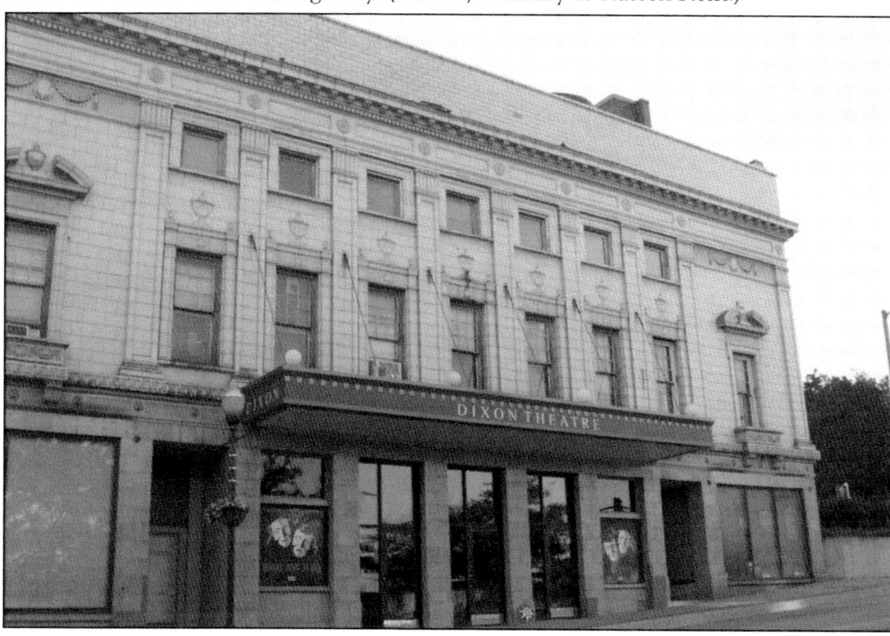

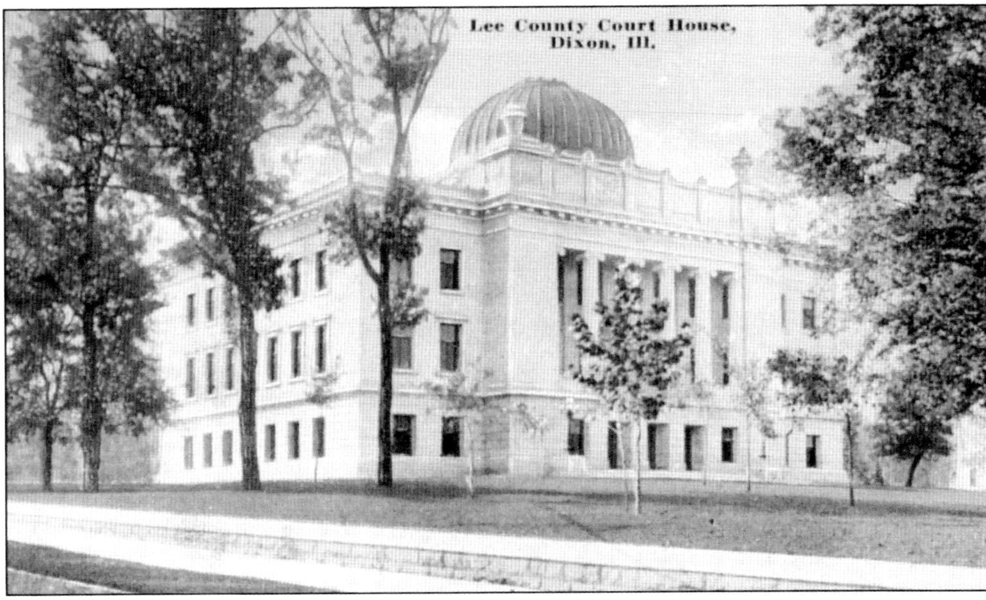

The old Lee County Courthouse is located on a block of land along the Lincoln Highway in Dixon. John Dixon, who founded the town in 1830, originally donated this block of land. Early maps have designated this land as a "Public Square," and three different courthouses have been erected on this site. Construction began on the third Lee County Courthouse in 1899, and the cornerstone was laid on July 17, 1900. The courthouse was dedicated and opened in 1901 and has served the public needs for many years. This postcard shows a view of the old courthouse from the highway. (Courtesy of Russell Rein.)

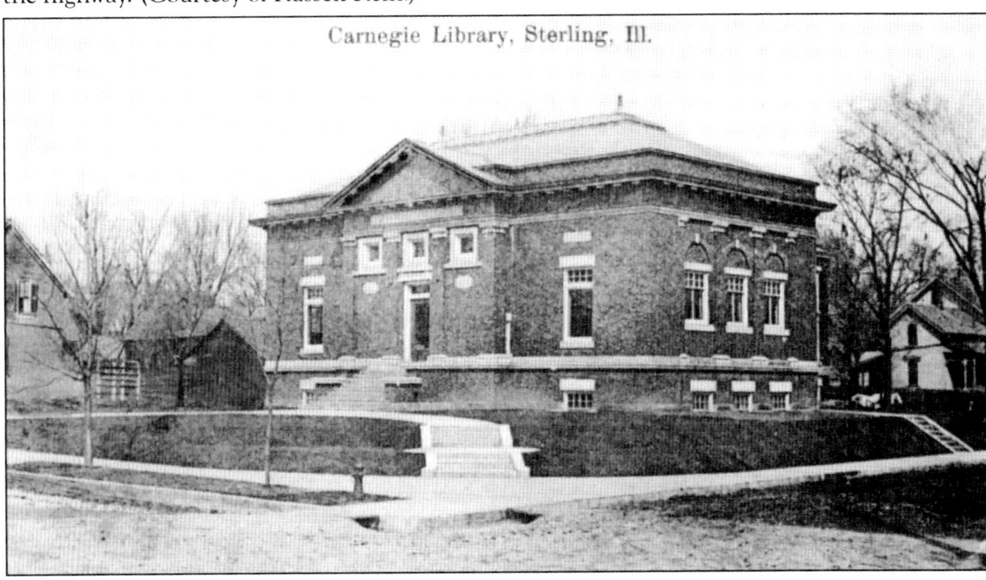

One of 19th-century industrialist Andrew Carnegie's greatest philanthropic efforts was to provide a funding source for many local libraries across the country. Between 1886 and 1919, Carnegie's financial donations helped to build over 1,600 new library buildings in small and large communities across America. The Sterling Public Library, located along the old Lincoln Highway, was constructed with Carnegie support and opened its doors to the public on November 22, 1905. (Courtesy of Russell Rein.)

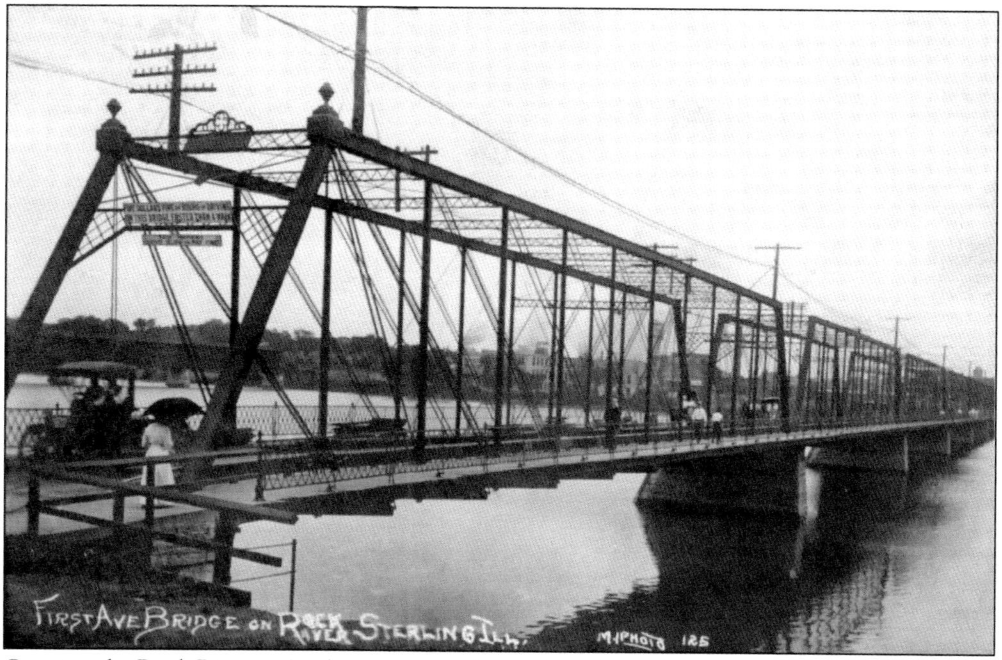

Crossing the Rock River in Sterling was a challenge for early settlers, as many had to ford the river until a rope ferry service began near Avenue B. Over the years, other ferries operated between Sterling and Rock Falls, including a steam tug that was run by George Barr. By 1878, an iron bridge was constructed across the river at First Avenue, and passage across required no toll. The original bridge, shown in the top photograph, included six spans stretching 170 feet each with an iron structure that suspended the roadway 20 feet above the river. Note the fair warning sign above the roadway, which reads: "Five Dollars Fine for Riding or Driving on this Bridge Faster than a Walk." This original bridge served the area until 1923, when it was replaced by a newer version, shown in the bottom postcard image. (Both, courtesy of Russell Rein.)

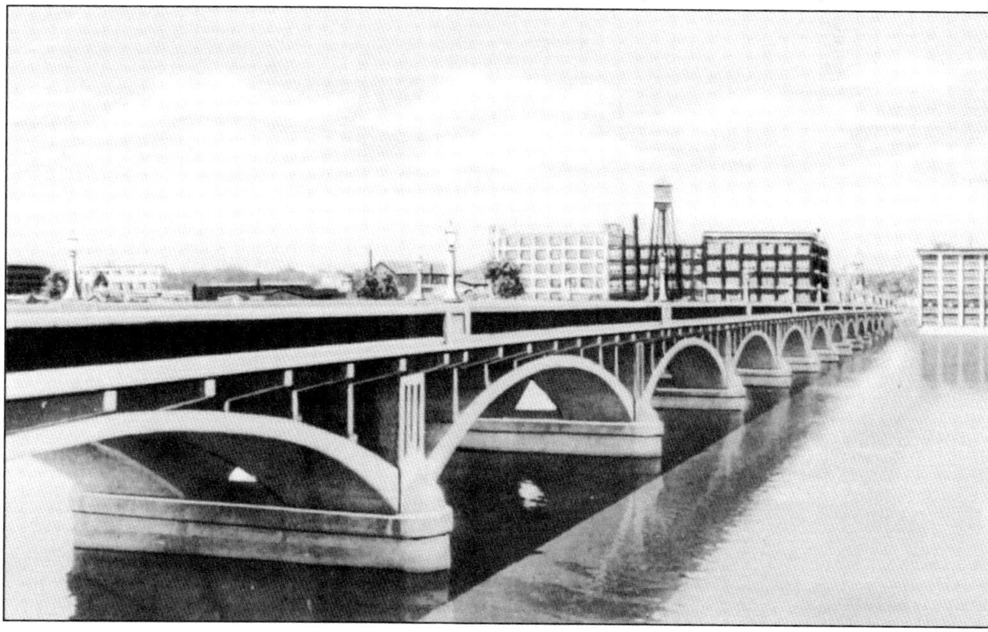

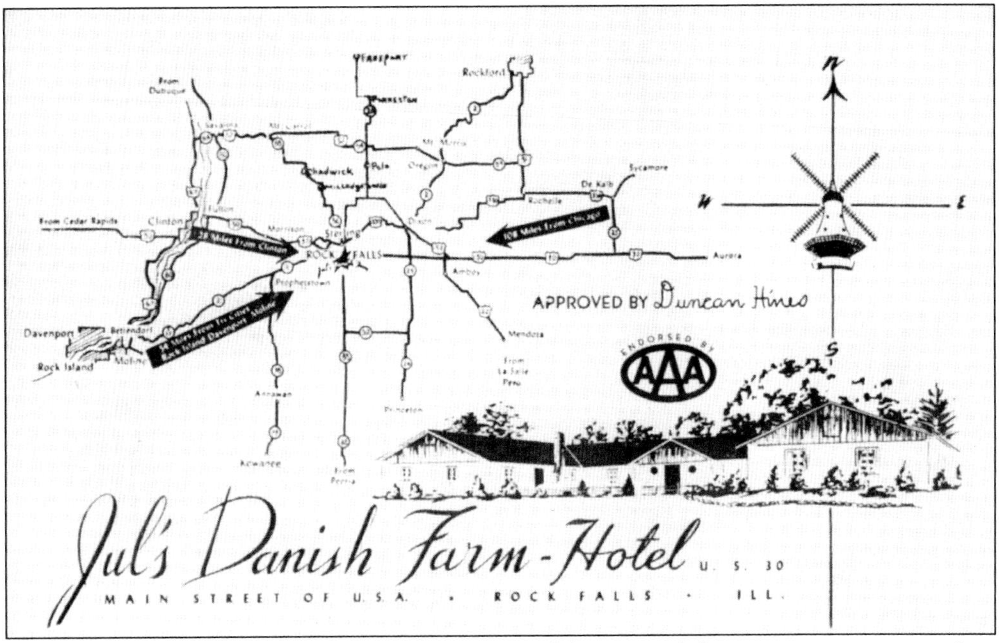

The trend of adding themes to motel signs, architectural designs, and illustrations was commonplace by the early 1950s. Another type of symbol or theme to appear on signs and postcard images by the early 1950s was a recommendation service or referral chain. For example, if the American Automobile Association (AAA) approved a motel, it meant that it met customers' standards. This postcard for Jul's Danish Farm Hotel, located along the Lincoln Highway in Rock Falls, indicates that both Duncan Hines and the AAA approved it. (Courtesy of Russell Rein.)

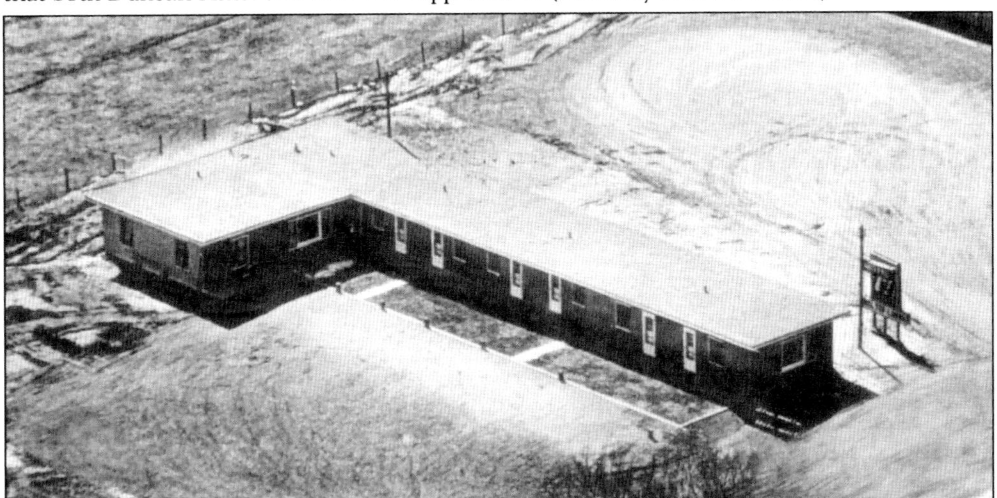

Being a small entrepreneur in the motel industry meant direct involvement with every aspect of the motel. Owners knew from the start that running a motel was hard work, entailing long hours seven days a week. Early motel owners had to learn that sweat equity also involved being knowledgeable in financing, bookkeeping, housekeeping, construction, and even allied services such as restaurants and service stations. This aerial photograph shows the Hillcrest Motel, located along the Lincoln Highway in Morrison. Phyllis and Warren Cent operated a year-round motel for many years. (Courtesy of Russell Rein.)

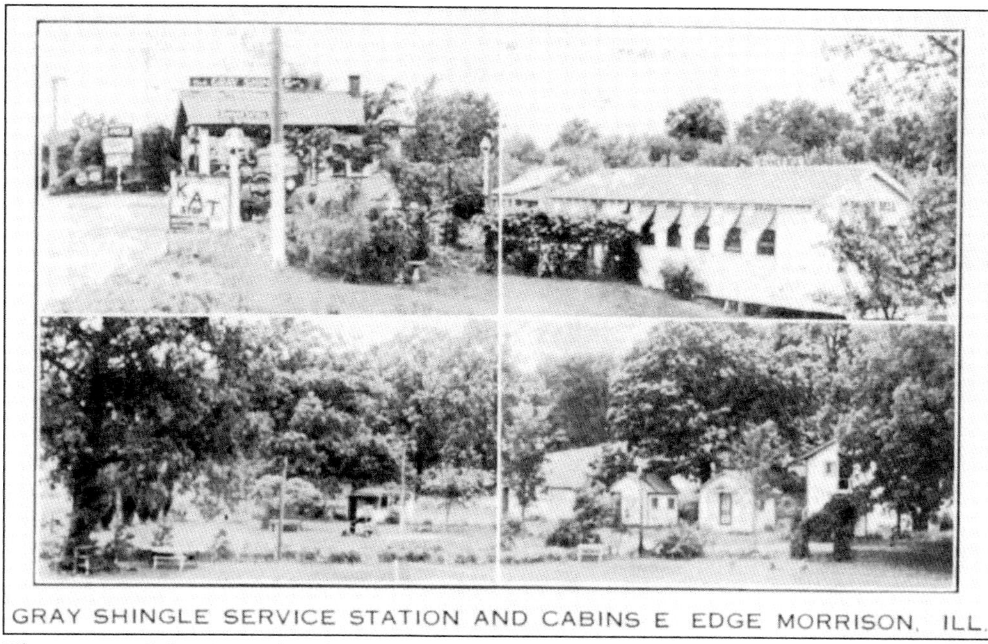

This image of the Gray Shingle Camp along the Lincoln Highway in Morrison provided the passerby with an isolated sanctuary to stop and unwind. Roy G. Smaltz, who owned and operated the Gray Shingle Service Station east of town, conceived this tourist camp. To complement the service station, Smaltz built a series of cabins beginning in 1928 to house motorists on the highway. The cabins were outfitted with some of the modern conveniences of the time, including Simmons beds, electric stoves and lights, running water, and hot and cold showers. Smaltz operated the business until the late 1940s, when it was sold. Today, the Parkview Motel operates on the site of the old auto camp. The top postcard shows views of the Gray Shingle Service Station and Cabins. The bottom photograph shows a view of the Parkview Motel from the Lincoln Highway. (Both, courtesy of Russell Rein.)

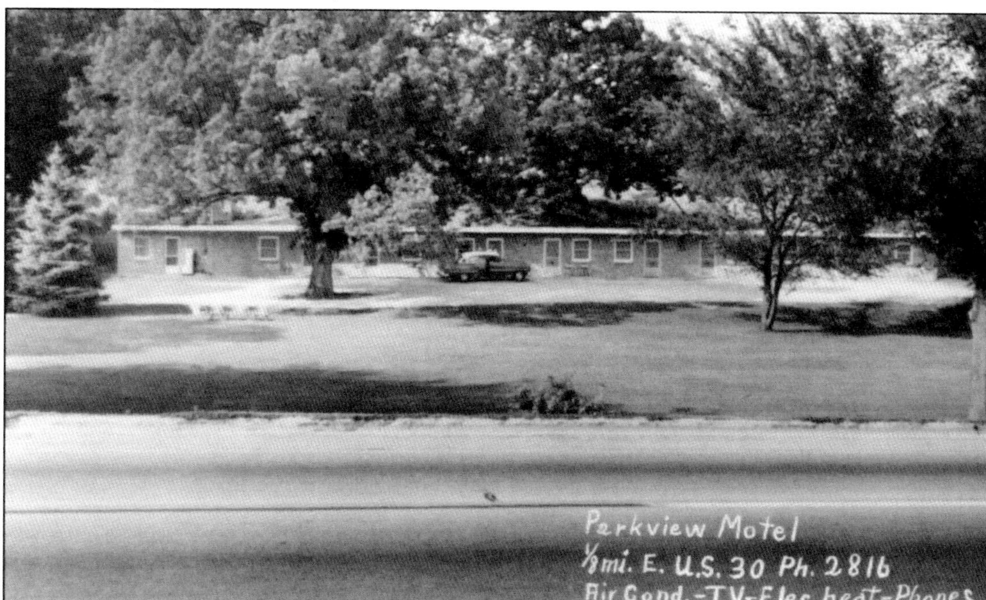

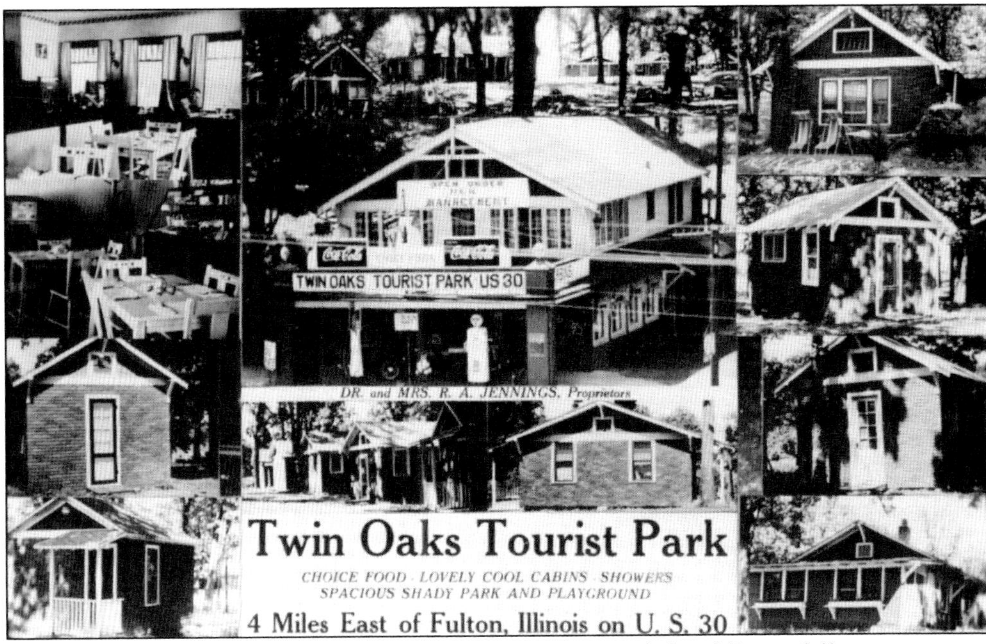

The names of tourist courts and motels in the postwar era tended to fall into different categories. Some used the names of owners, others incorporated the name of the town, and still others focused on a unique local feature. Also common was to use a name that was based on the actual location of the motel, such as the terrain, a geographic nuance, or even a particular specimen tree. In this picture postcard, the Twin Oaks Tourist Park, located along the Lincoln Highway in Fulton, focuses on nature as a way to get tourists to stop for the night. (Courtesy of Russell Rein.)

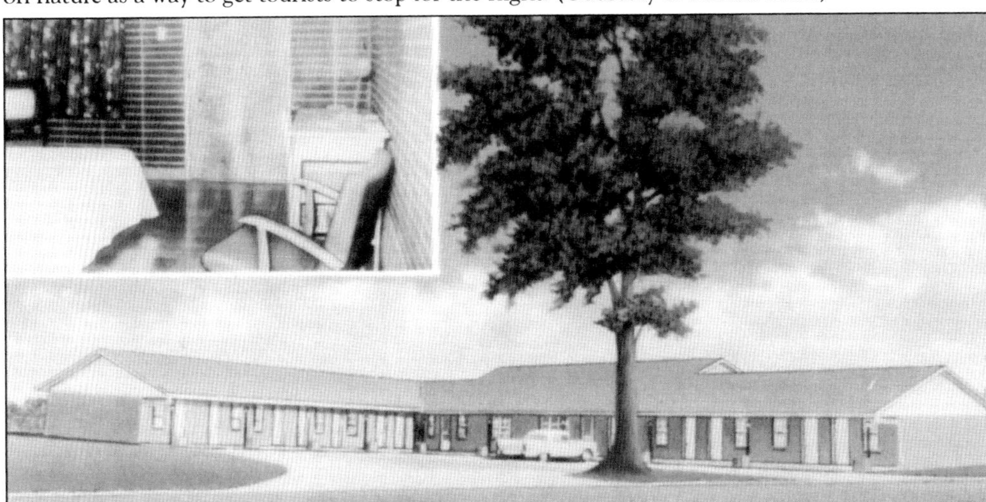

The more modern, photochrome postcard actually transports the viewer directly into the motel, often a guest room or a restaurant. The bottom frame of the image is saved for the highway or road bringing the viewer to the motel. The presence of the road in the image helps to convey a sense of mobility, and the hope is to urge the viewer to pay attention to the motel while traveling down the road. The c. 1955 postcard image shows the Maple Lane Motel along the Lincoln Highway in Fulton. Notice the framed insert image of a typical room in the upper left corner. This motel is still standing today. (Courtesy of Russell Rein.)

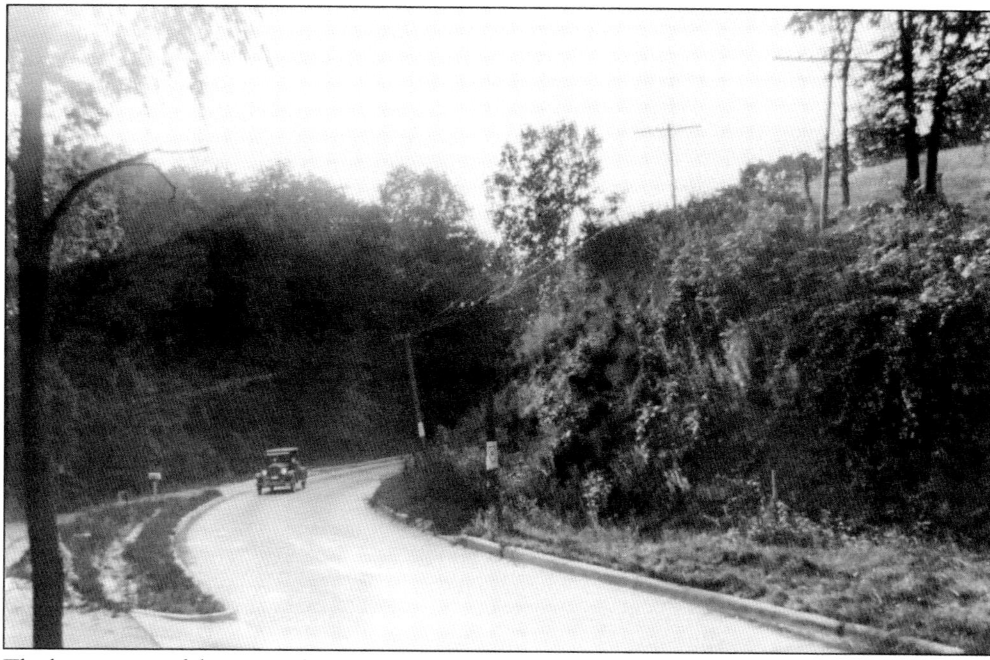

The beginnings of the town of Morrison can be traced back to 1854, when Lyman Johnson and H.S. Vroom came to town as contractors and builders for an early railroad line that was slated for the area. By 1877, the town had numerous businesses, including dry goods and grocery stores, hardware houses, and tailor and clothing establishments, among others. In the 20th century, the Lincoln Highway came through the town and brought tourists and businesses to the area. Morrison also became the site for two concrete Seedling Miles, which served as a prototype of what an improved highway could do for the nation. An interpretive Lincoln Highway mural depicting the 1921 Whiteside County Fair is located at 208 East Main Street. As the mural suggests, the newly paved Lincoln Highway gave motorists the opportunity to travel out of town for events like the county fair. These two images show sections of the Lincoln Highway between the towns of Morrison and Fulton.

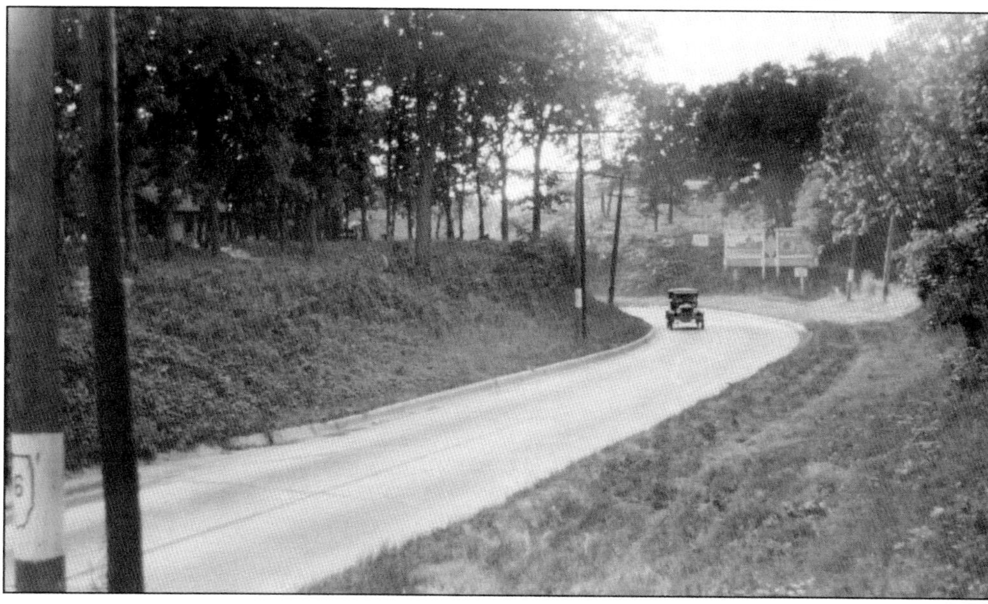

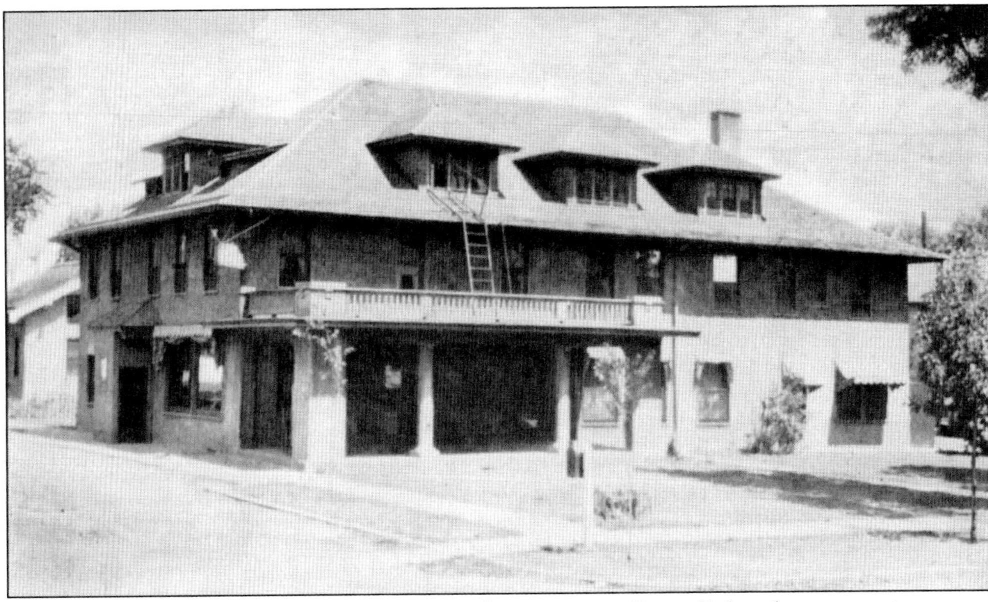

During the early years of steamboat traffic on the Mississippi River, Fulton became an important transfer and warehouse port between the upper and lower portions of the great river. As a transportation hub for travelers along the Mississippi River and motorists along the Lincoln Highway, the town of Fulton has always catered to the needs of temporary visitors. The Hotel Marin, shown here in the top image, has had a long history of serving a steady customer base. Know by a variety of names over the years, the hotel's location along Eleventh Street near the river helped to meet the growing demands and the economic boom of the town. Transcontinental travelers who preferred the outdoors, however, were more inclined to stop for the night at the Fulton Tourist Camp, located just north of the Fulton-Lyons Bridge. The tourist park, shown in the bottom image, offered plenty of shade trees, artesian water, stoves, modern toilets, and showers. (Above, courtesy of Russell Rein.)

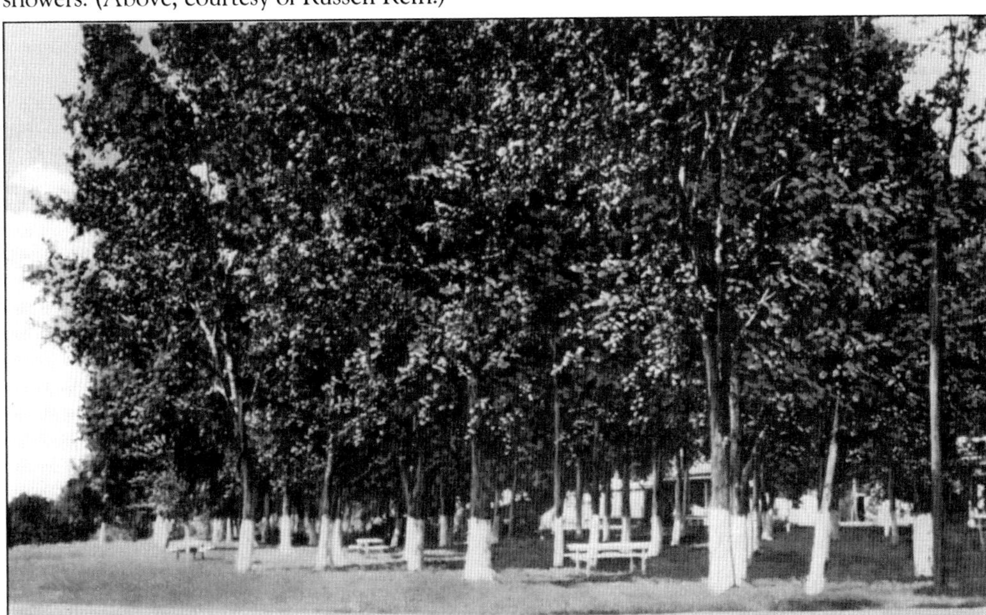

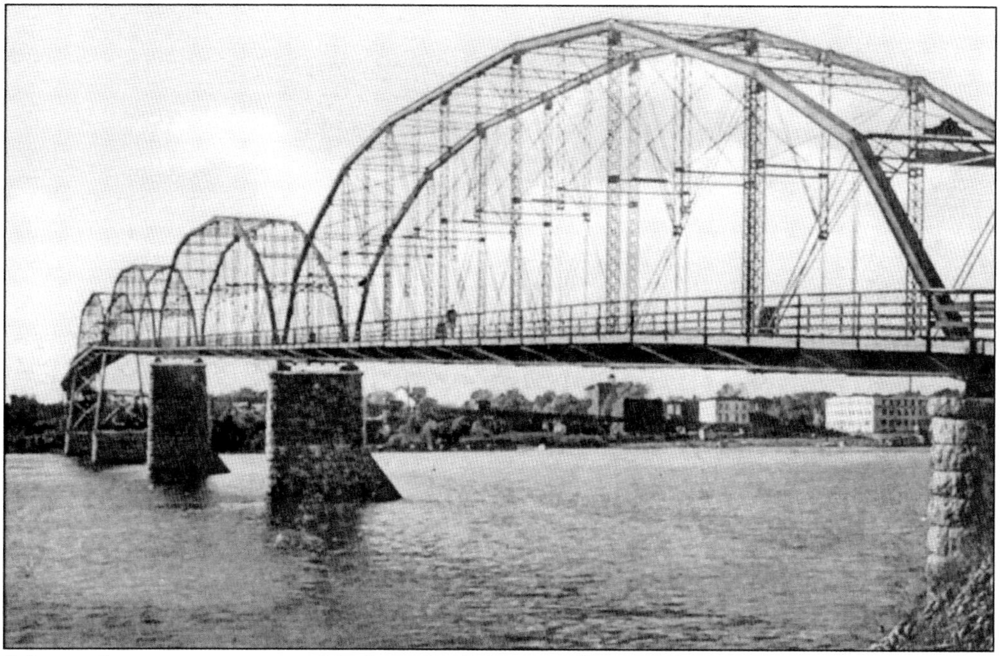

Fulton is the western terminus of the Lincoln Highway in Illinois and is often known as the "Gateway to the West." In Fulton, the Lincoln Highway crosses the Mississippi River into Clinton, Iowa. For a modest toll, motorists could cross the river on the Fulton-Lyons Bridge. Constructed by the Chicago Bridge Company, the Fulton-Lyons Bridge was opened on July 4, 1891, with fanfare and celebration. Built in nine months, the iron bridge included five spans stretching 2,617 feet and supported on six stone piers. In November 1975, the Fulton-Lyons was demolished using dynamite one span at a time. An interpretive mural featuring the former Fulton-Lyons Bridge, connecting Illinois to Iowa along the Lincoln Highway, is located at the corner of Tenth Avenue and Fourth Street near where the old bridge crossed the Mississippi River. (Both, courtesy of Russell Rein.)

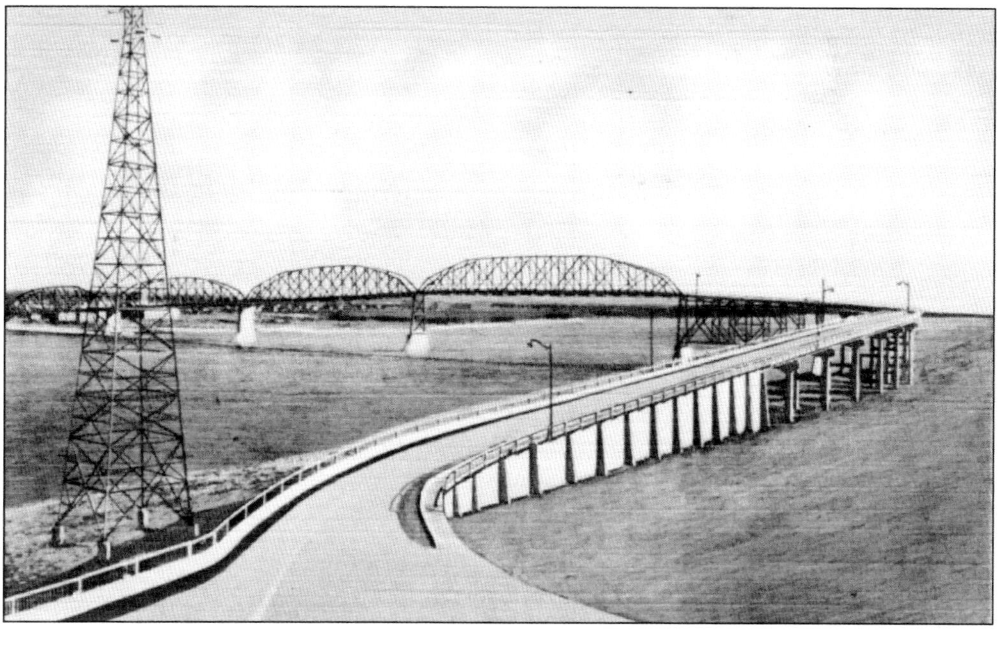

BIBLIOGRAPHY

The Complete Official Road Guide of the Lincoln Highway. 5th ed. Tucson: The Patrice Press, 1993. Republished in facsimile from the 1924 edition.

Genealogical and Biographical Record of Will County, Illinois. Chicago: Biographical Publishing Company, 1900.

Heimann, Jim. *Car Hops and Curb Service, A History of American Drive in Restaurants 1920–1960*. San Francisco: Chronicle Books, 1996.

Hokanson, Drake. *The Lincoln Highway, Main Street Across America*. Iowa City: University of Iowa Press, 1988.

Jakle, John A., Keith A. Sculle, and Jefferson S. Rogers. *The Motel in America*. Baltimore: The Johns Hopkins University Press, 1996.

The Lincoln Highway: The Story of a Crusade that Made Transportation History. Sacramento: Pleiades Press,1935.

Sterling, Robert E. A *Pictorial History of Will County*. 2 vols. Joliet: Will County Historical Publications Company, 1975, 1976.

———. *Joliet: Transportation & Industry, A Pictorial History*. St. Louis: G. Bradley Publishing, 1997.

Wallis, Michael, and Michael S. Williamson. *The Lincoln Highway, Coast to Coast from Times Square to the Golden Gate*. New York: W.W. Norton & Company, Inc., 2007.

Witzel, Michael Karl. *The American Drive-In, History and Folklore of the Drive-In Restaurant in American Car Culture*. Osceola, WI: Motorbooks International, 1994.

Woodruff, George H. *Forty Years Ago! A Contribution to the Early History of Joliet and Will County*. Joliet: Joliet Republican Stream Printing House, 1874.

INDEX